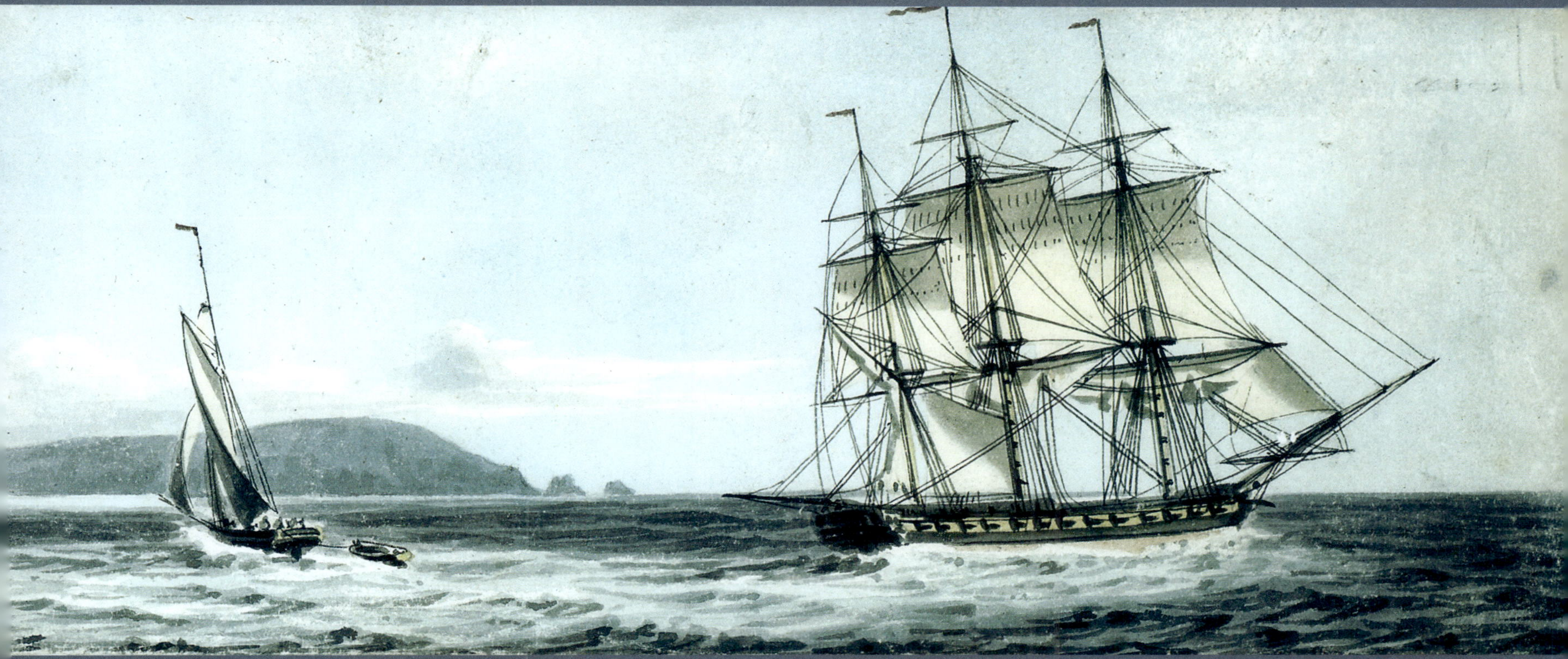

EYES OF THE ADMIRALTY

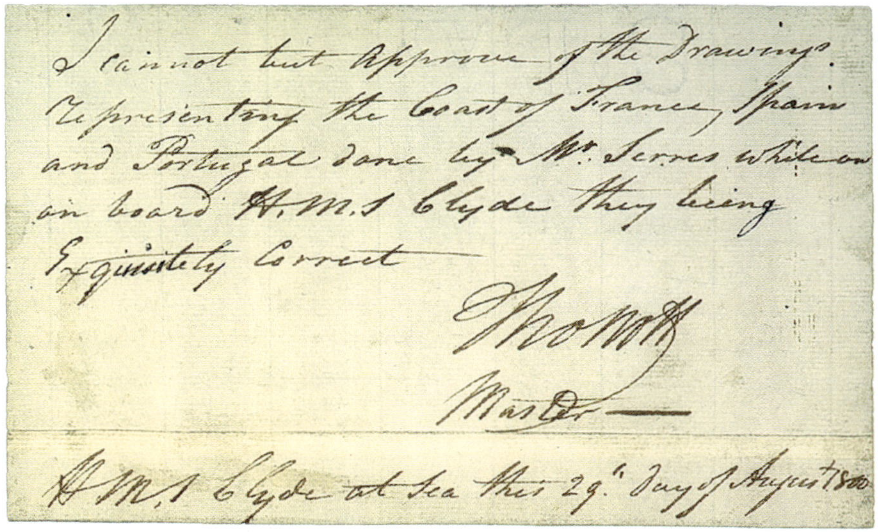

I cannot but Approve of the Drawings
Representing the Coast of France, Spain
and Portugal done by Mr. Serres while on
on board H.M.S Clyde they being
Exquisitely Correct

Tho Mott
Master

H.M.S Clyde at Sea this 29th Day of August 1800

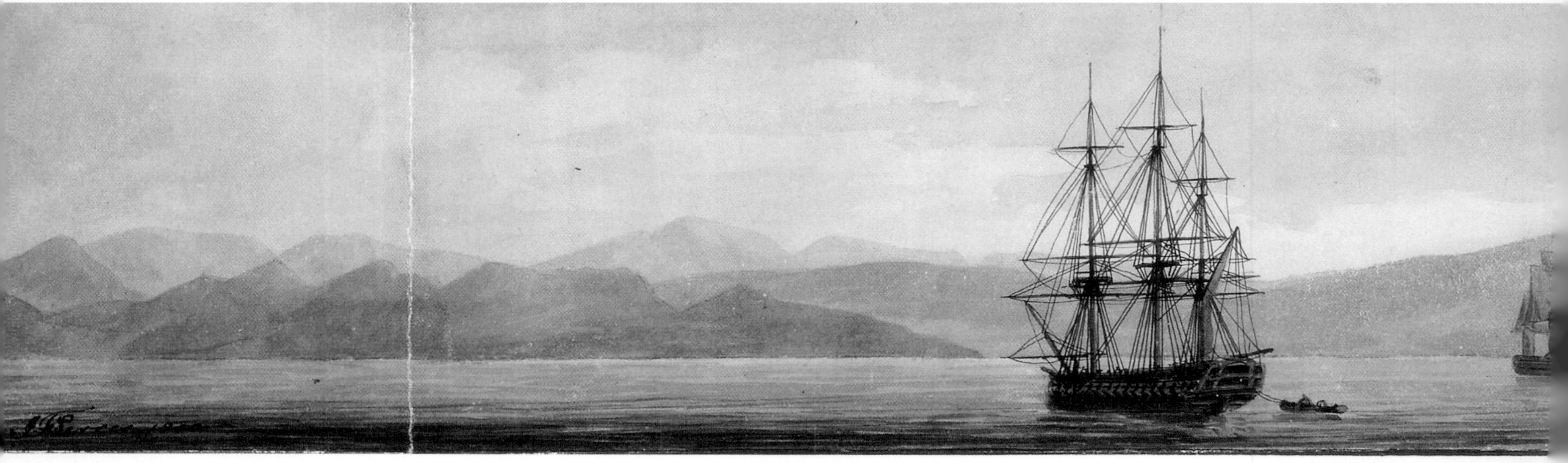

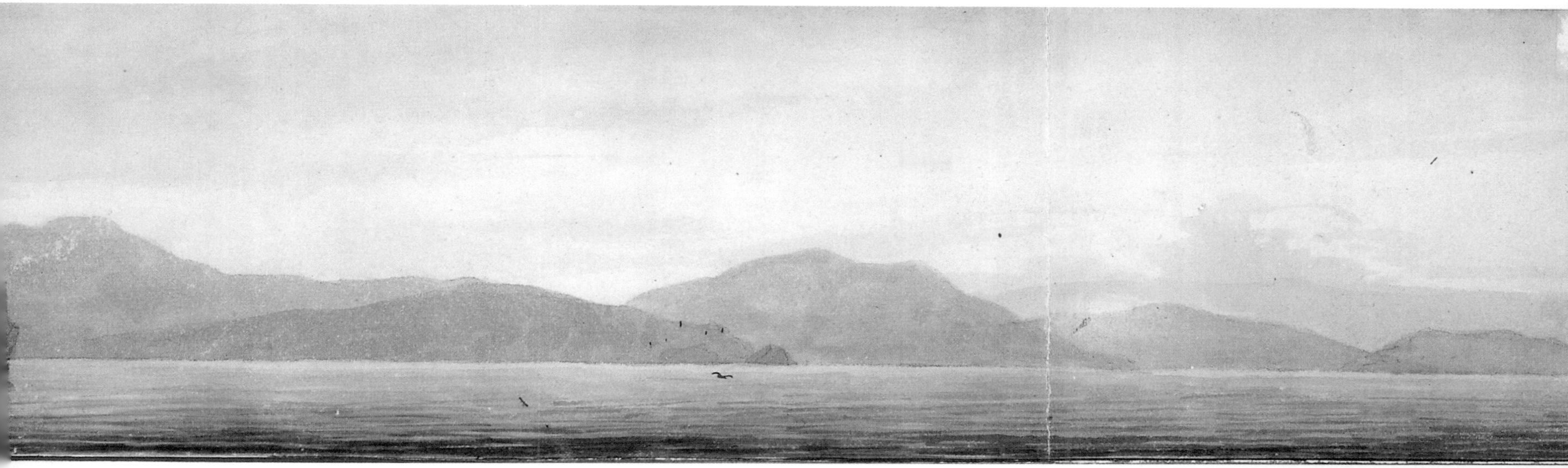

Eyes of the Admiralty
J.T. Serres
An Artist in the Channel Fleet 1799–1800

NATIONAL MARITIME MUSEUM

THE UNITED KINGDOM HYDROGRAPHIC OFFICE

M. K. BARRITT

Dedicated to Mr John Dyer, Mr Thomas Nott and the other Masters of the Royal Navy

'He is to apply himself to observe the appearances of coasts and how they show themselves in different points of view and if he discovers any new shoals or rocks underwater, to note them down in his journal, with their bearings and depth of water.'

Regulations and Instructions relating to His Majesty's Service at Sea, Part III, *The Master*, Article VII (Admiralty, 13th edn., 1790)

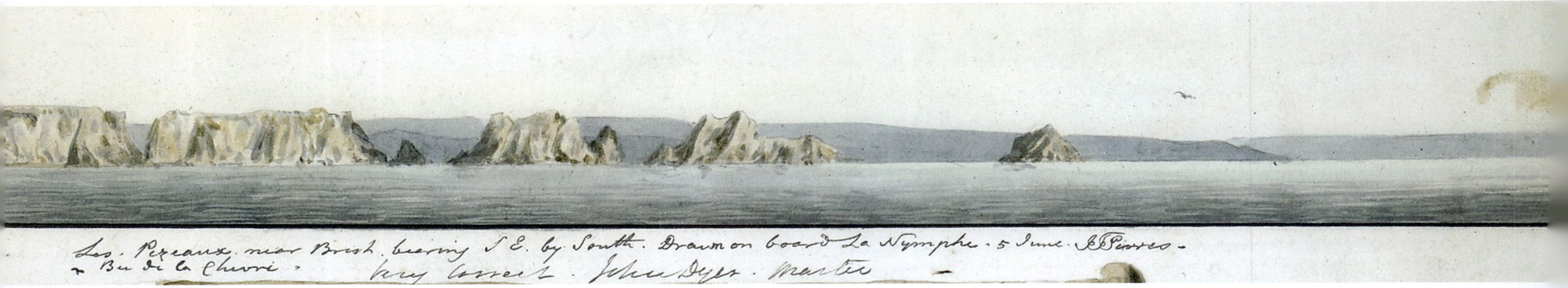

ISBN 978-0-948065-79-8

First published by the National Maritime Museum, Greenwich, London SE10 9NF

www.nmm.ac.uk/publishing

A CIP catalogue record for this book is available from the British Library.

Design www.studio-mark.co.uk
Production management by Geoff Barlow
Printed and bound in China

Above **J.T. Serres' appearance of Les Pezeaux, near Brest, approved by Mr John Dyer, Master, HMS *La Nymphe*.**

Front end-paper **An appearance of the Spanish coast made by J.T. Serres towards the end of his service in the Channel Fleet in 1800.**

Title page **View by J.T. Serres of 'Continuation of the coast of Spain towards Bilbao, including Cabo Machichaco . . . Drawn on board HMS Clyde, 14 July 1800'.**

CONTENTS

ACKNOWLEDGEMENTS

John Serres' remarkable views came to my notice when, on my retirement as Hydrographer of the Navy, I was presented with a copy of the fine panorama shown on the front end-paper of this book. This set me off on a research trail to find out more about the genesis of Serres' work, the circumstances in which it was conducted, and the subsequent use of the visual navigational information which he submitted to the Admiralty.

With the expert assistance of Philip Clayton-Gore, Adrian Webb, Guy Hannaford and Anne Brown, I was able to identify additional primary material in the archives of the UKHO, while Jane Postins in the UKHO Library obtained even the most obscure secondary sources. At the Royal Geographical Society, Francis Herbert gave me early access to a copy of *The Little Sea Torch*. Nigel Rigby, Daphne Knott and Gloria Clifton lit my path through the records at the National Maritime Museum, and Pieter van der Merwe pointed me to records of Serres' career. I have been voyaging in the wake of Alan Russett, whose second volume on the Serres family will be eagerly awaited, and I am indebted to him for

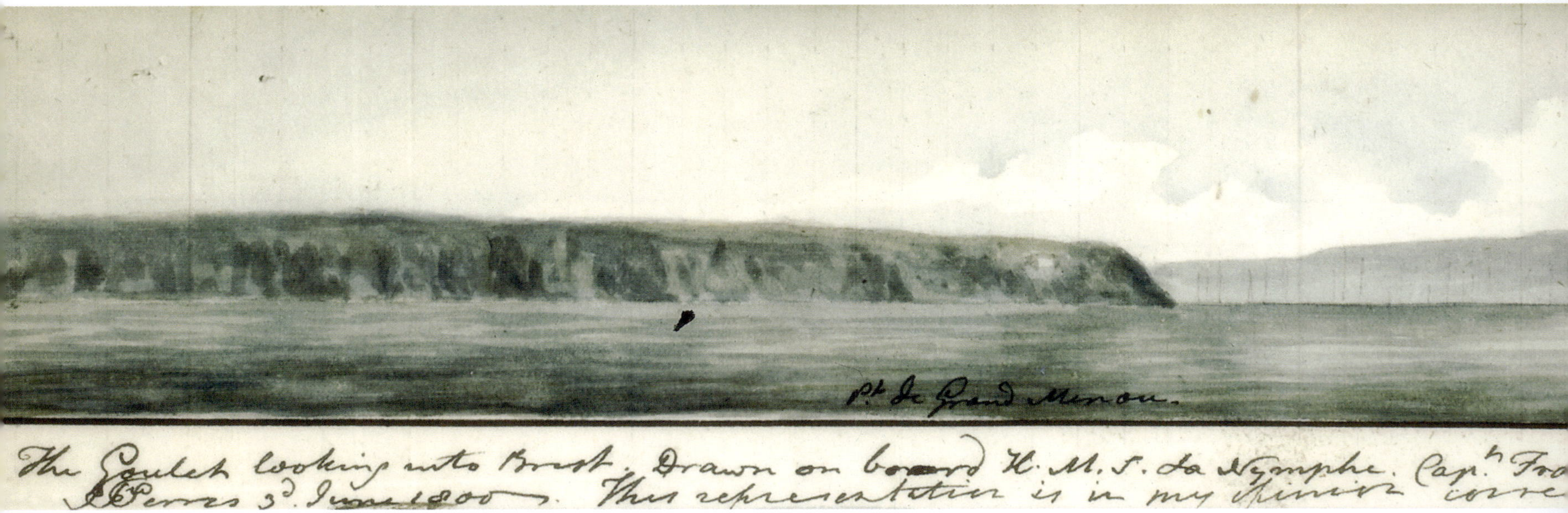

his generous advice. Members of staff at the National Archive have been unfailingly helpful, and the smooth delivery system has been vital for the work of a provincial visitor during precious research days.

The appearance of a third Navy Records Society (N.R.S.) volume on the Blockade of Brest, covering the years 1793–1801, not long before I began this research, provided a firm foundation. The analysis of Richard Saxby and Roger Morriss is essential reading for anyone seeking further elucidation of the strategy and tactics of the campaign. Similarly, for the hydrographic background, Andrew Cook and Adrian Webb have been never failing sources of guidance. Ingénieur en Chef de l'Armement Michel Huet of the International Hydrographic Bureau gave me the benefit of his knowledge of Brittany. Nicholas Rodger's *The Command of the Ocean* also appeared during my research and his extraordinary mastery of sources and rigorous testing of received wisdom have provided constant inspiration and discipline. Piers Mackesy's history of the period provides the definitive analysis of the

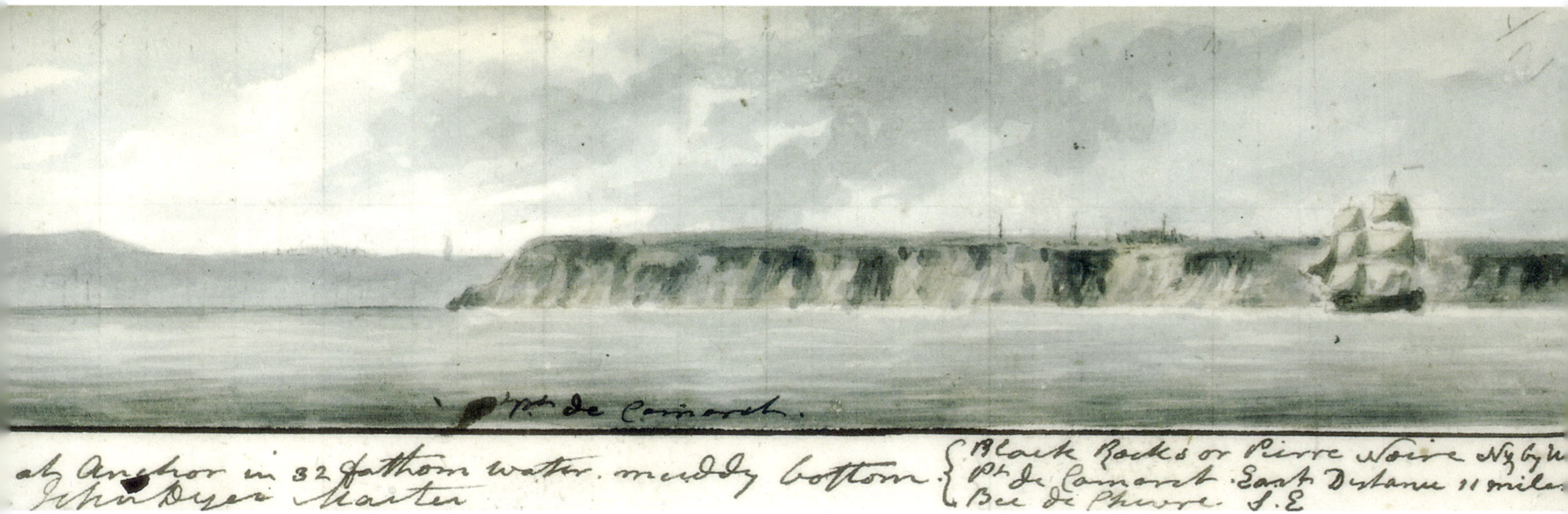

The blockading fleet's view of the entrance to Brest.

workings of Pitt's administration. I have looked back with great affection to his wise tutelage in my undergraduate days, and especially to the lesson that a text will always emerge stronger from critical expert reading. I am grateful to those who took on this commitment. Most important of all, without the loyal support and constant encouragement of my wife Rosanne, this book would not have seen the light of day.

Finally, the aim of making Serres' work available to a wider public has depended crucially on the skills of editor and publisher. All credit for the results must go to Rachel Giles, Emily Winter, Sarah Thorowgood and Sara Ayad at the National Maritime Museum and Benedict Richards and Mark Jones from Studio Mark.

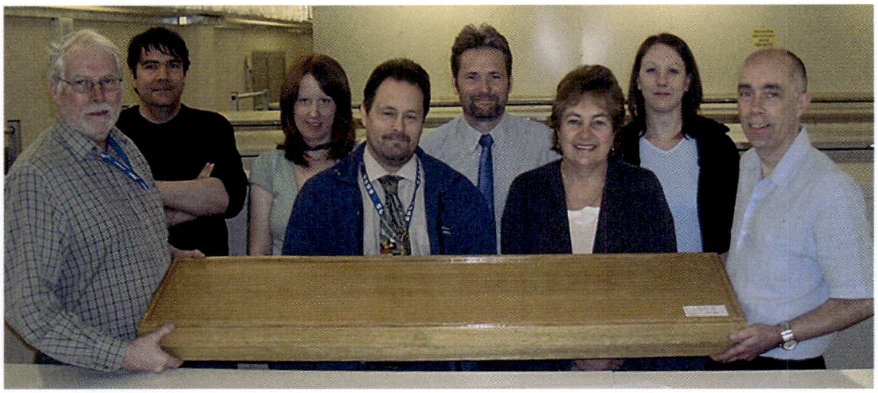

UKHO Archives staff with 'the coffin'.

PREFACE

The archives of the United Kingdom Hydrographic Office (UKHO) contain charts and other documents amassed over the course of three centuries. Here will be found the working records of the famous exploring voyages, traces of the eighteenth-century *Endeavour* and the twentieth-century *Endurance*. Mixed in with these are the routine Remark Books and sketches of less well-known captains and navigators, a treasure trove of glimpses of seafaring life in the days of sail and early steam. Much space is taken up by hundreds of painstaking survey sheets from which the published Admiralty charts have been compiled.

Among the shelves and presses lies a long wooden box, known affectionately to the staff as 'the coffin'. Inside, carefully mounted and protected, are 26 watercolours, two letters of commendation, and a sketchbook. On top, a short note gives a hint of the remarkable story of their production.

This book attempts to tell that story, and to give as many people as possible the opportunity to see some fascinating images of a dramatic period in the history of the Royal Navy. In 1800, the command of the Channel Fleet, with its vital role of watching and containing the French and Spanish navies, passed from Lord Bridport to Earl St Vincent. This account draws on St Vincent's copious correspondence, especially to a former protégé, Evan Nepean, once his Secretary and Purser in the ship of the line *Foudroyant*, now continuing a highly successful career in the civil service as First Secretary to the Admiralty Board. Other voices from the fleet add their colourful testimony to the realities of service in the challenging waters of the Breton and Biscay coasts, including the young William Cathcart, serving in the frigate *Triton*. Throughout the account runs a sombre thread, as dark clouds fall over the career of the man who produced the illustrations which form the core of this book.

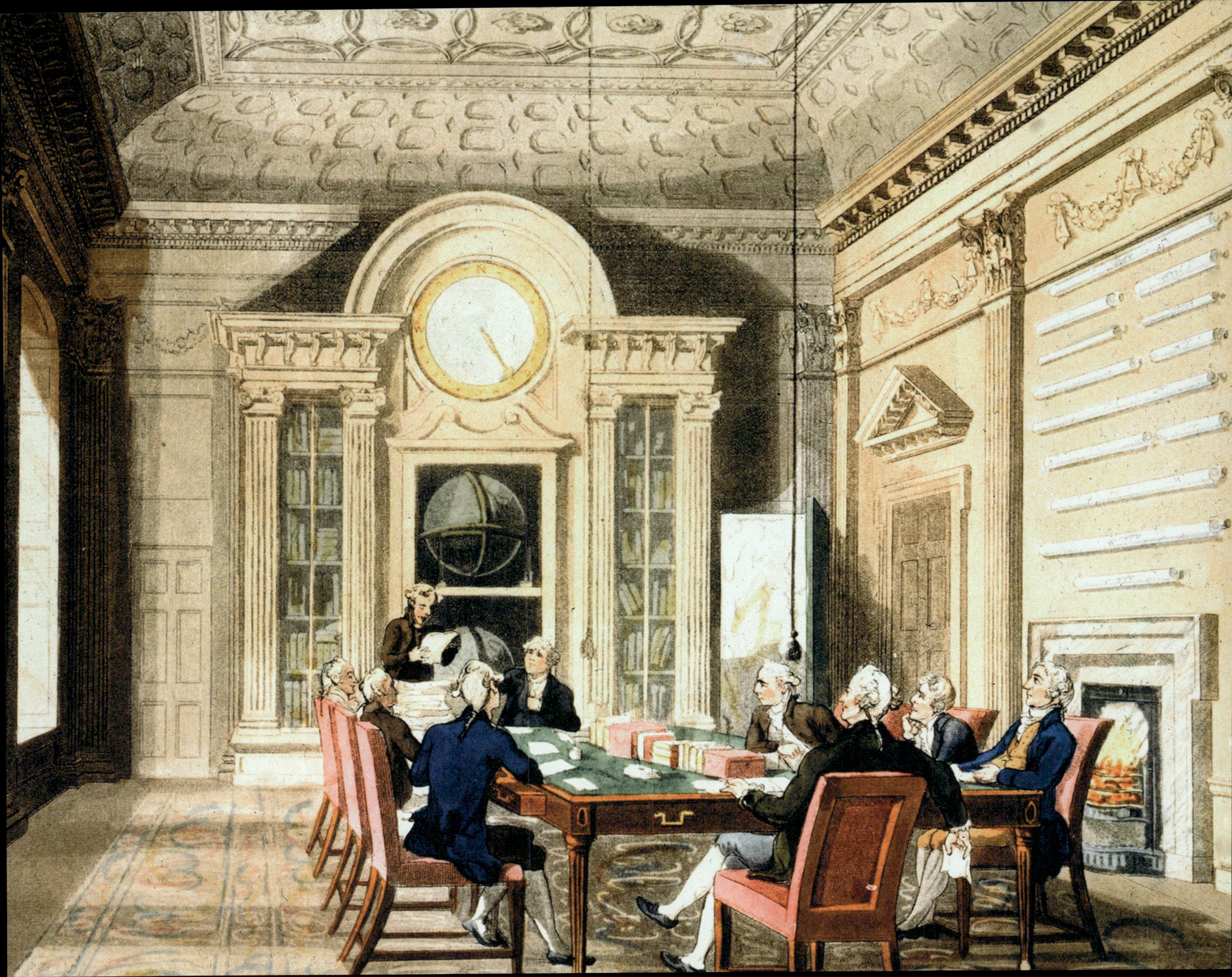

CHAPTER ONE

Britannia at bay

It was a chill, autumnal Monday morning in Whitehall. The mood in the grey streets of the capital was sombre. During the weekend there had been much discussion of an anonymous satirical poem which had appeared in the *Morning Post* on the previous Friday, 6 September 1799. 'The Devil's Thoughts', a production of Robert Southey and Samuel Taylor Coleridge, pilloried the government and bemoaned the dissipation of 'England's commercial prosperity'. It was now six years since the new French Republic had invaded Holland and declared war on Britain. As the century drew to a close, the conflict seemed as interminable and grim as the prevailing weather. The drenching rain which had set in at the end of June was to persist until mid-November, ruining the harvest.

In the first campaigns of the war in 1792–4, the new Revolutionary army of France had swept aside the forces of the other continental powers with their choreographed style of warfare. The Prime Minister, William Pitt the Younger, had reverted to his famous father's strategy. Sea power would be used to secure the country's trade, and to transport troops to defend the colonies and seize French possessions overseas. Direct intervention on the continent was limited to amphibious raids. But one by one Britain's allies came to an accommodation with France. In 1797 Britain stood alone and the threat of war came home to many people for the first time. Exports slumped, European corn supplies for the rising population were disrupted, prices soared, and the Bank of England suspended cash payments. Mutinies in units of the fleet based at Spithead and the Nore rocked the complacent trust in naval superiority. Never were victories more sorely needed than Jervis's at Cape St Vincent, Duncan's at Camperdown, and Nelson's at the Nile in the following year.

Opposite **In the Board Room the First Lord sits at the near end of the table, and the First Secretary at the far end, with the tell-tale dial of the wind-vane above him. The other Commissioners of the Admiralty, three civilians, and three naval officers, sit on either side of the table.**

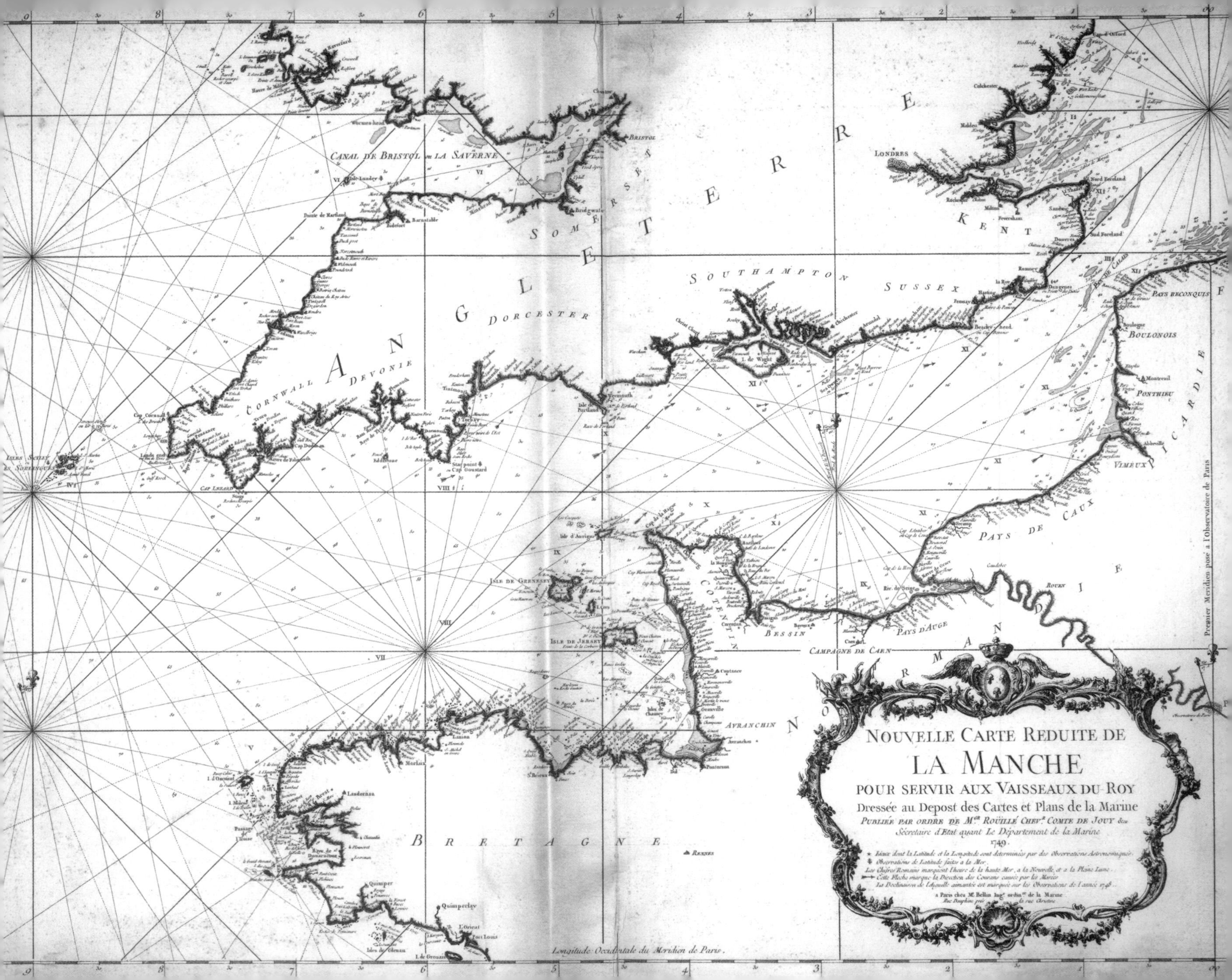

NOUVELLE CARTE REDUITE DE
LA MANCHE
POUR SERVIR AUX VAISSEAUX DU-ROY
Dressée au Depost des Cartes et Plans de la Marine
PUBLIÉE PAR ORDRE DE Mgr ROÜILLÉ CHEVr COMTE DE JOUY &ca
Sécretaire d'Etat ayant Le Département de la Marine
1749.
★ Lieux dont la Latitude et la Longitude sont determinés par des Observations Astronomiques.
Observations de Latitude faites a la Mer.
Les Chifres Romains marquent l'heure de la haute Mer, a la Nouvelle, et a la Plaine Lune.
Cette Fleche marque la Direction des Courans causés par les Marées
La Declinaison de l'Aguille aimantée est marquée sur les Observations de l'année 1748.
a Paris chez Mr Bellin Ingr ordinre de la Marine
Rue Dauphine près la rue Christine
Longitude Occidentale du Meridien de Paris.
Premier Meridien posé a l'Observatoire de Paris
ANGLETERRE
CANAL DE BRISTOL ou LA SAVERNE
SOMERSET
KENT
SOUTHAMPTON
SUSSEX
DORCESTER
DEVONIE
CORNWALL
LONDRES
BRISTOL
BOULONOIS
PONTHIEU
PICARDIE
VIMEUX
PAYS RECONQUIS
PAYS DE CAUX
NORMANDIE
ROUEN
COTENTIN
BESSIN
PAYS D'AUGE
CAMPAGNE DE CAEN
AVRANCHIN
BRETAGNE
RENNES
ISLE DE GRENESEY
ISLE DE JERSEY
Isle d'Aurigny
I. de Wight
ISLES SCILLY ou SORLINGUES

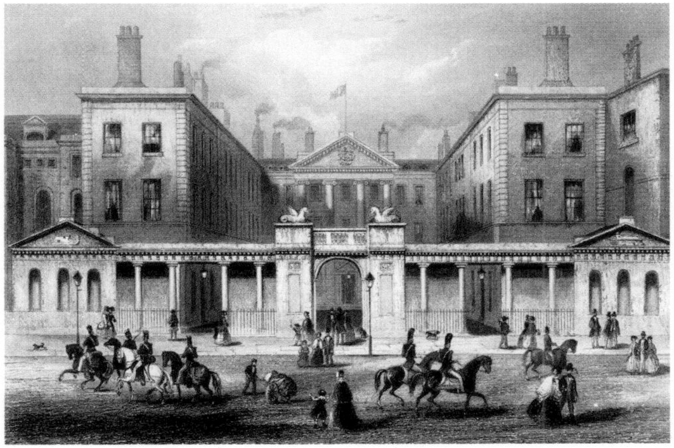

Under renewed pressure from King George III and from elements of his cabinet, Pitt had taken steps to construct a Second Coalition to contain France. An income tax was introduced for the first time in order to supplement the loan financing which furnished the subsidies for the continental armies. The raising of militias to counter the invasion threat had fuelled a new martial ardour in England, and loud voices called for a return on the massive cost of the war by direct involvement in Europe. Within the administration such a move was favoured by several ministers as a means of encouraging Austria and Russia to reopen the major war front on France's eastern borders. In August 1799 a British advanced force had landed in Holland and now people waited anxiously for news that the main Anglo-Russian army had joined them among the rain-swept dunes and dykes. The beleaguered administration badly needed a success on land; for, as the squibs of the opposition press revealed, the appetite for military engagement was shallow and war-weariness was not far below the surface. The threat of a renewed trade deficit was looming as reserves were again drained to purchase grain from the Continent.

Inside the Admiralty, the great wind dial on the wall of the Board Room rotated listlessly. A grave responsibility lay on the shoulders of the six Commissioners who met here under the firm leadership of Earl Spencer, First Lord of the Admiralty.[1] Not only the safe landing of the allied army in Holland, but a whole web of world-wide strategic interests, depended on the success of their direction of the Royal Navy. British sea power had frustrated a thrust into the Near East by the mercurial General Bonaparte but the ever-present threat of the substantial French forces in strategic Channel and Mediterranean bases had now been supplemented by those of Spain. In recent weeks fifteen Spanish ships of the line had joined the French in Brest, their major base at the mouth of the Channel, while another large squadron had been concentrated in Ferrol on the Atlantic coast of Galicia. Only the vigilance of Lord Bridport's Channel Fleet could prevent mischief from further enemy forays to Ireland, the Mediterranean or the West Indies, or to intercept British trade in the Western Approaches.[2] If the wind dial swung firmly into the east where would the combined fleet in Brest go, and would the blockading Channel Fleet maintain contact?

Above The Admiralty Building, Whitehall.

Left A chart of the Channel produced for the French navy in 1749 by the Dépôt des Cartes et Plans. The arrangements in France for the supply of navigational products to the French fleet were much envied in the Royal Navy.

The geography of Brest and Ferrol is very similar. Both bases lie in deep inlets in the rugged Atlantic coast of Europe. The dockyard of Brest is constructed in a river on the north side of a magnificent enclosed roadstead, with a narrow and easily defended entrance called the Gullet (le Goulet) (see chart p. 26). However, this doorway was effectively closed as an exit for square-rigged sailing vessels in westerly winds, and when the wind shifted back into the east or north the scouting vessels of the blockading British fleet closed in to keep watch. This was no light task, since the approaches to Brest are encumbered with submerged rocks and offshore skerries and fringed by two great promontories of islets and reefs. The northern of these extends from the Pointe de St Mathieu to the island of Ushant, while the Chaussée de Sein, known to the English as 'the Saints', stretches westwards from the Pointe du Raz. There are coastal passages at the inner ends of these promontories which were exploited by handy fore-and-aft sailing craft, such as the *chasse-marées* (literally 'tide-chasers'), to run supplies into Brest. However, the strong tidal streams presented a much greater challenge to the larger and less manoeuvrable warships. It might take one ebb tide to carry a French squadron from Brest Roads to Berthaume or Camaret Bay in the Avant Goulet. From there a dash could be made out into the Iroise, round La Parquette and the long finger of shoal rocks extending from the Pointe du Toulinguet, and then either to seawards of the Saints or through the Passage du Raz at its landward end. The inshore route would avoid an encounter with any superior British forces out of sight from the mainland in the outer part of the Iroise.[3]

Evan Nepean, First Secretary to the Admiralty Board, took stock. He was a tough and experienced public servant who was accustomed to dealing with threatening situations. His baptism of fire in the civil service had been in the new Home Office in 1782 when he had been plucked from the Royal Navy to become Under Secretary of State. He produced the plan for the penal colony in New South Wales to rid the kingdom of its surfeit of criminals and he established a secret service network to watch the radical elements that had caused turmoil in London and were suspected of liaison with French agents. He had now been at the Admiralty for five years, during which time the French navy had begun to recover from

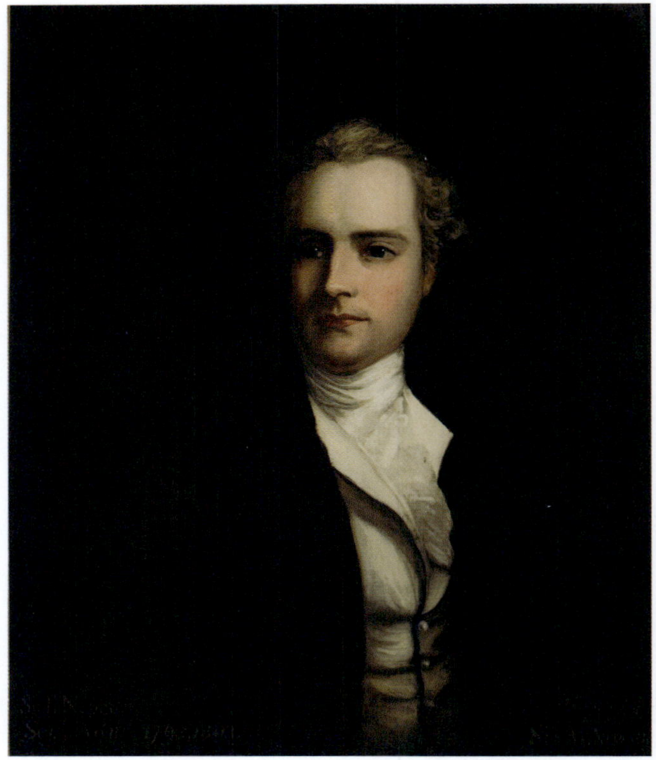

Sir Evan Nepean, 1751–1822, First Secretary to the Admiralty Board.

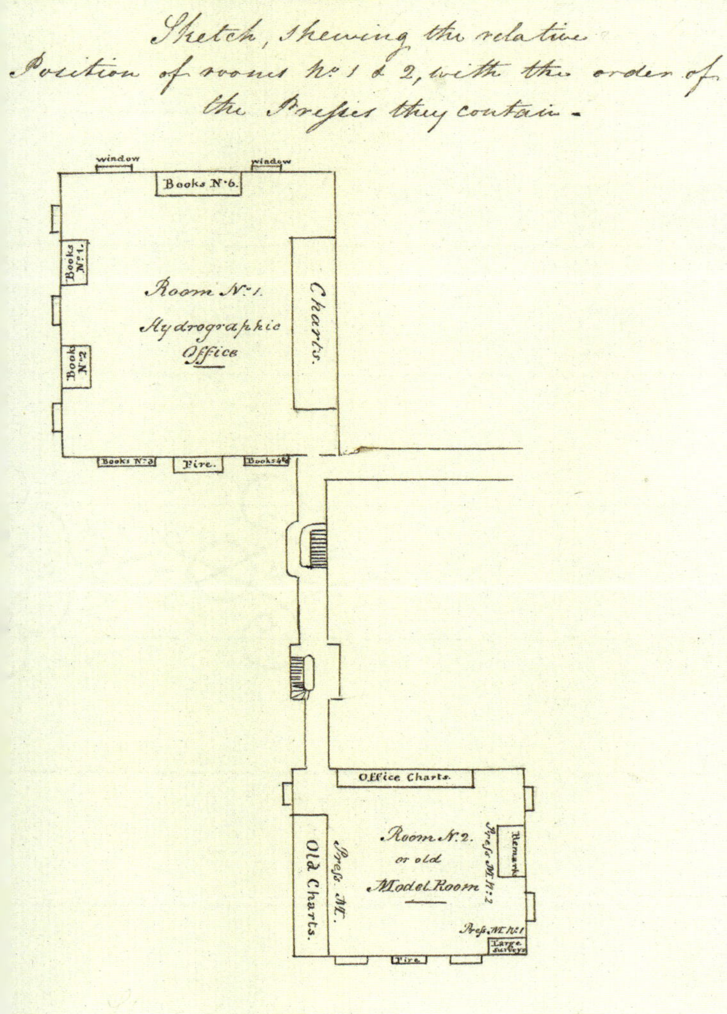

A sketch, dating from the early 1820s, shows the arrangements in the Hydrographer's attic offices in the Admiralty Building.

the impact of revolution. His spies kept a close watch on the enemy ports. His background of naval service as clerk, purser, and Admiral's secretary at Plymouth ensured that he shared with the three seamen on the Board a clear mental picture of the geography and weather off Brest whereas the three civilian Commissioners had no such first-hand knowledge.[4]

The Board was endeavouring to exert much tighter strategic control. Logistic arrangements had been made to allow the Channel Fleet to base itself at Plymouth and Torbay, rather than Spithead.[5] Now the focus was on potential measures to tighten the foothold off the French coast where enterprising commanders of cruising vessels had highlighted the possibility of strangling the passage of war supplies to the French fleet. Was it indeed possible to launch an amphibious operation to join Royalist insurgents and imperil the Combined Fleet in its very base? For Brest had one further drawback for the French: it was isolated by poor road communications at the extremity of one of the regions which was least loyal to the Republic. A series of Royalist risings had prompted the stationing of a British frigate squadron in Quiberon Bay, and these vessels maintained clandestine traffic with the dissident elements.[6] The First Lord was actively assessing the option of intervention, which would satisfy the most strident voices calling for action, but extremely good intelligence of enemy defences would be needed to support the planning.

The fleet was required to assist in this intelligence-gathering by rendering illustrated reports and plans. These, with the other navigational records which sea officers were under an obligation to deposit at the Admiralty, were stowed in attic rooms where skylights and light wells gave the best conditions in which to peruse them in the gloom of the capital. This repository would have been the first resort in the search which Nepean now ordered for material which could provide a picture of the theatre of operation of the blockading squadrons. As recently as 1795 Alexander Dalrymple, partly through Nepean's influence, had been installed there as the first Hydrographer to the Admiralty. By 1799 he had an assistant, two draughtsmen, three engravers and a copperplate printer. Also jammed into his attic were naval officers whom the Admiralty grudgingly permitted to make fair

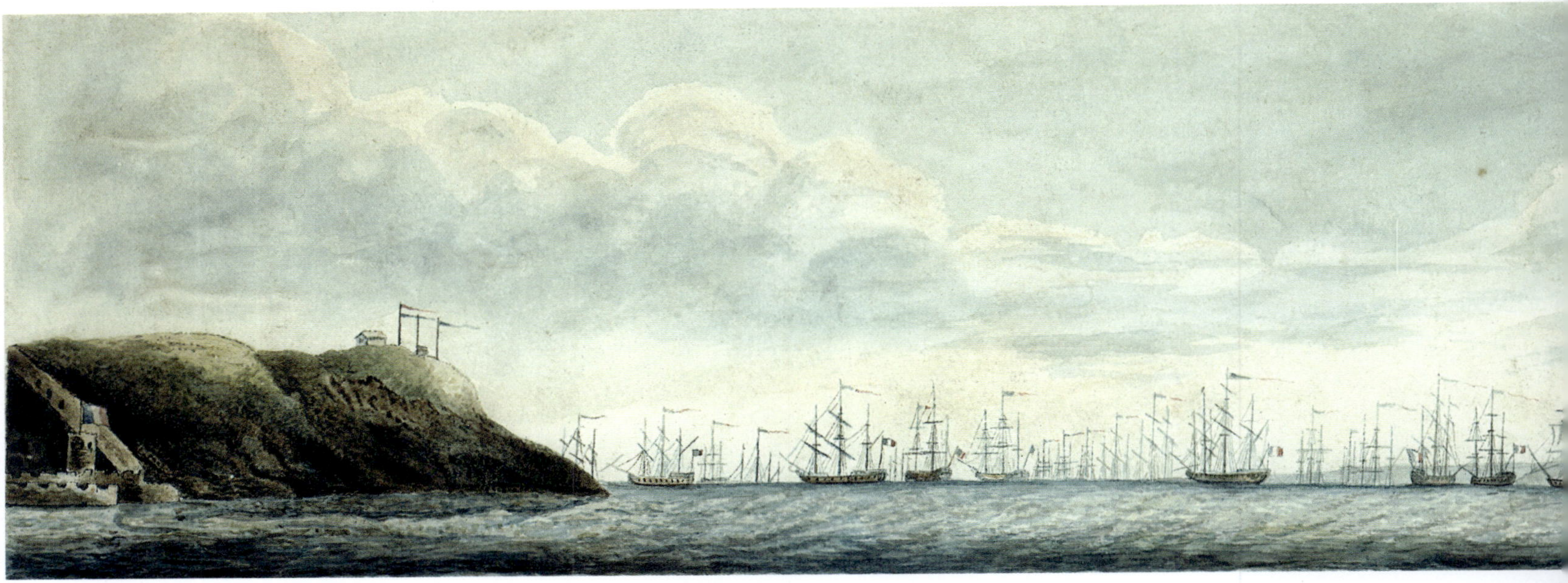

copies of their surveys. The whole arrangement was run most parsimoniously. Dalrymple's remit was 'to take charge and custody' of the material in the attics, and 'to select and compile' information which might assist war planning and improve navigation. Once he had persuaded the Board of the utility of a new proof chart, they would apply to the Navy Board to commission its production by a commercial chart-maker. Dalrymple brought with him to Whitehall a great collection of surveys of eastern waters amassed during his previous service as Hydrographer to the East India Company. He was now engaged in hunting down surveys made in other parts of the world, as well as some plans of Home Waters which, despite the fact that they had been commissioned by the Admiralty, had never been rendered to the office.[7]

As Dalrymple and his assistant John Walker made their search, they recalled one or two images which had been copied in 1798[8] but otherwise there was little to offer.[9] So, on 9 September 1799, Nepean composed a letter to Lord Bridport:

A view of le Goulet held in the Admiralty Hydrographical Office and annotated as copied by John Walker in August 1798. The original artist is unknown. It would appear to have been made from a frigate making a close reconnaissance. It is possible that the unnamed schoolmaster (mentioned in Nepean's letter to Lord Bridport) serving in the *Sans Pareil*, a large flagship, embarked in the cruiser to get a closer view of the enemy.

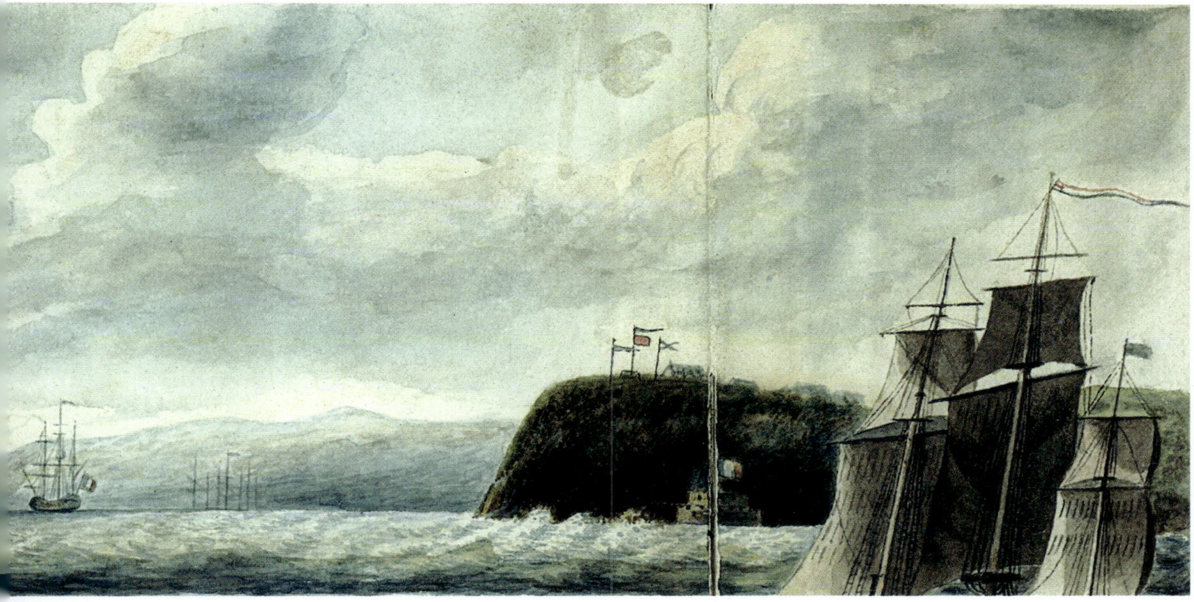

I have engaged Mr Serres, the marine painter whose father I dare say your Lordship well remembers, to go out in one of the ships from Plymouth for the purpose of taking views of Brest and the environs and to continue at sea during your present cruise. It is somewhat extraordinary that, excepting a sketch taken by the schoolmaster of the Sans Pareil there is not one view of that port or of any part of the coast in its vicinity to be found in this or any other of the public offices, though every possible search has been made, and it is not new for your Lordship to know that views of that description give landsmen a better idea than the best constructed charts. I flatter myself that your Lordship will receive Mr Serres kindly and that you will give him every opportunity of performing the service required of him by putting him on board the frigates and other ships you may order to reconnoitre and the more extended his views are along the coast the better. I am to give him a large sum for this purpose.[9]

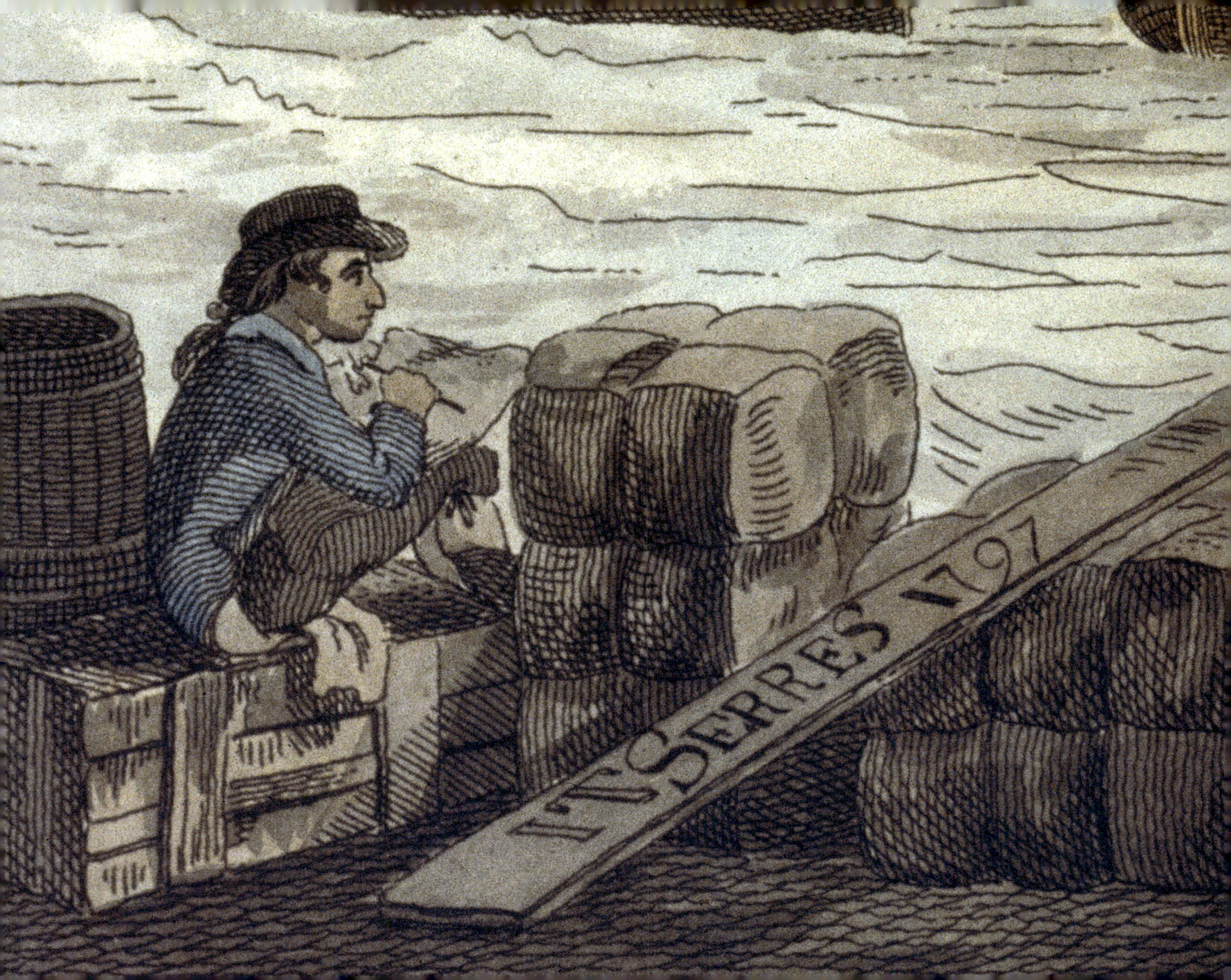
I T SERRES 1797

CHAPTER TWO

A wartime commission

A mile from Whitehall, at 81 Wimpole Street in the expanding and very fashionable residential district of Marylebone, John Thomas Serres, 40-year-old artist and drawing instructor, had watched the dreary summer blend into autumn. His circumstances matched the weather, for he was trapped in an unhappy marriage, and there can be little doubt that the Admiralty's commission represented a luring prospect. He would not be the first of his family to seek solace in this way. Family tradition held that his father Dominic, a native of Gascony, had escaped either from an ecclesiastical career or unrequited love by crossing the border into Spain in search of adventure at sea. The 23-year-old Dominic had first set foot in England early in the morning of Monday 31 May 1742 when he was marched to Plymouth Prison with the 93 other surviving members of the crew of the Spanish privateer *San Antonio* (14). Despite desperate attempts to escape, their ship had been overhauled and taken by the British frigate *Bideford* (24) in the Western Approaches, some 80 miles west of the Scilly Islands.[10] Stories circulating amongst Dominic Serres' friends suggest that he was subsequently exchanged and resumed his sea career. He is said to have lived for a few years in Havana before falling foul of the British fleet once more and being brought back to England.[11] During his subsequent internment he took up the precarious profession of painting, which is recorded in the registry entry for his marriage in London in 1749. He made one further voyage as Master of a merchantman on a round trip to Havana. His natural skill as a marine draughtsman, enlivened by his experience as a seaman, was noticed, and the Seven Years' War brought the beginnings of extensive naval patronage for commemorative paintings.

Opposite This self-portrait of John Thomas Serres in the corner of a view of Liverpool made in 1797 is the only image of him that has been traced. It shows that he inherited the strong features and compact frame of his father, Dominic Serres, whose eminence in London society ensured that he was well recorded by his fellow artists. A surviving engraved portrait of J.T. Serres' elder daughter Lavinia, who was born at this time and baptised in St Nicholas' Church on the waterfront, shows that she in turn inherited the aquiline Serres nose.

Although he was often referred to as 'the Gascon', Dominic Serres was an accomplished linguist who quickly spoke fluent English. He was high-spirited, convivial, and a popular figure in the artistic community of the capital, while being equally at home in naval circles. Surviving correspondence suggests that John, who was born in 1759, grew up in a happy and prosperous family. His elder sisters were introduced to society each year at Bath, and their mother appears to have had firm views on suitable marriages for them. The marine painter John Cleveley the younger courted John's favourite sister Sally in vain throughout his short life. Although father Serres assisted his younger son and namesake to try out a naval career, he does not seem to have deterred the talented John from following in his footsteps as an artist. He may, however, have detected an element of fecklessness and he schooled the young man to stand on his own feet financially. When John set his heart on a Grand Tour, he had to fund his travels by selling a substantial art collection. Armed with introductions, and blessed with his father's gift for languages, John set off in 1789 for what should have been a rich and profitable exercise. He was much taken with Italy and quickly picked up the language, with which he larded his happy letters home, frequently signing off as 'Giovanni'. However, a shadow soon fell across the happy scene.[12]

Amongst John's private pupils was a young lady, twelve years his junior, called Olive Wilmot.[13] She appears to have set her eyes on her tutor and to have insinuated herself into the Serres family. By the time John set off on his travels he had fallen for her charms. Olive was soon importuning him to return, using letters to Sally to reinforce her efforts. Despite the opposition of his family, John returned to England and married the under-age Olive by special licence in September 1791. Olive's own guardian shared the general misgivings and declared: 'Serres, she is now your wife; but mind me – keep her employed or she will be plotting mischief.'[14] These words were to prove prophetic. Olive, who had already begun to make a mark on London society, was to prove manipulative, extravagant, and devoid of domestic and maternal instincts. A wistful letter to Sally in 1797, urging that 'we must submit to be buoyed up alternately by hope and despair and snatch at happiness', speaks volumes of the impact of Olive's conduct on her generous if impulsive and trusting husband, who would never lose his first love, even when his wife tormented him with a series of affairs. Now he was writing from Liverpool, where perhaps he had hoped to remove Olive from the temptations of the capital. He was also doting on a new-born daughter Lavinia, and working hard on five views of the Merseyside scene.[15]

However, his best prospects undoubtedly lay in London. His father had been a founder member of the Royal Academy and in 1792 was appointed its Librarian. In 1780 Dominic had received the honorary appointment of Marine Painter to George III and was clearly well-placed to seek further patronage for other members of his family. John had been appointed Marine Painter to the Duke of Clarence in 1790, having made his reputation as Master of Drawing at the Marine School, Paradise Row, Chelsea. Dominic died in 1793, and on 20 November the President of the Royal Academy wrote to John Serres to inform him that it was the King's pleasure that 'you take the Title of Marine Painter to His Majesty, in succession to the same Title first granted by His Majesty to your late worthy Father.'[16] The royal appointment was strictly honorific and unremunerated, and it does not appear to have led to any official commissions even though the practice of employing artists ashore was well established in both the French and British naval administrations.[17] In France, Claude-Joseph Vernet, counterpart and correspondent of Dominic Serres, had been awarded a substantial royal commission in Louis XV's reign to produce a series of large topographical paintings of major military and commercial ports. He followed an official itinerary, and was required to report back from each port with details of the views he had chosen. He had covered ten ports before funding dried up at the close of the Seven Years' War.[18] Following the Revolution, Jean-Francois Huë was commissioned to continue the project. Meanwhile, in England Joseph Farrington and Nicholas Pocock were commissioned to produce large panoramas of the main naval bases.[19] By contrast, J. T. Serres' views of Liverpool and Merseyside were commercial ventures, dedicated to noble patrons, citing his honorary appointments to the Royal Family to underline his credentials.[20]

His employment in the Marine School at Chelsea did reflect the importance which was placed on draughtsmanship as part of a sea officer's education. A drawing master had

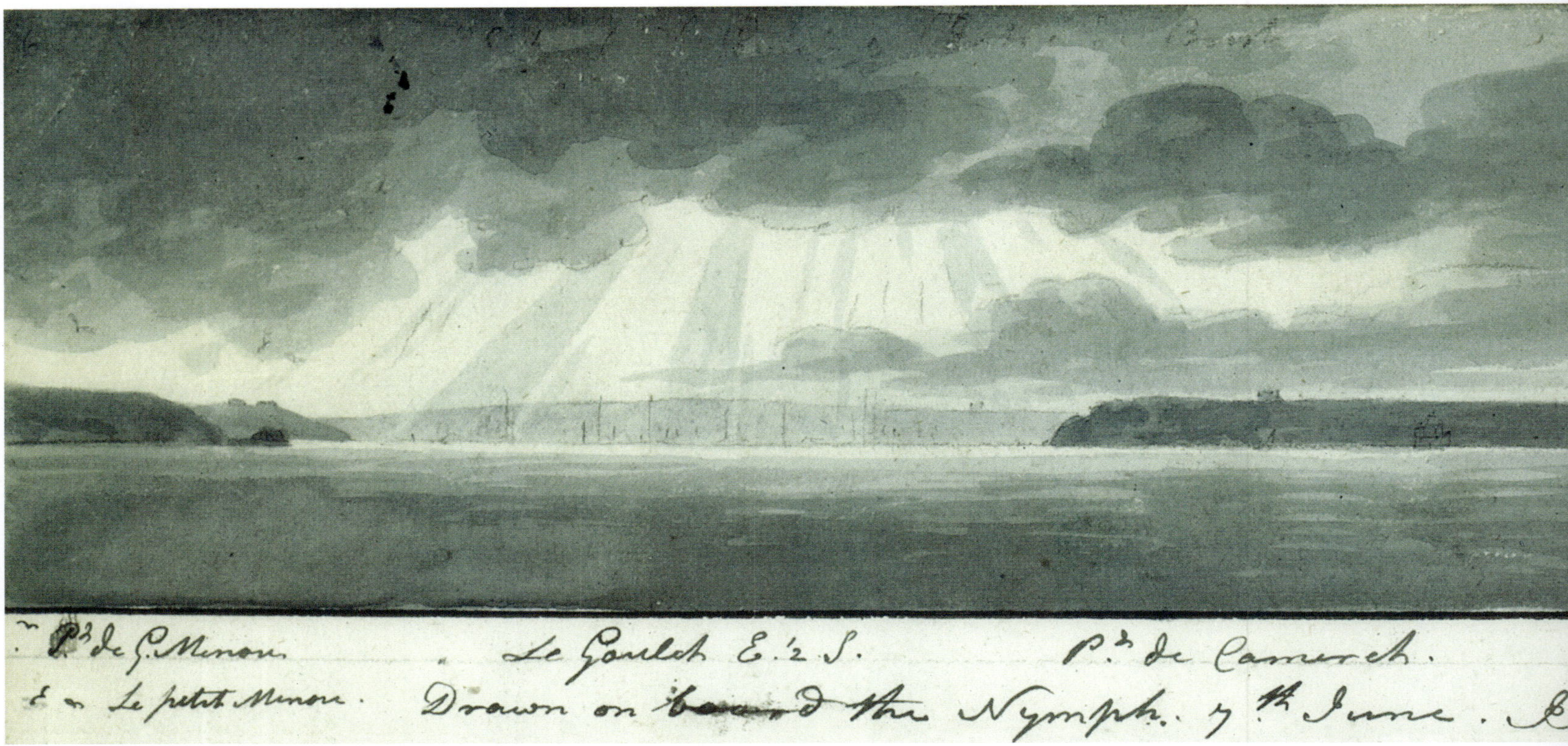

been included in the establishment of the Naval Academy in Portsmouth when it was opened in 1733. Admiralty instructions for the rendering of reports on enemy coasts and fortifications noted that 'where there shall be Artists on board sufficiently qualified, you are to add Drafts or Plans, for the better Illustration of the above particulars with proper References and Explanations.'[21] The artists referred to were officers or ratings with an aptitude for the task. Up to this time the employment of professional artists in the fleet had been confined to the voyages of exploration, notably the second and third voyages of Captain James Cook. These artists had produced many drawings specifically for navigational purposes and also tutored junior officers in the necessary skills. The primary purpose of these

One of J.T. Serres' coastal views of the entrance to Brest, approved by the ship's Master. The bearing of le Goulet at the time the sketch was made is recorded carefully. Serres cleverly draws attention to the strategic sector with the sun's rays, which break through the clouds directly over the opening in the coast.

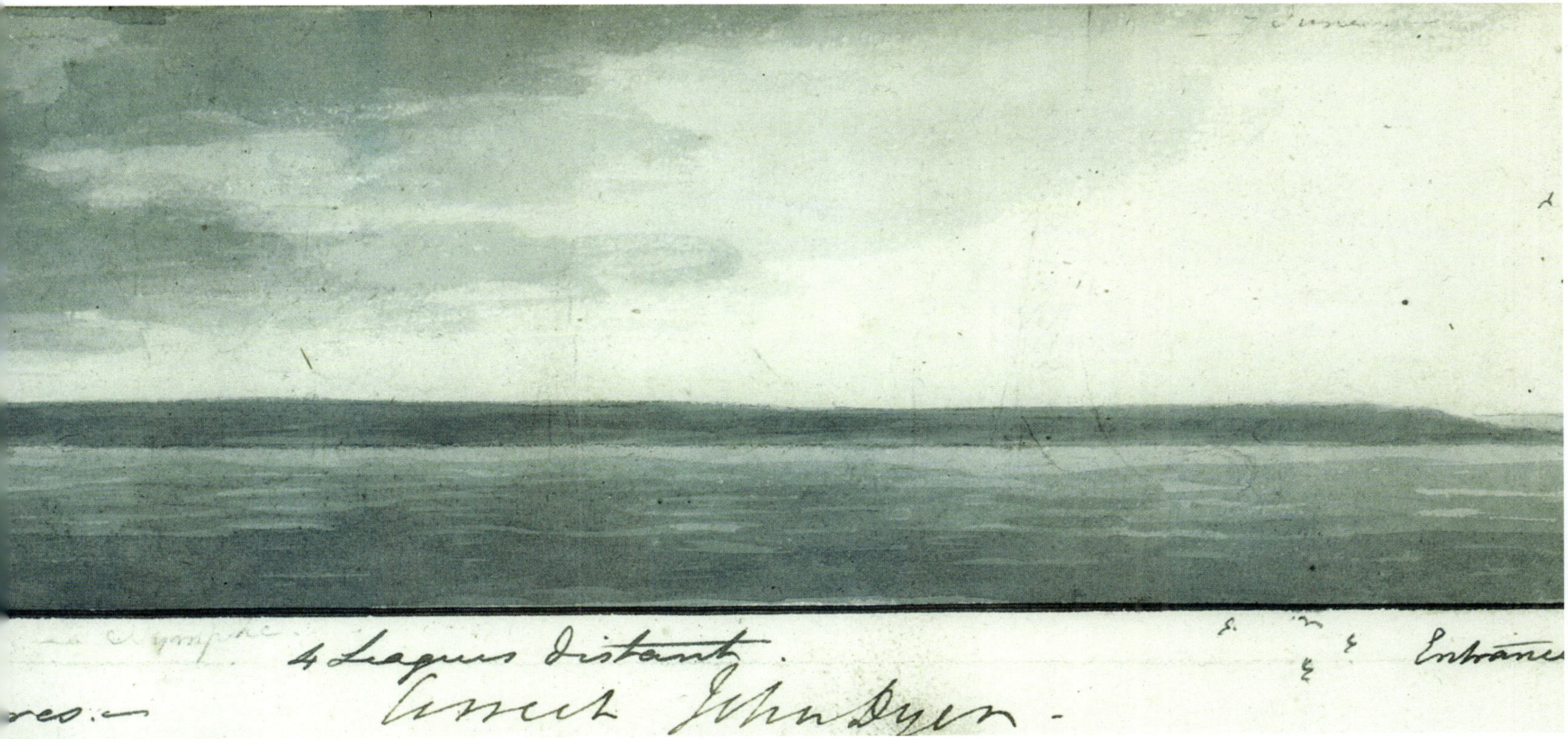

largely panoramic profiles was to assist a mariner to make a landfall on an unfamiliar coast. Following the wreck of a warship in the Mediterranean because of misidentification of a headland, Dalrymple remarked 'it . . . points out how expedient it is for views to be taken of all lands seen'.[22] To be of true worth to the navigator they had to be based on careful angular measurement between landmarks on the profile, and skill was also needed to apply an exaggeration to the vertical scale and to the representation of conspicuous objects to permit more detail to be shown. Too much artistic licence, however, particularly to match the expectation of prevailing taste, would detract from the faithful image which the seaman required.[23]

The value of up-to-date coastal views during hostilities, particularly to those charged with the political direction of the war, is clear. Although Spencer was accused by some Cabinet colleagues of being unduly deferential to the naval members of the Board, he and Nepean were firmly in control of the bulk of the correspondence of the Admiralty, and the plan to send out Serres appears to have originated with them.[24] The artist may have lobbied and influenced the extent of his work, for subsequently the Commander-in-Chief wrote to Nepean: 'Serres writes me that it was settled with Lord Spencer and you he should be sent along the Coasts of France, Spain & Portugal as far to the Southward as Cape St Vincent . . .'[25] However, the only contemporary correspondence from him in the Admiralty records relates to a request for information to allow him to work up a sketch of the Bay of Naples, made during his Grand Tour, so that it could be published as a depiction of the recent return of the Neapolitan court to the capital. His thoughts appear to have remained firmly on commercial matters rather than war service up until this point.[26]

Were there other motives for his despatch to the Breton coast? Is he the agent named in a letter from Henry Dundas, Secretary of State for War, to Lord Spencer, on 18 September 1799? The editor of the First Lord's papers tentatively suggested the identity of a trusted source in the following passage: 'Our information from Serres [?] with regard to everything relative to Brest has been so accurate during the whole of this war that I am strongly impressed with a notion that through that channel is the most certain and safest way of getting all the information to be expected.'[27] The Serres family retained some links with France, where John and his father had visited Vernet in 1785. Four years later, John began his Grand Tour in Paris, where he paid a ritual visit to the ruins of the Bastille. At this time Dominic Serres was helping *émigrés* who had fled to England.[28] But neither the personality of J. T. Serres nor the tenor of his correspondence suggest any involvement in clandestine work. Nepean was an experienced 'spy master' who had taken his agents with him when he moved with Dundas from the Home Office to the Department of War and the Colonies. His network was still exploited by both those departments when he subsequently moved to the Admiralty. There is no record of Serres in Nepean's meticulous record of secret service outlays, nor does the tone of his references to Serres suggest any involvement in such work.[29]

There seems little doubt, however, that the artist would commend himself to Spencer and Nepean. As the Secretary's letter indicated, the elder Serres' reputation opened doors to an influential circle, including prominent naval figures. John had also been given a good education and had inherited a charming manner and a gift for languages. His main failing was a not uncommon one in his day: a friend described him as one of those 'who always calculated, at least with respect to his pecuniary affairs, that the deficiencies of the present day would be supplied by the morrow'. Indeed, perhaps elated by the generous additional income from Nepean's commission, he was to leave at least one promissory note to fall due during his absence.[30] By the end of his life he had a poor reputation in business, and was said to promise much but to be slow to deliver. However, his commitment to his profession, and his love of the maritime scene were never in doubt. It would not be surprising if sea service in the fleet held great attractions for a man who had little taste for the gay life of London society and who found solace by immersing himself in his painting. His technical preparation by his seaman father had been thorough, and he was well qualified for the opportunity which now presented itself to use his skills in the service of his country. He seized it with alacrity.[31]

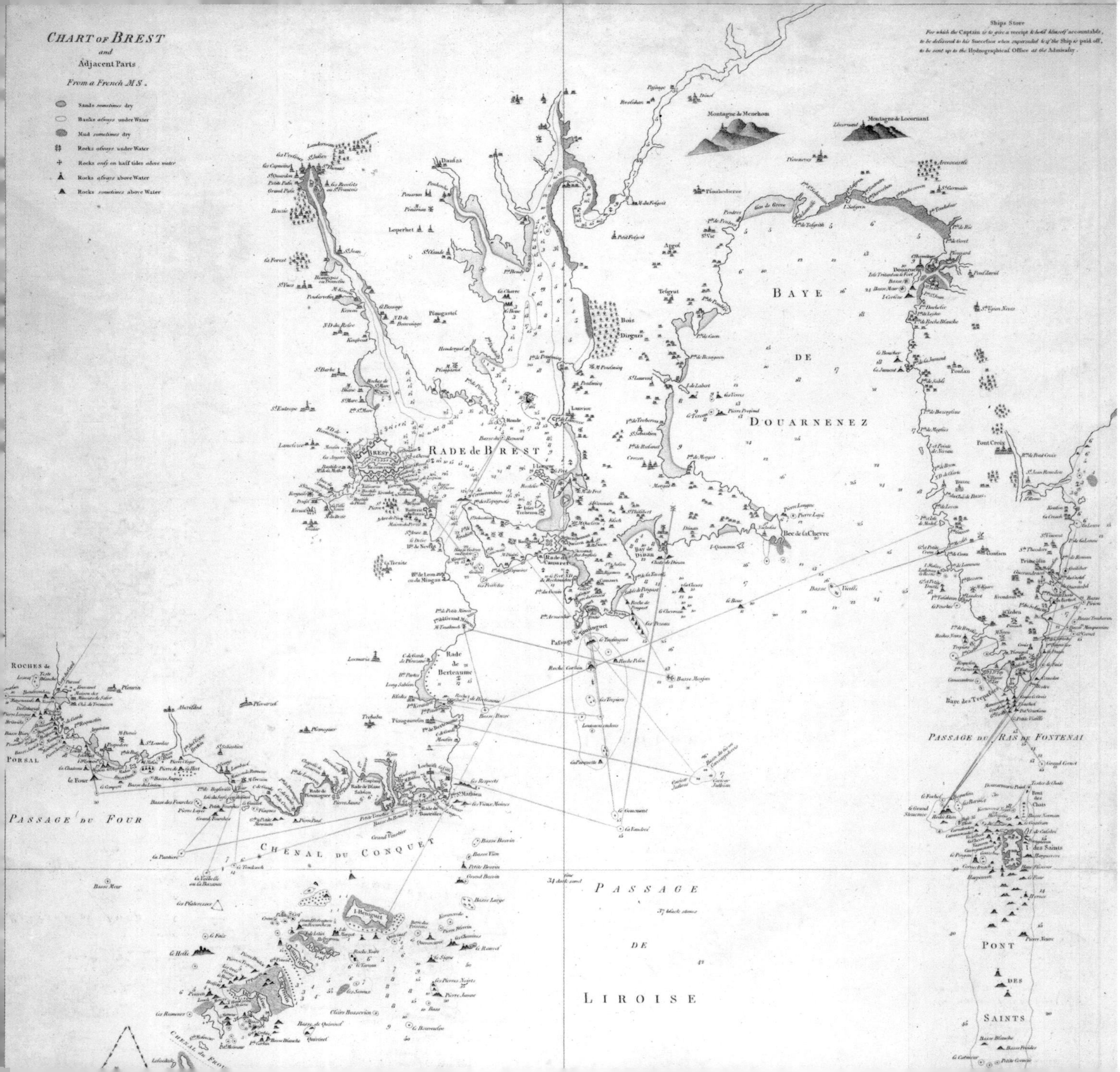
CHART OF BREST
and
Adjacent Parts
From a French MS.
Sands sometimes dry
Banks always under Water
Mud sometimes dry
Rocks always under Water
Rocks only on half tides above water
Rocks always above Water
Rocks sometimes above Water
Ships Store
For which the Captain is to give a receipt & hold himself accountable,
to be delivered to his Successor when superseded & if the Ship is paid off,
to be sent up to the Hydrographical Office at the Admiralty.
Montagne de Menehom
Montagne de Locornant
RADE de BREST
BREST
BAYE DE DOUARNENEZ
Bec de la Chevre
Bay de Dinan
Rade de Camaret
Rade de Berteaume
Baye des Trepassés
PASSAGE DU RAS DE FONTENAI
ROCHES de PORSAL
PASSAGE DU FOUR
CHENAL DU CONQUET
PASSAGE DE LIROISE
PONT DES SAINTS
I. des Saints
Pont Croix
Landerneau
Daulas
Douarnenez
Le Four
I. Beniguet

CHAPTER THREE

An artist joins the fleet

Opposite The first chart of the approaches to Brest to be published by the Hydrographer, in 1803, was based on a French manuscript of unknown provenance and which does not appear to have survived. The orientation, with east upwards, is particularly striking and may have been selected with the perspective of the blockading squadrons in mind. The chart is annotated with the firm warning: 'Ships Store. For which the Captain is to give a receipt and hold himself accountable – to be delivered to his successor when superseded and if the ship is paid off, to be sent up to the Hydrographical Office at the Admiralty.'

In fact, Serres had not even waited for his written commission. By the time Nepean dictated his letter to Lord Bridport, the artist had already embarked in the flagship *Royal George*. He had been preceded by the First Lord himself, who had paid a short visit a few days earlier to take advantage of a rare opportunity to see the large and 'very fine fleet' which the Commander-in-Chief Lord Bridport had been gathering in Torbay since 2 July, after the return of the Combined Franco-Spanish Fleet to Brest.[32] Intelligence from the frigates stationed off that port was suggesting that enemy units were growing bolder in their movements, especially to escort in much-needed supplies, and Spencer's naval colleagues were increasing the pressure on Bridport to put to sea as soon as his stores were complete. On 1 September, with the last victuals transferred from a stores lighter from Plymouth, the signal was hoisted to prepare for sea. Now Serres made the short boat journey from Brixham Quay to the great 100-gun ship in the designated anchorage for line-of-battle ships in the centre of the bay.[33] At 5 p.m. the fleet weighed anchor and sailed.[34]

The wind was variable and light, coming from the NNE and east. The next day, off the Eddystone, more ships joined company, and during the following 24 hours the fleet straggled towards the French coast. On the afternoon of 3 September, the island of Ushant with its prominent lighthouse, the turning point off the tip of the Brittany peninsula, was sighted from the masthead. Serres must have shared the excitement as they rounded the island and began to sight the British frigates inshore. One of them, thought to be the *Triton* (32), was chasing a cutter. Bridport was admired in the fleet for taking his flagship far into the hazardous coastal waters.[35] Now he was clearly determined to make a personal estimate of

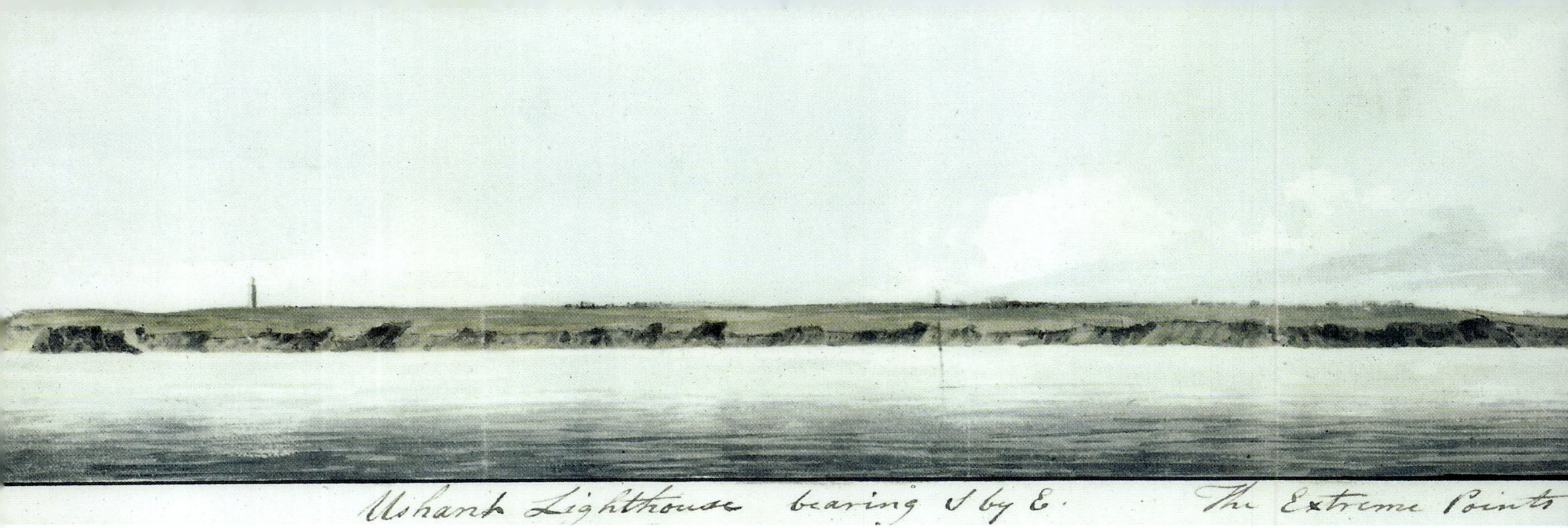

the situation, as well as to make contact with his advanced force, and he closed to within sight of the north arm of the entrance to Brest and the extensive islands and shoals extending westwards to Ushant. The ship's logs record that a number of small vessels were seen 'burning on the shore, set on fire by the frigates'.[36]

Serres got down to work, and there are five views dated 1799 in the collection which he subsequently passed to the Admiralty.[37] Four of them are classic views made to assist the mariner to make a landfall. Two,[38] labelled with compass bearings of the lighthouse, depict Ushant and nearby islets with a 74-gun ship and a frigate in the foreground, manoeuvring in the light airs (see above and p. 42). A third[39] adopts an artistic device whereby five panoramas of the island from different points of the compass are enclosed within a scroll (see p. 110). All these views were made from the main fleet's normal station in the outer part of the Iroise. Here the frigates and smaller vessels of the inshore force would come and go, their captains reporting to the Admiral. When westerly gales set in, the main fleet would move out into the Channel, and on 20 September it was forced back to anchor in Torbay, where it remained for a whole month. The Muster Book of the

When J. T. Serres first arrived off Ushant in the flagship *Royal George*, the winds were light, and this 74-gun ship is depicted with main topgallant studding sails set.

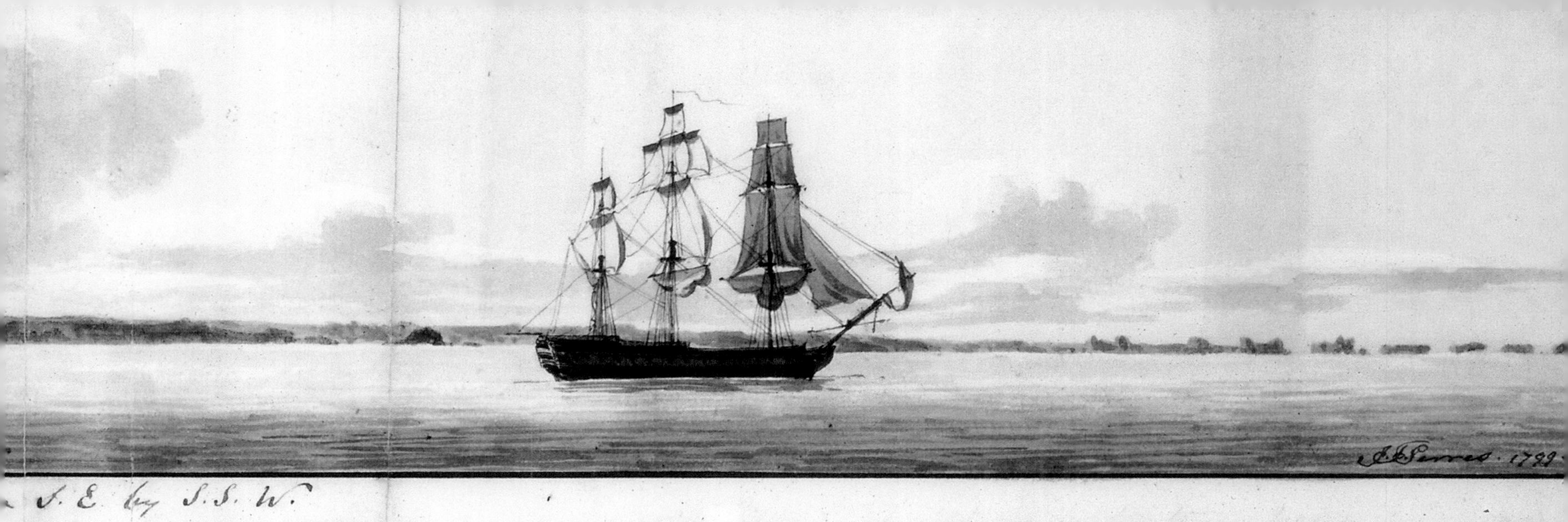

Royal George shows the number of supernumeraries borne for victuals dropping sharply at this time, and it may be that Serres went ashore during this period, escaping the round of the ship's routine in which he could only be an observer: punishments for drunkenness, sometimes on spirits smuggled from ashore; the embarkation of stores; exercise of the great guns, enlivened by the firing of volleys of small arms. There is certainly no surviving evidence that he used the time to record his surroundings, though he may well have taken sketches of the ships to use in future publications.

On the 24 October the wind swung back into the east, and at 6.30 a.m. the flagship made the signal to weigh, unmoored and sailed. Two days later John Douglas, the Master, recorded 'set fore sail standing in towards Brest. Saw several ships getting underway, working in. At 11 made the signal and tacked, up fore sail . . . Fresh breezes and clear. All the Fleet in company. Several ships looking into Brest water.'[40] A three-point fix placed the *Royal George* some 4 leagues off the entrance to Brest. It was at this moment that Serres made a quick sketch of the coast which he was to see at much closer quarters at a later date (see p. 30). Overall it is clear that the busy master of a flagship had little time to give to the

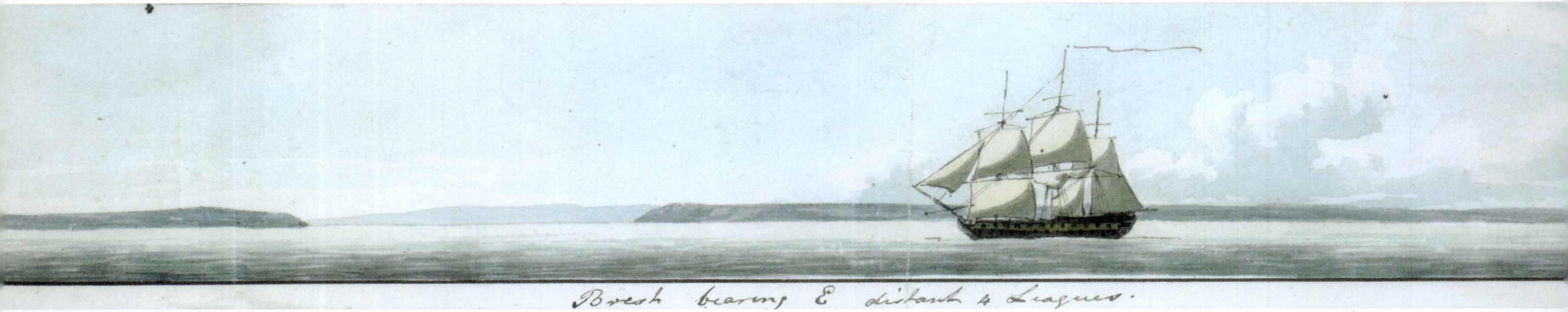

artist passenger, and there is a marked contrast between these first efforts of Serres and the sketches which he produced as soon as he returned in the following year.

The fifth sketch with a date of 1799 presents a mystery. It purports to have been made in the very mouth of the narrow entrance to Brest Roads (see p. 34). It is annotated in French, with some idiosyncratic spelling. However, despite the instructions from the Admiralty, there is no indication that Serres was transferred to any of the frigates and smaller vessels until 31 October. On that day the fleet was on station in the southern part of the Iroise, from where a close eye could be kept out for any supply vessels moving up from the southwards in the inshore waters. At 1 p.m. Captain Charles Cunningham of the *Clyde* (38) was summoned onboard the flagship, and Serres returned with him to the frigate. Cunningham was senior officer of the inshore squadron at this time, and the *Clyde*'s log records close reconnaissance of Brest on 18 and 25 October and 19 and 23 November, but not during Serres' time onboard. Indeed, the beginning of what was to be a very fruitful association was inauspicious. Strong gales set in on 1 November with thick weather and the fleet was driven back to the English coast, experiencing a heavy swell. The *Clyde*, which had been left with the *Fisgard* (38) to keep a watch off Brest,[41] was also driven off. Her first landfall was Pendennis Castle. On 6 November she anchored in Plymouth Sound, from whence Cunningham wrote to Bridport: 'Nothing but the improbability of getting to the Westward with the present weather and such as is to be expected from appearance,

J.T. Serres' sketch of his first sighting of the entrance to Brest is annotated with the bearing and distance which the Master, John Douglas, had computed and recorded in his log.

would have induced me to put into port at this time, and I shall seize the first opportunity of a suitable wind to return to my station.'[42] The gales continued until 15 November, and it was not until the following day that the *Clyde* resumed her vigil off Brest. Serres was not onboard, for he had gone ashore the day after the frigate's arrival in Plymouth.

It seems clear, however, that he had begun to discuss his task with Cunningham, who had a lively interest in the production of hydrographic information. Though his commission was intended to assist the strategic planners in Whitehall, Serres' practical companions were determined to benefit as well. Their task regularly took them over the landfall threshold into coastal waters where danger lurked. To keep clear of rocks and shoals, the mariner might be assisted by natural or man-made marks and transits, where these were available. Terrestrial or floating aids to navigation could assist him to 'get his bearings', but they were vulnerable to weather damage and might be removed in time of war. 'Clearing' compass bearings of prominent objects could keep him a safe distance from danger, provided that he was supplied with a reliable instrument for which he knew the appropriate corrections. In the waters of north-west Europe where thick weather and low visibility were commonplace, the lead-line was the most important equipment. Depths and nature of the seabed in the Channel form one of the earliest known written records of navigational information for the mariner. However, the lead would not save him from an unknown and unmarked rock or shoal which was steep-to all round.

There is general agreement that the chart was as little favoured by north-west European seafarers as it was by Nepean's landsmen of the Admiralty Board. The strong tidal streams and currents of the region are usually cited as one factor. They certainly complicated the process of dead reckoning, i.e. the estimation of track made good with allowance for leeway and water flow. A want of knowledge of the rates of tidal streams recurs frequently as an extenuating factor in records of courts martial of the period. Many mariners favoured a pilot book which encapsulated the oral record of marks and soundings, and which might include some primitive panoramic coastal silhouettes.[43] Surviving records and illustrations suggest that coastal charts were most often rolled and stowed, or bound in atlases. They were another source to be consulted for soundings, coastal views, leading lines and clearing bearings, rather than forming a plotting surface on which the navigator would record position and project a course to follow. It was not till 1808 that Captains Columbine and Hurd of the Admiralty Chart Committee urged that single charts should be mounted on coarse brown linen and stowed in boxes to facilitate their use.[44]

In the fleet which Serres joined in the autumn of 1799, navigational products were treated as just another item of naval stores, purchased and issued by the Navy Board from the available stock of private publishers. Commanding officers and masters were responsible for identifying the material they needed. Those like Cunningham with a more acute interest would often purchase charts and publications on their own initiative. Dalrymple's duties as Hydrographer extended beyond the assessment of the original material in the Admiralty's possession to the appraisal of the commercial charts. He later complained that this inspection process was bedevilled by the failure of many English cartographers to provide a Memoir on the chart describing its construction. He also lamented the absence of a requirement for official examination of charts together with the survey data on which they were based. It was to be some years, however, before Dalrymple's stringent standards were to benefit the fleet with the publication of accurate, detailed charts, issued in practical single sheets. The private publishers continued to reprint general charts in 'Pilots' which appeared to offer economical and comprehensive coverage. One gifted hydrographic surveyor lamented that when he first went to the Mediterranean only a portion of the many extant surveys were known to the Royal Navy, '. . . and the miserable charts of Heather, Norie, Blachford, and other ship-chandlers, were officially used in our ships of war'.[45] The unsatisfactory provision of navigational guidance for the close blockade of the French coast had long been especially notorious. During the Seven Years' War an Admiralty circular had noted that 'The King's Service has suffered very much . . . for want of due information and knowledge of harbours, roads and accessible places on the coast of France', and instructed that captains and masters were to keep a book of sketches with pertinent hydrographical information.[46] Admiral Hawke, who was already demanding such information from his squadron off Brest, attributed the loss of the two Royal Navy ships wrecked during the Battle of Quiberon Bay to the deficient arrangements for supply of charts and navigational publications to the fleet.[47] Admirals Howe and Kempenfelt also urged the establishment of an effective hydrographic organisation. At a later date Admiral Collingwood wrote of '. . . tides and rocks, which have more danger in them than a battle once a week'. Weather and grounding continued to account for more losses than enemy action.[48]

There is little coverage of coastal pilotage in eighteenth-century manuals.[49] The French Academician Pierre Bouguer noted how two bearings taken with a compass, or a bearing and a horizontal sextant angle, could be used to plot position on a chart. Such compass cross-bearings are regularly recorded in the logs of the vessels employed on the Brest blockade; but only for anchorages, and for flagships when marking important manoeuvres such as an alteration away from the point of closest approach to land, is there a third bearing. When the third bearing line in such a fix does not pass through the same intersection as the first two, leaving a triangle, known to navigators as a 'cocked-hat', one source of the misclosure is unknown compass error. At this date the Navy Board and Royal Dockyards were only just awakening to the need to employ copper nails and fixtures in the vicinity of the steering compasses. The cumbersome bearing compasses of the day were contained in wooden boxes with carrying handles and glass windows with a vertical hair sight, and they were moved to positions around the ship where a line of sight could be obtained clear of sails and rigging. They were principally designed for the measurement of the azimuth of a heavenly body and priority was given to vessels proceeding overseas, especially on scientific voyages. In the majority of vessels it was necessary to unship one of the binnacle compasses from the helmsman's position to obtain a bearing. In the first volume of the *Naval Chronicle*, published in 1799, Joseph Whidbey, Master Attendant at Sheerness Dockyard, who had extensive experience as the master of Captain George Vancouver's exploring ship *Discovery*, had noted the wide variation in readings depending on the amount of iron in different parts of a ship.[50] Ignorance of the deviation error induced by iron in the ship's structure contributed to at least one grounding during the long Brest blockade.[51] It would need significant advances in

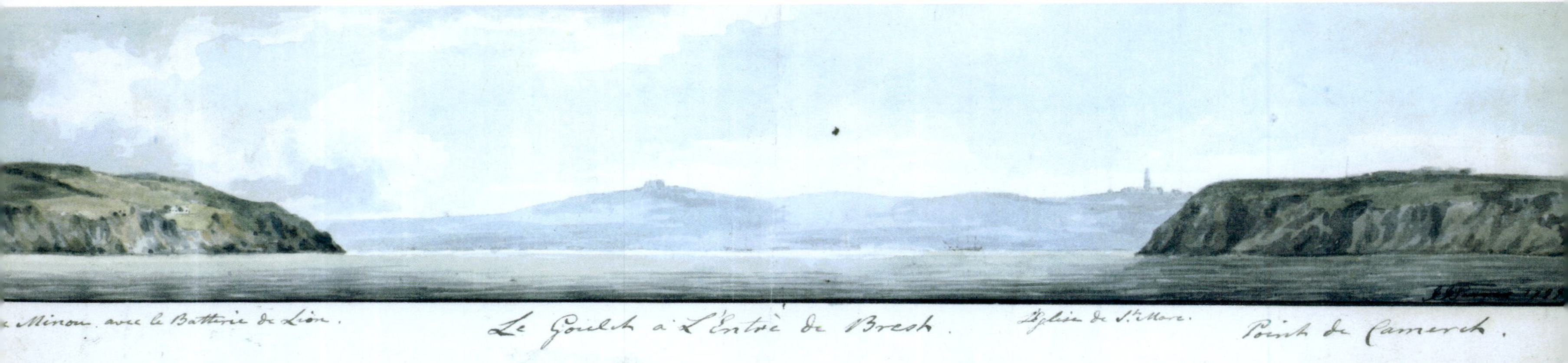

compass theory and the technology of instrument manufacture before the chart could be used to plot a continuous record of past and projected movement as became the drill in the fast power-driven warships of the late nineteenth century. In Serres' day it would seem that, as in many merchant vessels right up to the present, no graphic record was maintained, and coastal navigation was done by a loose form of visual pilotage.

This practice of visual pilotage is illustrated in Serres' mysterious 1799 view of le Goulet, which almost certainly represents a test piece produced from information dictated by Cunningham together with the embarked Breton pilot, Yves Cormat.[52] It includes St Marc's church in Brest as a leading mark. If a navigator kept the church just in sight round the headland he would stay in the channel to the south of the Plateau des Fillettes which obstructs the middle of le Goulet. The view is evidence that, though their first cruise had been a short one, Cunningham had recognised the contribution which the official artist could make and had begun to instil in Serres the importance of close teamwork with the ship's navigation team. This drill was to pay off when the artist eventually got closer inshore in the smaller vessels of the fleet.

Meanwhile, Serres remained on the books of the *Royal George* and is not recorded as discharged from the flagship until 26 December, some eleven days after she returned

Serres did not get this close to the entrance to Brest Roads in 1799, the date recorded on this sketch. It is almost certainly a rendering of information given to him by the senior officer of the inshore squadron of frigates and his embarked Breton pilot. The spire of St Marc's church in Brest in line with the Pointe de Camaret leads safely through the south passage in le Goulet.

to Spithead after one final period off the French coast. There are no indications that Serres had rejoined the *Royal George* for this final cruise. Indeed, during November, both he and the brilliant young painter William (J.M.W.) Turner, fresh from election as an Associate of the Royal Academy, were negotiating for rented rooms at number 64 Harley Street. Turner, who was notoriously private, made no secret of his unhappiness at the prospect of sharing the house, and it was surmised that he feared frequent descents by Olive Serres from the nearby family home in Wimpole Street. She herself had developed into a competent landscape artist who had already exhibited at the Royal Academy in 1794. Serres would require every ounce of his good and generous nature to reconcile the touchy young man to the arrangements, building on the foundation of common interests and enthusiasm. Both men admired the work of the French-born marine painter Philippe-Jacques de Loutherbourg, who had advised Turner in techniques for his first sea-piece in 1796. De Loutherbourg had been lured to London in the 1770s by lucrative employment as a scenic director at the Drury Lane theatre. In the wake of the Revolution his work, like that of other painters of French origin, fell out of fashion, but he was now emerging as a leading light of the Romantic movement. All in all, with these preoccupations and the winter setting in, Serres' task at sea was better left to the following year.[53]

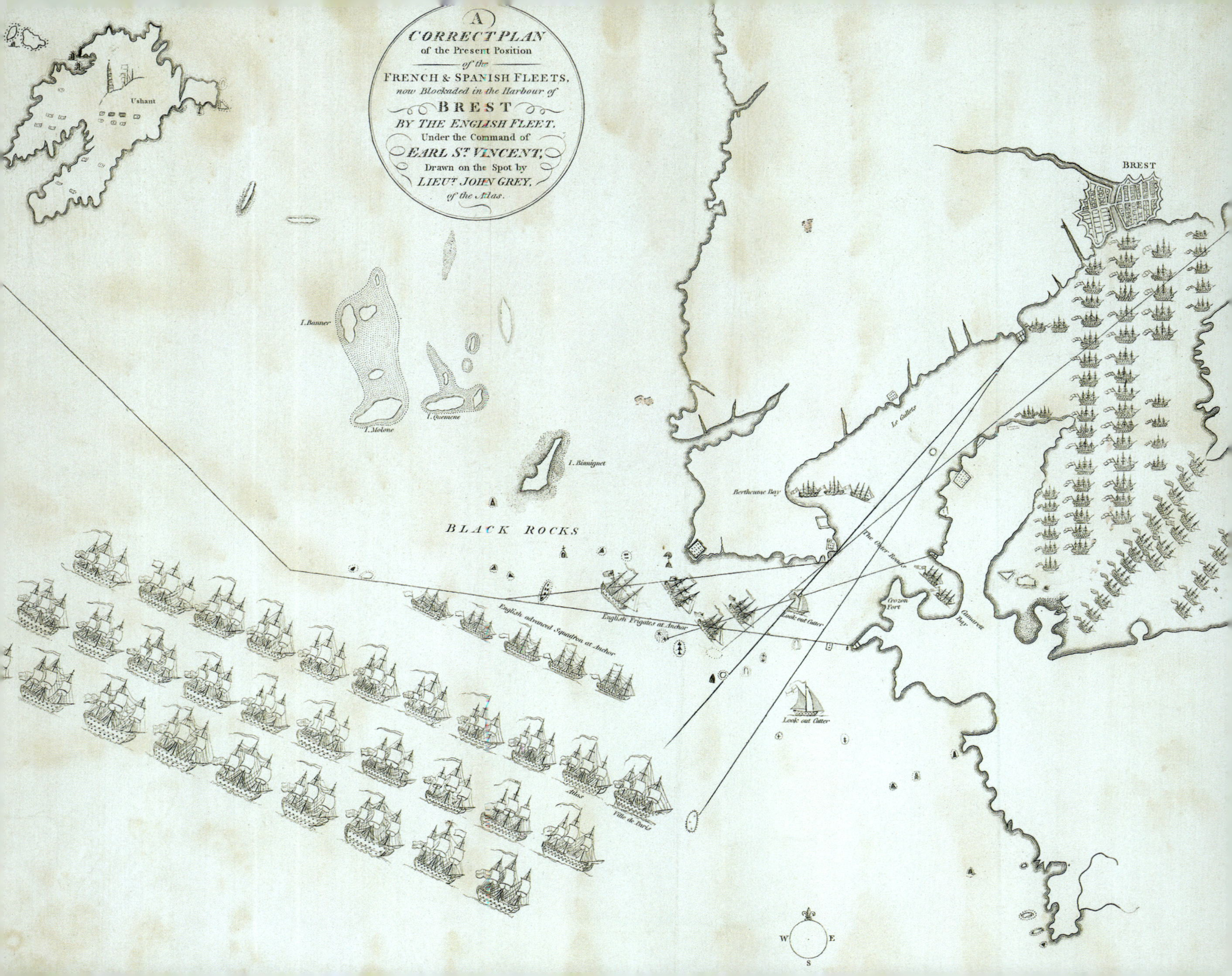
A
CORRECT PLAN
of the Present Position
of the
FRENCH & SPANISH FLEETS,
now Blockaded in the Harbour of
BREST
BY THE ENGLISH FLEET,
Under the Command of
EARL St. VINCENT,
Drawn on the Spot by
LIEUt. JOHN GREY,
of the Atlas.
Ushant
BREST
I. Banner
I. Molone
I. Quemene
I. Binnignet
BLACK ROCKS
Le Gullets
Bertheume Bay
The Outer Roads
Crozon Fort
Camaret Bay
English advanced Squadron at Anchor
English Frigates at Anchor
Look out Cutter
Look out Cutter
Atlas
Ville de Paris
W
E
S

CHAPTER FOUR

The blockade of Brest

While Serres worked to establish harmony in his domestic and business life in London, the Channel Fleet was severely shaken by an event in the very approaches to Brest. On the evening of 15 March 1800, part of the ship's company of the frigate *Danae* mutinied and seized the ship, while it was in pursuit of a convoy in Camaret Bay. The ringleader, one of the captains of the foretop, who had been secretary to Richard Parker, the leader of the mutiny at the Nore (1797), took the ship inshore under the guns of Fort Conquête and surrendered to the corvette which had been escorting the convoy. Opinion was strongly divided as to whether Lord Proby, the young commanding officer, was too lenient or, as Admiral Collingwood concluded, too severe. Earl St Vincent, who took command in the Channel in the following month, held the firm opinion that poor conduct on the part of the officers had been a prime factor in the breakdown of discipline in the Channel Fleet in 1797, and he reflected this conclusion in stern demands on his commanding officers.[54] He placed particular stock by the calibre of the inshore frigate captains, including Charles Cunningham of the *Clyde*, and John Gore of the *Triton*.

By now the Admiralty's instructions for the blockade were taut. They laid great stress on immediate information which would enable an engagement before the French could clear the coast with their destination and intentions undetermined. This could only be done if the inshore squadron of frigates and smaller vessels was constantly watching the Passage du Raz and le Goulet. Nothing must distract them from this task, although, as much as it allowed them, they were to take or destroy the supply convoys bound for Brest. If sufficient cruisers were available, some senior officers would station one or two to the

Opposite **A plan of the blockade of Brest drawn during 1800 by Lieutenant John Grey.**

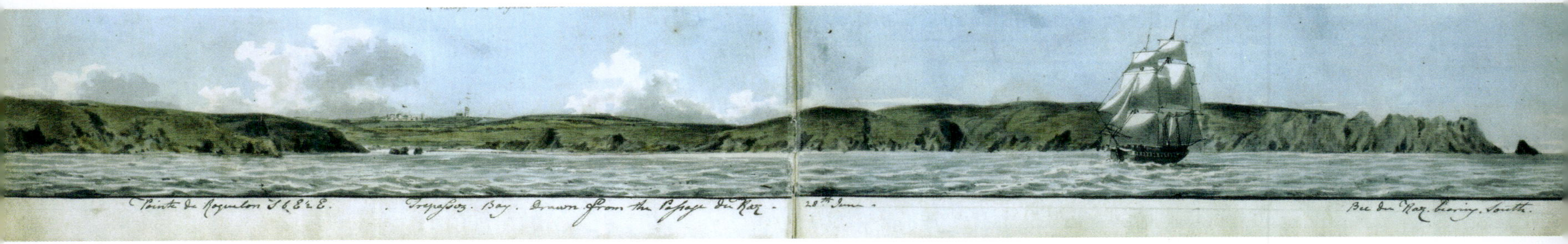

south of the Saints or in Hodierne (Audierne) Bay to get an earlier sight of coasting convoys heading for the Passage du Raz. The blockading captains reported that local knowledge allowed the convoys to slip through the narrow channels in the rock reefs between the Pointe du Toulinguet and La Parquette shoal when the weather did not make them impassable. This also happened with supplies from Lower Normandy, where the intricate coastline and uncertain tides made it difficult to intercept the French seamen. The Admiralty instructions to the Commander-in-Chief for this inshore task concluded that 'their Lordships do not doubt but that you will see the propriety of employing upon it the most active, audacious and intelligent captains under your orders.'[55] Now John Serres was to be at their side, contributing to measures to address another obstacle to the success of the blockade.

Back in the 'mad March days' when the *Danae* had passed into French hands the fleet had lost an even larger vessel. During a violent gale on the night of 10 March, the 64-gun ship *Repulse* ran onto one of the rocks of the Saints. Her captain had been thrown down the companion ladder during a severe roll on the preceding day, and was confined to his cabin. The master and watch-keeping officers had lost their reckoning during the thick weather, but had not hove to. The ship was proceeding at about six knots when she struck, and it was some three-quarters of an hour before they could wear the ship and sail her clear. By then irreparable damage had been sustained and the lower deck was flooded. The *Repulse* was kept afloat long enough to close the French coast and to allow the ship's company to take to the boats. At the subsequent court martial, the first lieutenant and master were found guilty of disobeying the Captain's orders and were dismissed from His Majesty's service.[56]

The *Unicorn* (32) is depicted on patrol in the Passage du Raz. In the view Serres carefully records the conspicuous marks which the officers onboard would need to master, including the village of Plogoff, a signal station behind the marshland of Trépassés Bay, and the tower of a windmill above the Bec du Raz.

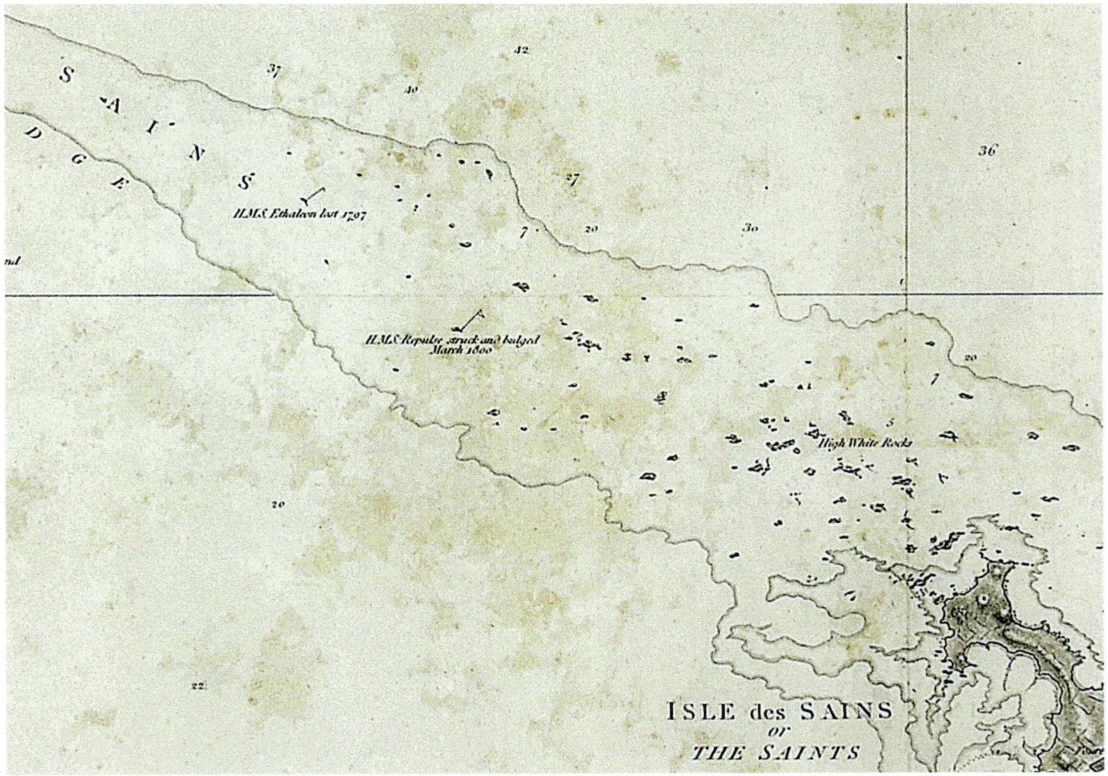

The great promontory of the Saints (Chaussée de Sein) was a major danger to the blockading squadrons. The positions where the frigate *Ethalion* and the ship of the line *Repulse* ran aground are recorded on this large-scale chart drawn up during summer 1800 by Captain John Knight, senior officer of the advanced squadron.

The inshore waters of Brittany were a most demanding station for ships of the line like the *Repulse*, and some senior officers considered the wear and tear on ships and their companies to be too great to be acceptable. In 1804, Admiral Cornwallis dismissed the tactic of anchoring off the coast '. . . as a few chosen two-decked ships have occasionally done when called the advanced squadron. Some of our bravest captains in the last war, I have been told, got into three-decked ships to avoid such service . . .'[57] In 1800 the scouting frigates were supported by an advanced squadron of four to five manoeuvrable, third-rate 74-gun ships of the line stationed near Les Pierres Noires, the dreaded Black Rocks, 'which from its peculiar terrors, at that time was commonly known in the fleet by the name of Siberia'.[58]

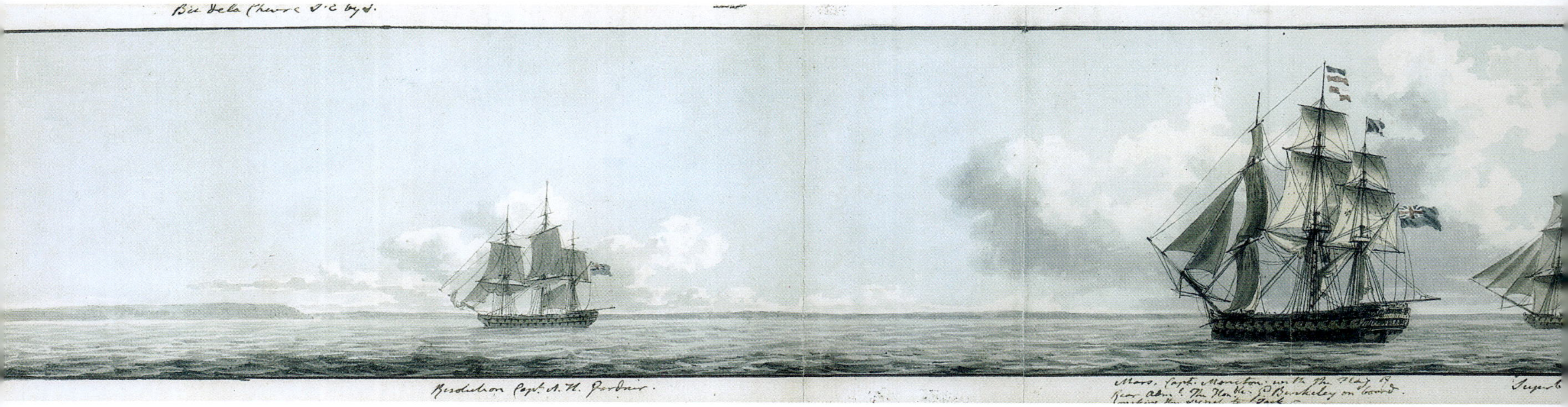

This tactic had been developed by Admiral Hawke during his close blockade in 1759. He anchored his whole squadron off the Black Rocks in high summer when conditions allowed.[59] St Vincent expected the squadron to remain at anchor in their station in an east wind 'winter or summer'.[60] The lighthouse on Pointe St Mathien was kept burning throughout hostilities, and, when underway at night, the squadron had clearing bearings until fog clamped down. The main peril was a shift of the wind into the west with the rapid building of a swell. The dangers of a lee shore were illustrated when the *Mars* ran foul of *Centaur* on 10 April 1801, and subsequently had a narrow escape from stranding on the north coast of Brittany.[61] Both ships are shown in more clement weather conditions in Serres' magnificent panorama of the inshore squadron, under the command of William Berkeley, Rear-Admiral of the Blue.

Great reliance was placed on local pilots such as Yves Cormat, Serres' companion in the *Clyde*. The 74-gun ships and frigates in the advanced squadron off Brest almost invariably embarked a 'Pilot for the coast of France',[62] probably a Breton with little liking for the Revolutionary regime.[63] These pilots were usually transferred to relieving ships as they joined the squadron.[64] Their guidance was not infallible, and they showed indifferent

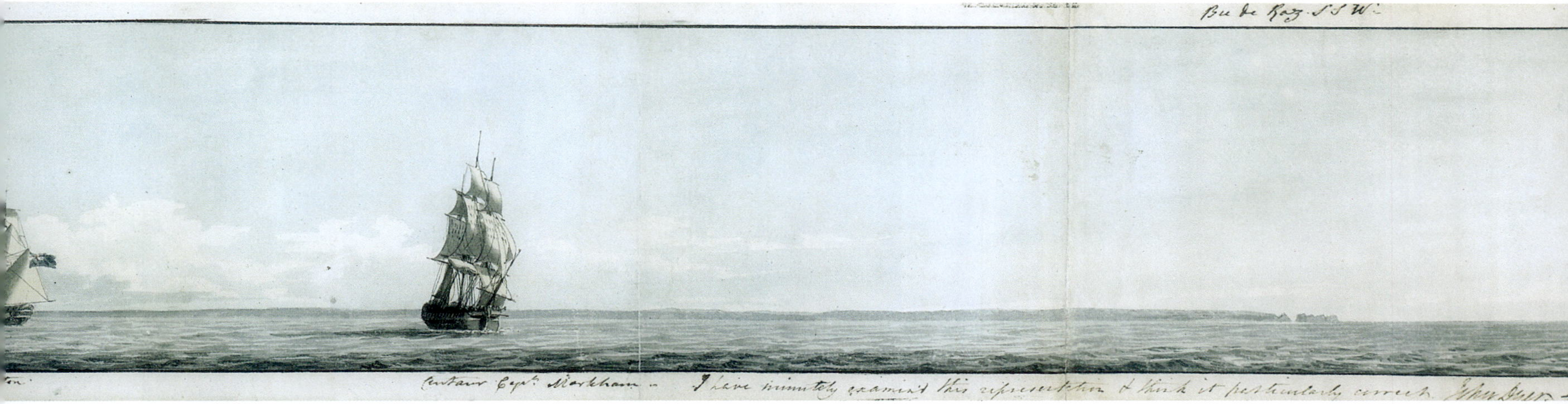

Resolution, *Mars*, *Superb* and *Centaur* of the advanced squadron manoeuvre in the approaches to Brest in fine summer weather. The *Mars* and *Centaur* were sister ships built during a period when admiration of French designs led to expenditure on larger, faster 74-gun ships. The *Superb*, even larger than them, was actually built to a French design. The flagship, the *Mars*, was a veteran of these waters, where she had defeated the brand-new *Hercule* (74) in a famous single-ship action in 1798. Serres records that the flagship had made the signal to tack and she and the *Superb* are shown paying off to starboard with their foreyards braced to bring the sails aback. The three-panel triptych from which this image is taken amply demonstrates Serres' contention in the 'Address to the Amateurs of Marine Drawing' in the *Liber Nauticus* that success in that medium depended as much on an 'acquaintance with seamanship' as mastery of naval architecture.

knowledge of the navigational information published by their own government. They were as liable as the naval officers they served to underestimate a safe offing from danger. Indeed the greatest contemporary challenge was to estimate distance. The frigate *Ethalion* had been under pilotage when she struck on the Saints while on patrol in the Iroise in light airs on a dark Christmas night in 1797.[65] Experienced officers used their Remark Books to urge their counterparts to anchor in the Iroise at night or in low visibility. One wrote: 'I should recommend to all officers not thoroughly acquainted with its navigation and the different set of the tides, rather to drop an anchor underfoot during the night, in calms, light airs, and fogs (particularly at the Springs), than risk being driven about at the mercy of the tide.'[66] It was failure to observe this precaution which had resulted in the *Repulse* (64) ripping her bottom open on the Saints, less than a mile from the wreck of the *Ethalion*.

St Vincent was characteristically dismissive of the performance of his predecessors: '. . . in old times a sight of Ushant from the deck was considered a near approach . . .' The demanding seamanship which was required in manoeuvring inshore gave him the opportunity to drill his new command. He endeavoured to be close under Ushant with the main body of the fleet every morning at daylight when the wind was in the eastward.

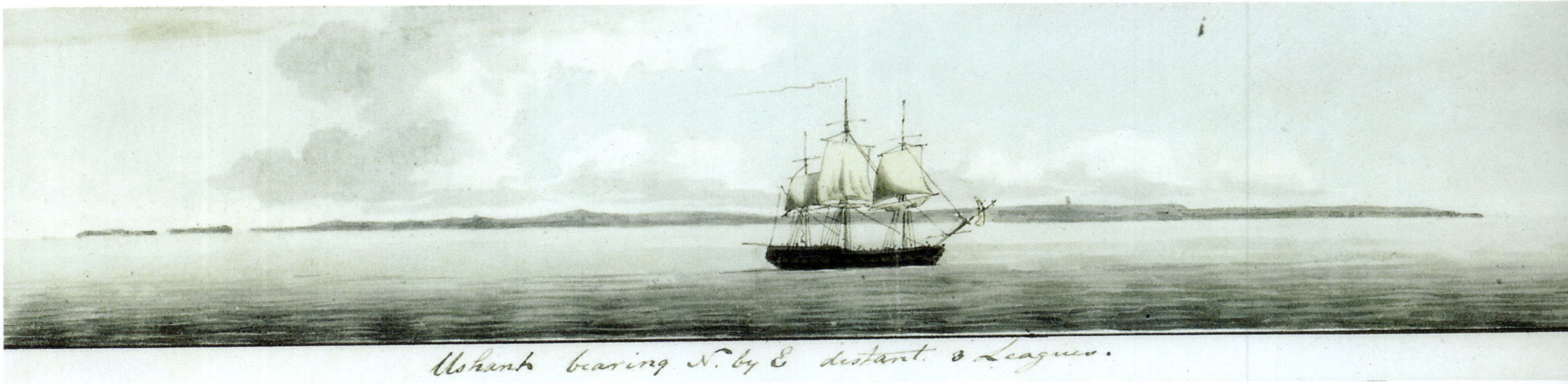

He was 'upon deck at 3 o'clock a.m.' and was quick to spot when his advanced squadron was to seawards of him. On 12 May 1800, off Ushant, he wrote: 'Both wind and weather are favourable to the departure of the enemy and the tides are so rapid and troublesome that it is with some risk I keep the Squadron so near Ushant. Captain Keats is very masterly in his conduct and Rear-Admiral Berkeley is active and vigilant, yet finds it difficult to preserve a position so near the Black Rocks as he and I are equally desirous he should maintain.' In fine summer weather he wrote almost exultantly: '. . . we are standing by the wind in a line of bearing between the Black Rocks and Ushant the water as smooth as a Mill Pond under 3 single reefed tops'ls, mizon and fore topmast staysail . . .' Provocatively, he called this cruising ground 'the Elysian lake'![67]

St Vincent's opinions were certainly backed up by solid experience. In the years of peace in the 1770s he had spent a year in France, and had also gone on a yachting cruise during which he had studied the approaches to Brest and other key ports to the south on the Biscay coast.[68] At the outset of his command in the Channel he shared the general view that the management of navigational publications in France was on a much firmer footing than in Britain. This was the claim of Jacques Nicolas Bellin in his introduction to the revised edition of *Le Neptune François*, published in 1753. He stated that the charts in this official

A heavy frigate lies hove to in light airs in the main fleet station south of Ushant.

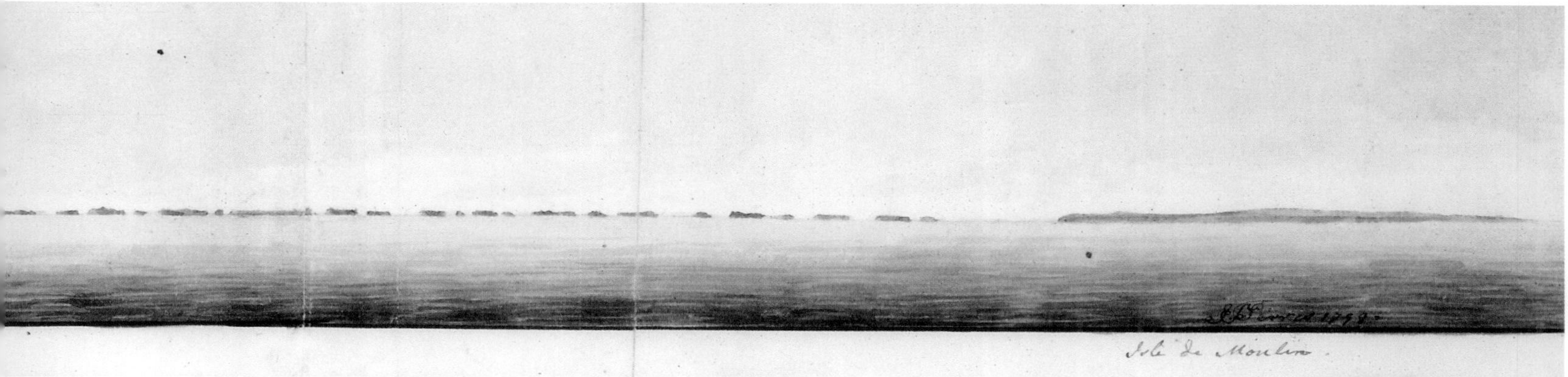

publication, which had been available to the French navy since 1693, had now been corrected to reflect meticulous determination of the latitude and longitude of the most important landfalls together with the results of coastal surveys conducted by 'able engineers and pilots'. When the Admiralty eventually established a Chart Committee, its members noted the superiority of the French list of accurate positions, *La Connaissance des Temps*, compared to the *Requisite Tables* produced by the Astronomer Royal. The introduction to the *Neptune* also included detailed instructions for use of the charts, and these include warnings against the inaccuracies in unofficial pilot books, especially the use of positions which were not based on precise astronomy. In 1800 an even more superior French production was issued: *Le Neptune François* now covered the whole world in eleven volumes.[69]

In contrast to Dalrymple's cramped quarters, the French Dépôt des Plans, Cartes et Journaux de la Marine had been established in its own spacious accommodation in Paris since 1720. By the late 1790s it had advanced from the collection of documents to publication and dissemination of official charts. In addition, the Director, Rear-Admiral Rosily, with the active encouragement of the powerful minister, Decrés, was taking the first steps to create a corps of field surveyors to conduct wartime surveys. Auxiliary chart depots had been created in the main naval ports some 20 years earlier. A prisoner of war in Brest in 1794

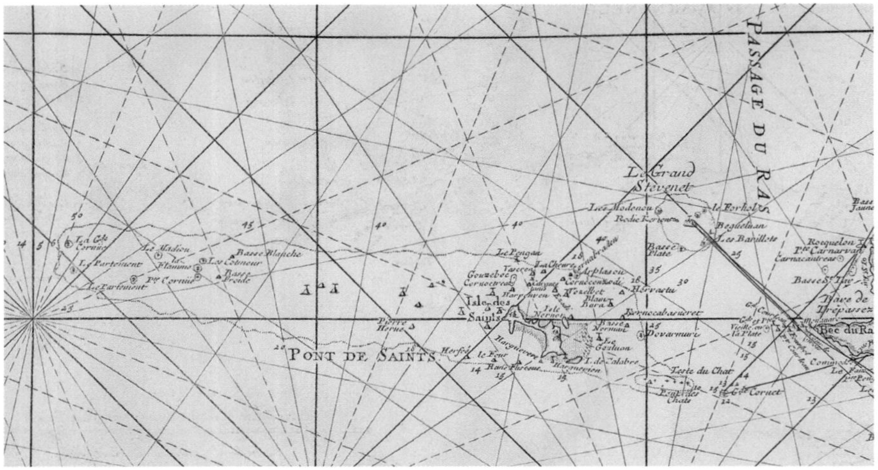

This extract from the ***5ième Carte Particulière de Bretagne*** in the ***Neptune François*** shows the Passage du Raz and the Pont de Saints extending out to the westwards.

remarked enviously that: 'Every ship is furnished, at the public expense, with a superb set of charts of every part of the known world: those of our country are particularly excellent; there is scarcely a little harbour in Britain or Ireland which is not laid down in them. With us this important charge is left to the prudence and honesty of a master; and how many accidents have befallen our ships by a neglect of it, need not be here enumerated.'[70]

Dalrymple had built up particularly close links with Jean-Baptiste D'Après de Mannevillette, his counterpart in the Compagnie des Indes, who had produced another superb atlas, *Le Neptune Oriental.* Dalrymple respected French hydrographic accomplishments[71] and these views were shared in the fleet. The master of one of the frigates in the inshore squadron opened his remarks with the comments: 'as the Navigation between Ushant Brest the Saints etc. is so well known, and has been so often represented, I beg leave only to recommend in Foggy weather, and night time, strict attention to the different depths of water and Kind of soundings round that part of the Coast, which I found when compair'd with the French Charts of that Place Published by order of that Government to be perfectly correct.'[72] This testimony was echoed by no less a man than the Commander-in-Chief himself, in an outburst to Rear-Admiral Berkeley on 19 July 1800: 'Captain Knight will love the *Montague* if he is permitted to make use of her in surveying, which I very much disapprove; a cutter and his own boats in the day are *tante* to all his views . . . all he has done and will do is not worth, to the public, a coil of twice laid rope . . . do you think the French during the reign of Louis Quatorze under the auspices of le grand Colbert did not make a better survey of Brest than Captain John Knight will do and have you not got it in the Neptune?'[73]

St Vincent had a reputation as an intemperate critic. In 1800 the Admiral's health was frail, and the balance of some of his judgements of fellow officers has been questioned.[74] A contemporary noted that once he had formed a bad opinion of an officer he could not readily overcome a prejudice against them.[75] John Knight was a favourite of Admiral Lord Hood, and had been serving as his flag captain at the time of the admiral's controversial replacement by Jervis (St Vincent) in the Mediterranean Command in 1796. The incoming Commander-in-Chief never overcame a suspicion of his predecessor's protégés.[76] Knight's reputation among his fellow officers also suggests that his leadership style was very different to that approved by St Vincent, who certainly regarded the *Montagu* (74) as a slack ship.[77] Additionally, St Vincent was always alert for ships with large numbers of Irishmen on board which might spread the contagion of mutiny. Nearly a quarter of the men under Knight's command hailed from Ireland. In June 1800 St Vincent reported that: 'I have tacked the *Montagu* to Admiral Berkeley's Black Rocks Squadron, which her Captain did not like, but the admitting the crew of her to familiar intercourse with several ships in this squadron would be dangerous.'[78]

To St Vincent's discomfiture, when Rear-Admiral Berkeley obtained leave later that summer, the much-maligned Captain Knight took command of the advanced squadron for a short period as the senior officer. It was not long before St Vincent was expressing dissatisfaction with his performance, and declaring, somewhat disingenuously, that 'accident, not design, placed Captain Knight at the advanced post: he was ordered into the Bay of Brest for the sole purpose of surveying, in the performance of which I believe him to be the most accurate in H.M. service.'[79] Knight certainly had a reputation for his 'peculiar scientific

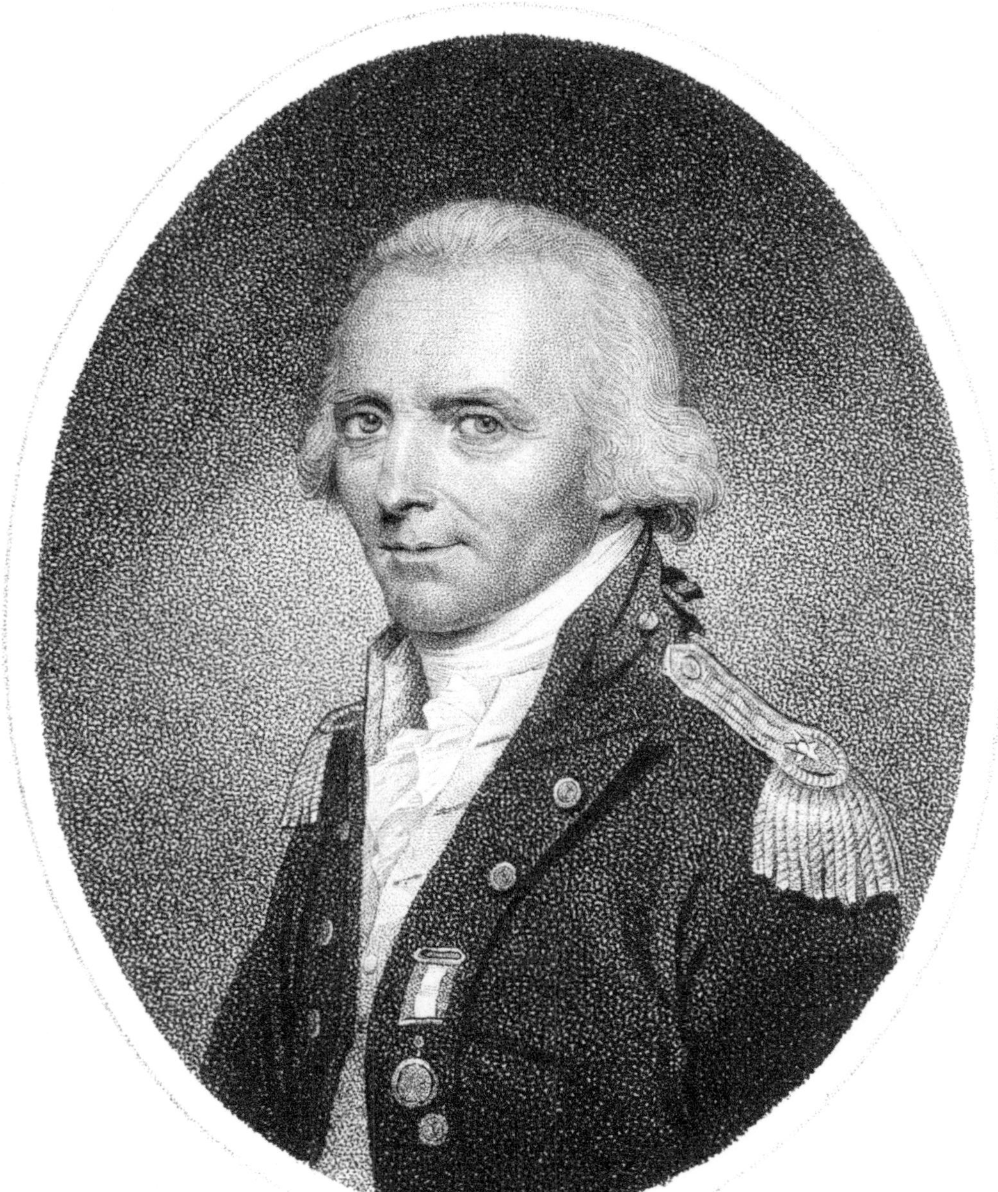

abilities' and his commitment to improving the charts of those waters in which he served. He was one of several naval officers who learnt surveying skills on the coasts of North America before and during the War of American Independence, and he was bold and accomplished in inshore operations.[80] He ejected the French frigates which were stationed, when the weather permitted, in Berthaume or Camaret Bays to counter the intelligence-gathering tactics of the Royal Navy's frigates. Contemporary biographical records also list a series of boat operations in these months, during which the *Montagu* provided close fire support.[81] Towards the end of the year he requested a docking to repair and inspect the keel of his ship of the line, which had been damaged by grounding on a 'sand knowl' while covering his boats under a battery. A high degree of seamanship was particularly necessary for the surveying work. The log of the master records a narrow escape in haze when the ship, with all its boats deployed, came within a ship's length of the Mare (Jument) rock off the west end of Ushant.[82] It is interesting to speculate whether, had he been aware of Serres' presence in the fleet, Knight might have sought to add him to his team.

St Vincent's confidence off Brest illustrated an essential difference between the eighteenth-century British and French navies. Whilst some small French squadrons had made good use of their navigational information to achieve landings on the complex coasts of Ireland and Wales, major fleet operations off the English coast had revealed a real timidity and a lack of confidence in their much-vaunted chart supply organisation. By contrast, despite the shortcomings in hydrographic support, British ships had at various times operated in French inshore waters as boldly as if they were their own. Offshore islands in view of the mainland were occupied in support of amphibious descents, as sources to supplement food and water supplies, and even as recreation grounds for cricket matches![83] But, as the fate of the *Repulse* had shown, there was a cost, and even St Vincent could not dismiss the efforts of Knight and the commission of Serres too lightly, particularly if they tightened his sea control.

Opposite **Captain John Knight was renowned among his contemporaries for his efforts in gathering hydrographic information for the benefit of the fleet. He began this work long before the Hydrographical Office was established and he published his results through the commercial outlet of William Faden. During his time with the Channel Fleet he produced a series of charts covering the most complex areas of its inshore operations.**

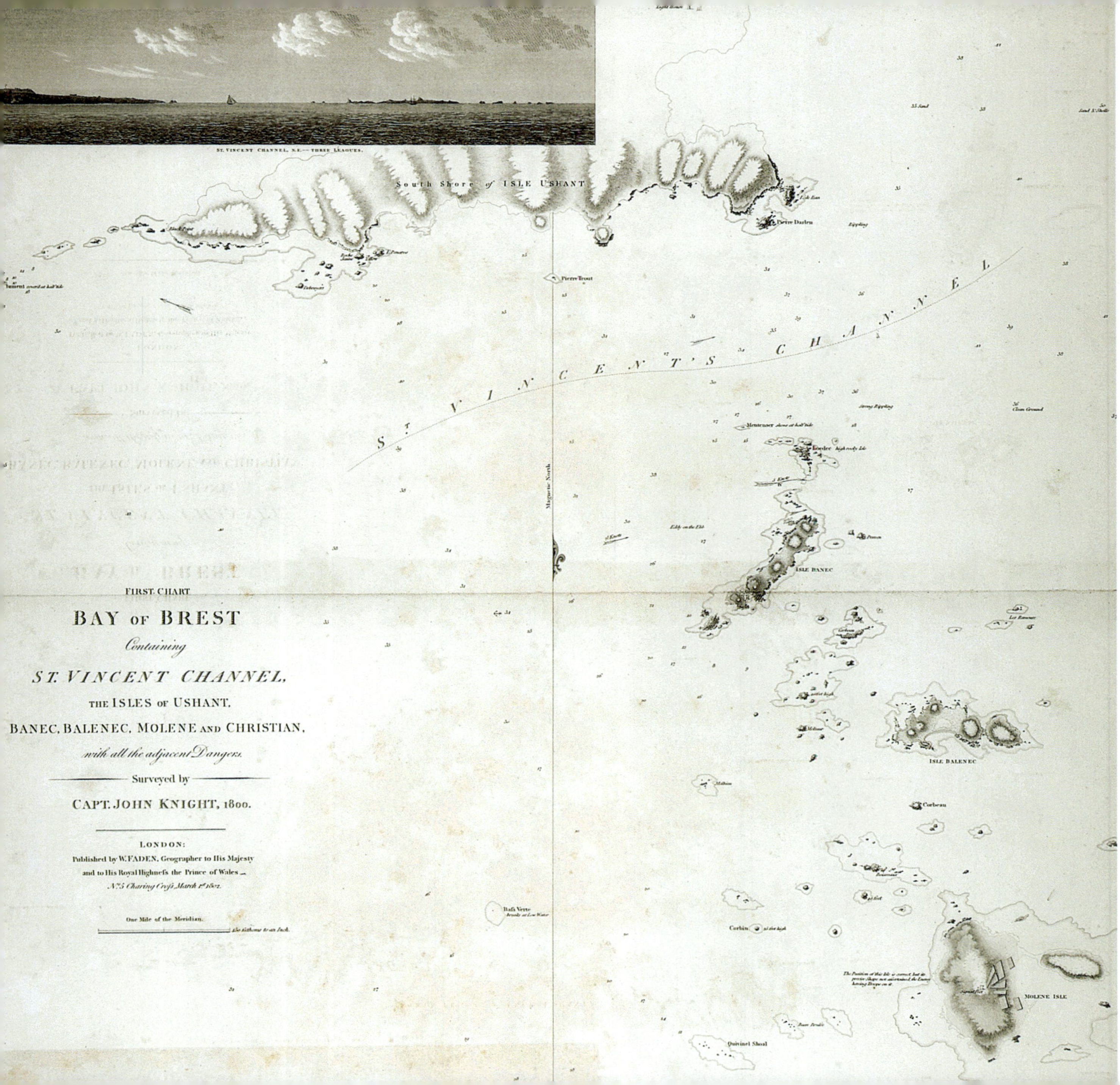
ST. VINCENT CHANNEL, N.E.-- THREE LEAGUES.
South Shore of ISLE USHANT
Pierre Darlen
Pierre Trout
ST. VINCENT'S CHANNEL
Magnetic North
Strong Rippling
Clean Ground
Kedec
Eddy on the Ebb
ISLE BANEC
ISLE BALENEC
Corbeau
Corbin
Basse Verte
Quivinel Shoal
MOLENE ISLE
FIRST CHART
BAY OF BREST
Containing
ST. VINCENT CHANNEL,
THE ISLES OF USHANT,
BANEC, BALENEC, MOLENE AND CHRISTIAN,
with all the adjacent Dangers.
Surveyed by
CAPT. JOHN KNIGHT, 1800.
LONDON:
Published by W. FADEN, Geographer to His Majesty
and to His Royal Highness the Prince of Wales
No. 5 Charing Cross, March 1st 1802.
One Mile of the Meridian.

Opposite **Captain John Knight's large-scale charts gave the blockading fleet more detail of their operating area than they had ever had before. They also aimed to give prominence to the vital information, such as the set of the tidal stream, which facilitated swift decisions under the pressure of action or pursuit of the enemy. Knight was conscious that he had to overcome the antipathy of his Commander-in-Chief, and the naming of the channel inside Ushant after St Vincent was a clear attempt to win the old admiral over. The limitations of Knight's wartime surveys are clearly acknowledged, e.g. the inability to delineate Île Molène accurately while it was occupied by French troops.**

CHAPTER FIVE

In action

The monthly muster book of HMS *Indefatigable* (44) records that 'J T Serres, Marine Painter to Admiralty, Passenger to the Fleet' joined in Plymouth on 26 May 1800. The frigate sailed on the following day. Off the Devon coast between Bolt Head and Start Point a rendezvous was made with the fleet, which had been sheltering from westerly gales in Torbay. The captain of *Indefatigable*, the Hon. Henry Curzon, was summoned onboard the flagship. In his swift pencil sketch (pp. 50–1), which he never found time to work up, Serres caught this moment as the frigate, under full sail, closed the flagship, the *Ville de Paris*, while the rest of the fleet spilled out from behind the Start. Perhaps retrospectively, Serres labelled another frigate which was to feature prominently in his work in the days ahead.

In light airs, the fleet now sailed in close company towards Ushant. At 4 a.m. on 31 May they stood in with the advanced squadron ahead. The meticulous log of David Stewart, the Master of the *Ville de Paris*, records that in fresh breezes and hazy conditions they 'made and shortened sail as necessary to keep the fleet in their stations and to keep close in to Ushant'. St Vincent estimated that the fleet had arrived 'in the very nick of time' since French ships had moved out into Camaret and Berthaume Bays, and ships of the line had driven off the lookout frigates. During his few days in the *Indefatigable*, Serres worked with the Master, John Gaze, to produce the first of a number of much more detailed panoramic sketches 'drawn by compass bearings', showing the island and the offshore rocks among which John Knight would labour. In the course of the summer more and more evidence reached the blockading fleet that the work of the inshore ships was starving the markets of Brest, and that this stranglehold was tightening as their confidence inshore increased: 'the

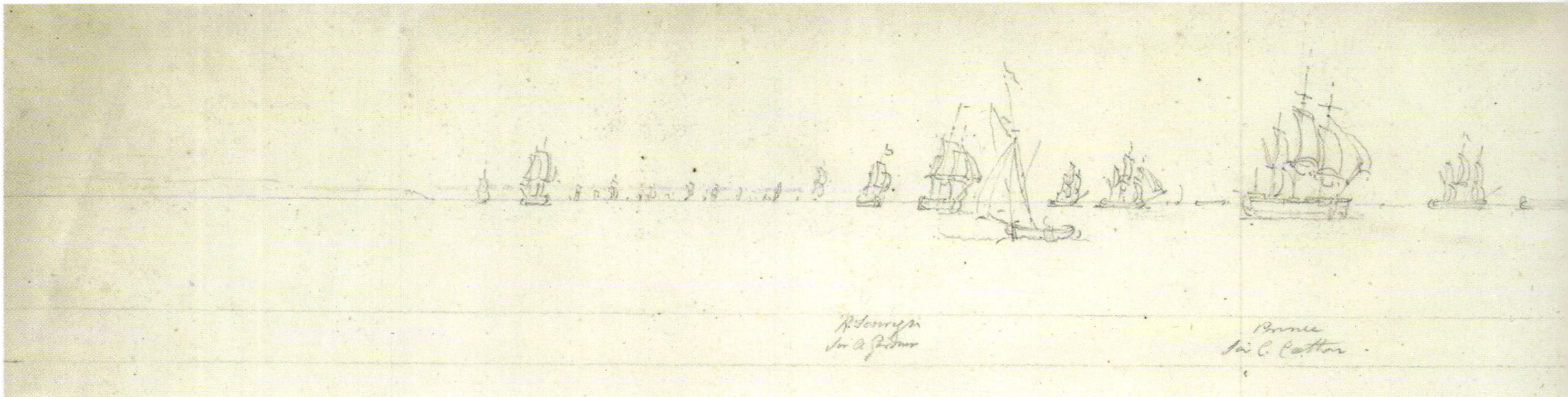

advanced squadron is now commanded by Captain Knight, who has been able, from the very extraordinary long run of fine weather to survey almost all the small islands and rocks within Ushant and the Isle of Molene.'[84]

Despite the widespread approbation of 'the Neptune', its limitations were becoming evident, and Knight's hydrographic efforts began to earn some acknowledgement from St Vincent: 'I return you many thanks for your observations on the bay of Brest and I take the liberty to send you a copy of a chart lent me by Sir James Saumarez which was taken out of a French ship in the year 1747 by his intrepid uncle, Captain Philip Saumarez of immortal memory, and you will oblige me very much by filling it up with soundings, views of headlands, etc.'[85] Instead Knight produced a set of four new charts which were eventually

Above **Start Point is at the left side of the drawing, with the Channel Fleet deploying from Torbay, as sketched by J. T. Serres on 26 May 1800. Two of the flagships are labelled, and an armed lugger is positioned at a focal point. Serres has depicted his ship the *Indefatigable* under full sail to close St Vincent's flagship, the *Ville de Paris*. At the right-hand extremity he has labelled the frigate *La Nymphe*.**

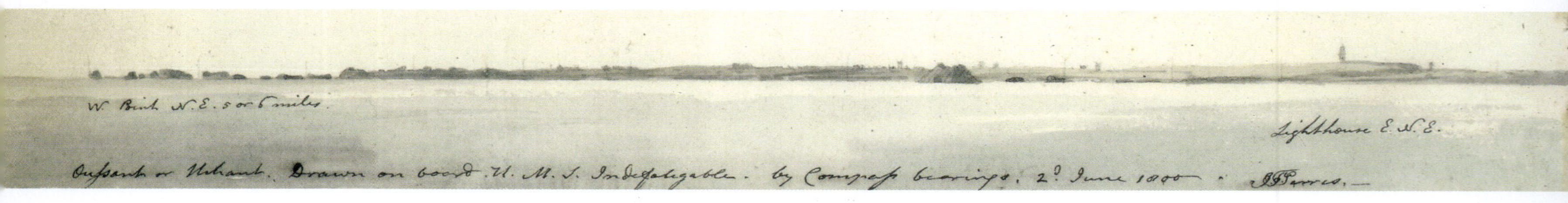

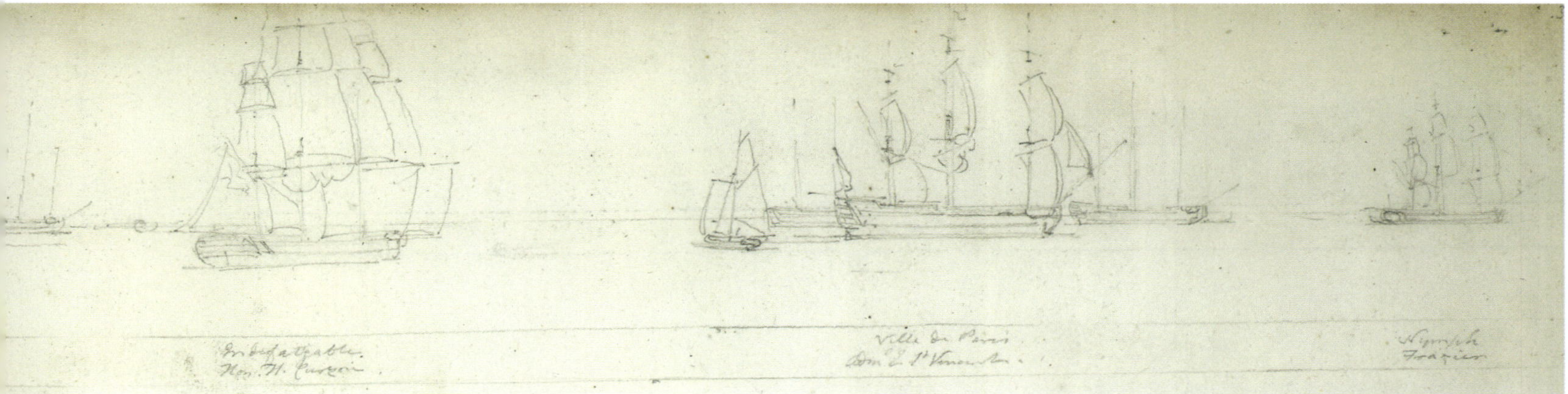

printed privately in 1802. These reflected the content of the illustrated observations on the area of the blockading operations which he had sent to the Commander-in-Chief.[86]

Knight's general chart carries the prominent dedication: 'Surveyed by Directions of The Right Honourable ADMIRAL EARL ST VINCENT'. The other three were at a larger scale, and intended to assist the pilotage of the fleet in several of the most complex areas of the approaches to Brest. Indeed the major outcome of Knight's persistent effort had been the sounding of a passage inside Ushant which he named St Vincent Channel (the Passage du Fromveur), and which is illustrated in Serres' view on pp. 52–3. Knight reported that 'a knowledge of this Channel may be of infinite advantage to ships beating out of the Iroise, as also to those in the British Channel not able to weather Ushant in a Northerly Gale'.[87] The Commander-in-Chief noted: 'Captain Knight has deserved well of his country for ascertaining the passage between Ushant and Banec which the French have taken great pains to keep us in ignorance of . . .'[88] The passage is certainly not evident in the *Neptune*. Knight's charts included views illustrating prominent marks and leading and clearing lines. While not as artistically accomplished as Serres' efforts, they would have provided the newcomer to this genre with excellent models of the type of information which the practical navigator required.[89]

Left **The rocks at the west end of Ushant mark the beginning of the first detailed panoramic view sketched by Serres from the *Indefatigable*. This was so well executed that it was picked out later in the Hydrographical Office for engraving and use on an official chart. The compass bearings on which it is based are all carefully recorded.**

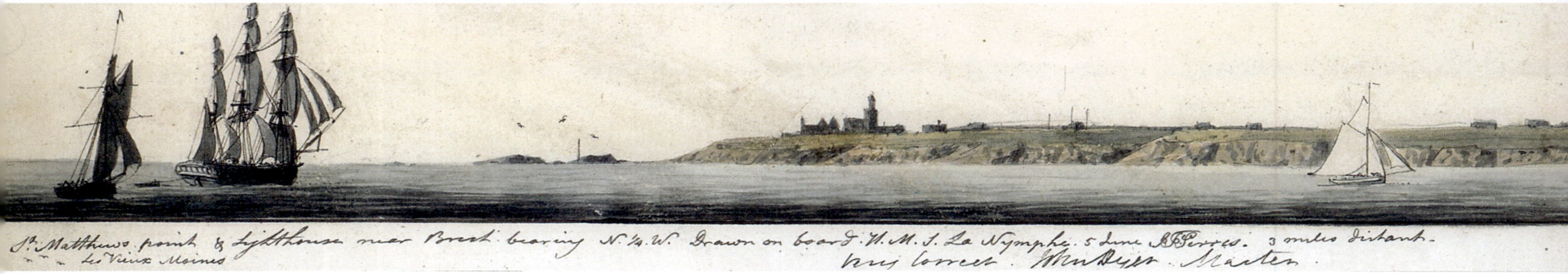

Serres continued the detailed panorama in his sketchbook in company with another captain who was to influence his techniques. St Vincent had intended to place Serres with John Gore in the *Triton*. However, on 2 June Captain Percy Fraser of HMS *La Nymphe* (36), after having been summoned on board the flagship, collected Serres from the *Indefatigable*. At 9 p.m. onboard the flagship Mr Stewart recorded that 'The *Nymph* made sail from the fleet standing to the SSE.'[90] Percy Fraser had obtained his first command in 1791 with only two years' seniority as a lieutenant. He had been promoted to post-captain in 1795, and *La Nymphe* was his second command in that rank. He had just joined the ship in April 1799, and was alone in the close inshore station when Admiral Bruix's squadron left harbour in thick

Above **The reality of the close blockade is tellingly illustrated by this image of *La Nymphe* and two armed cutters in the Avant-Goulet of Brest. Serres has labelled Les Vieux Moines rocks close off Pointe de St Mathieu.**

Below **The continuation of Serres' panoramic view in his sketchbook illustrates the complex area of the St Vincent Channel (Passage du Fromveur) and the annotation by John Gaze, Master of the *Indefatigable*, attests to its accuracy.**

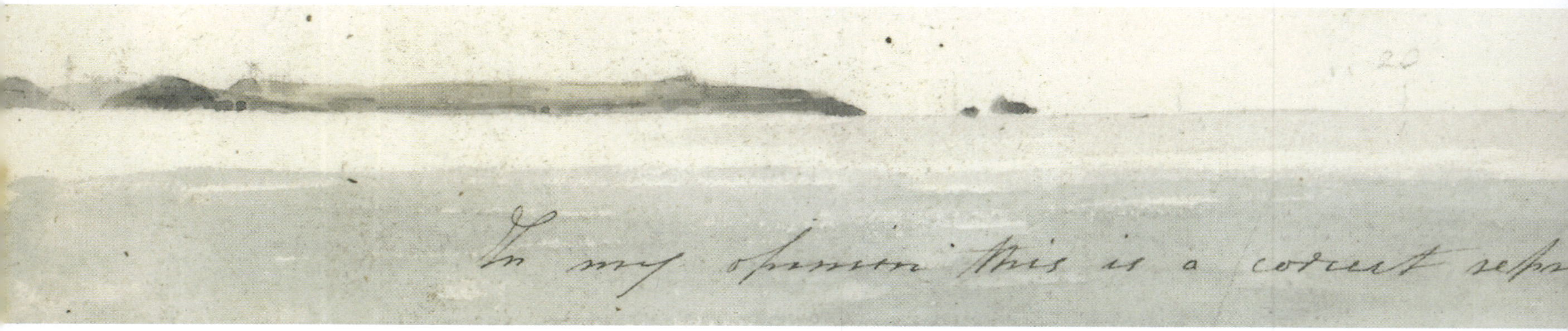

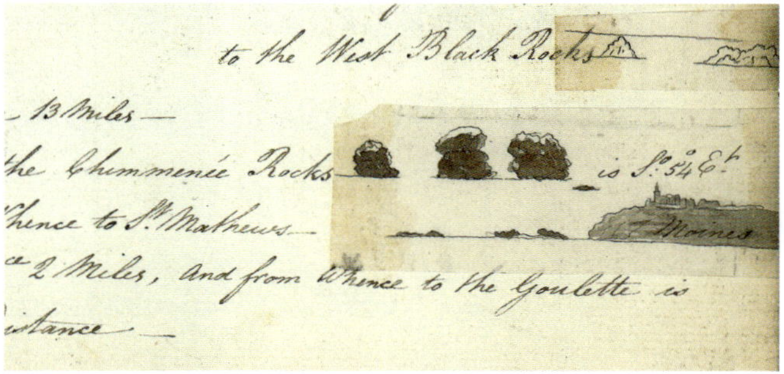

Above Les Trois Cheminées, well known to William Cathcart and his fellow officers in the *Triton* during their service inshore, was listed by John Knight as one of the conspicuous marks for the advanced squadron, 'being mostly white topped by the dung of sea fowl'. This sketch was included in the notes which he made for St Vincent, later passed to the Hydrographer.

weather. Fraser's judgement that the French had subsequently turned back to Brest led Lord Bridport to call off a general chase.[91] It was this excursion which had enabled the French and Spanish squadrons to return together to Brest, to constitute the force of more than 40 sail which St Vincent was now expected to contain. Fraser's part did not go unnoticed in the Admiralty,[92] but in the summer of 1800 he remained with Gore as one of St Vincent's chosen captains for the inshore task of watching the combined fleet. He now took Serres into his patrol area to sketch 'the continuation of the French coast' round to the Bec de la Chèvre, highlighting such dangers as 'Le Parquet ESE at Low Water Spring Tide' (see p. 54).

William Cathcart, 18-year-old acting lieutenant in the *Triton*, described the inshore routine to his father, a Privy Counsellor and distinguished major general, in this same summer of 1800. 'I shall now briefly give you an idea of our advanced position . . . We were stationed between the Chéminée and Parquette, and used to stand within gunshot of Toulinguet Point every evening to reconnoitre. They frequently threw shells close to us from St Mathew's, till we got marks of their range, which we found to be a mile and a half. At night our sole guidance was the light of St Mathew's . . . We were obliged to tack every two hours; and if it came calm, with a flood tide, to anchor; if a westerly wind we had to anchor. You may guess what a harassing station that was for the captain and us all for a spell of thirteen weeks.'[93]

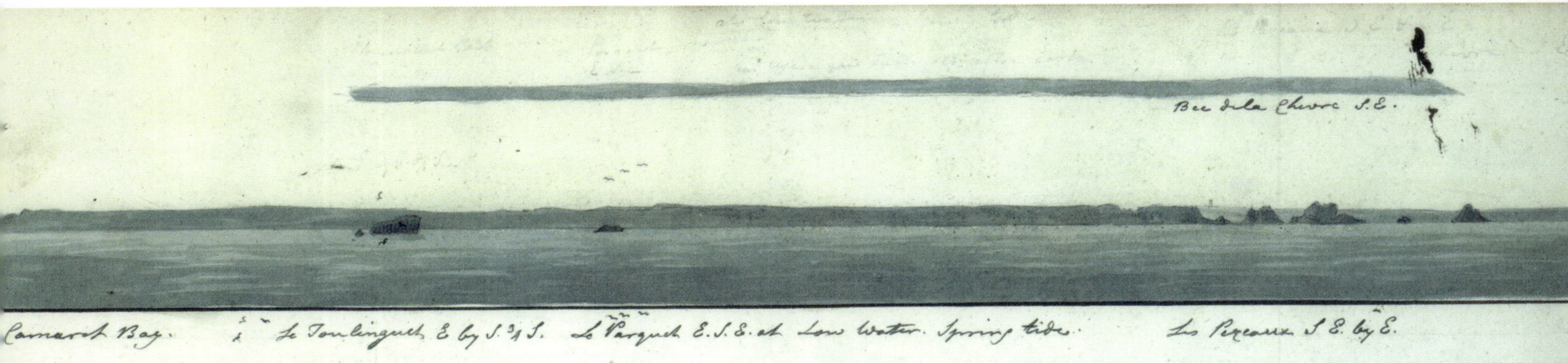

Serres quickly got a taste of action. Rear-Admiral Berkeley described the events of 10 June 1800 as follows: 'The frigates made sail close in this evening covered by the *Centaur*; the enemies batteries fired at them from each side, as they made the best use of the opportunity the weather gave of pushing their reconnoitring very far up the Goulet . . .' One aspect of the tension between central instructions from the Admiralty and the judgement of the Commander-in-Chief was the balance of information from Royalist agents and the counts by the officers of the frigates. As St Vincent observed, the task of the latter was testing: 'I know from experience how difficult it is to ascertain precisely the number of ships crowded together into port, and the discrimination between large Frigates and Ships of the Line is still more difficult when they intersect each other as must be the case in Brest . . .' Nonetheless, he placed great store on a frequent count, particularly during the favourable summer months. Gore was well practised in looking into Brest, and retained this task through most of the summer of 1800.[94] St Vincent wrote that Bridport's frigate captains '. . . had merits in the Bay of Brest but nothing compared with what Captain Gore exhibits daily, which is in no wise inferior to his great predecessor, Keats.'[95] As Serres depicts, Gore has taken *Triton* under easy sail right up to the mouth of the Gullet itself, within close range of the Lion battery on Pointe du Petit Minou and the Cornouaille battery

Above John Dyer, Master of *La Nymphe*, is now working in close concert with Serres to ensure that not only the controlling bearings but the state of the tide at the time of each drawing are carefully recorded. This information was vital to the identification of the dangerous rocks off this rugged coast.

on the southern shore.[96] *La Nymphe* is shown on the port tack, working up under full sail to support her consort.

The frigates of the inshore squadron were always alert for other opportunities to gain intelligence, including interrogation of the Breton fishermen. However, this source required careful assessment. In June 1800 St Vincent noted: 'I believe all the intelligence we have obtained, on the state of the ships in Brest, to have been erroneous, and there is reason to suspect the fishing boats which Captain Keats laid hold of were sent out with a tale to deceive us.' There were other expedients. Captain Keats had sent a young officer from his ship inshore in a fast four-oared rowing boat which had to fight its way back out. Cathcart told his father of an adventure under flag of truce when he and the first lieutenant went into le Goulet in an eight-oared, lug-rigged cutter, with despatches and a box of cigars from St Vincent for the Spanish admiral. They were taken onboard *La Furieuse*, flagship of the commodore in Berthaume Bay, where they enjoyed 'an indifferent supper' while awaiting the reply of the French admiral. Perhaps suspicious of another ruse to obtain intelligence, he answered that the box had been received out of respect for the Spanish, 'but that if we attempted to send a flag of truce on a bagatelle like that to any officer under his command, he would seize the boat'. In Serres' watercolour sketch overleaf, the boat secured astern of *Triton* may well be the cutter used in Cathcart's adventure.[97]

The officers and men who knew these waters best served in the *Joseph* and *Lurcher* cutters and other small vessels shown in Serres' views. The armed cutters were responsible

Below **On the evening of 10 June 1800 Captain John Gore of the *Triton* wrote to inform St Vincent that 'I this afternoon availed myself of a steady breeze to reconnoitre the enemy's combined fleet in Brest and find them as per enclosed report which I took on the spot.' Serres records this dramatic scene, with his own ship *La Nymphe* and the cutter *Joseph* in close support.**

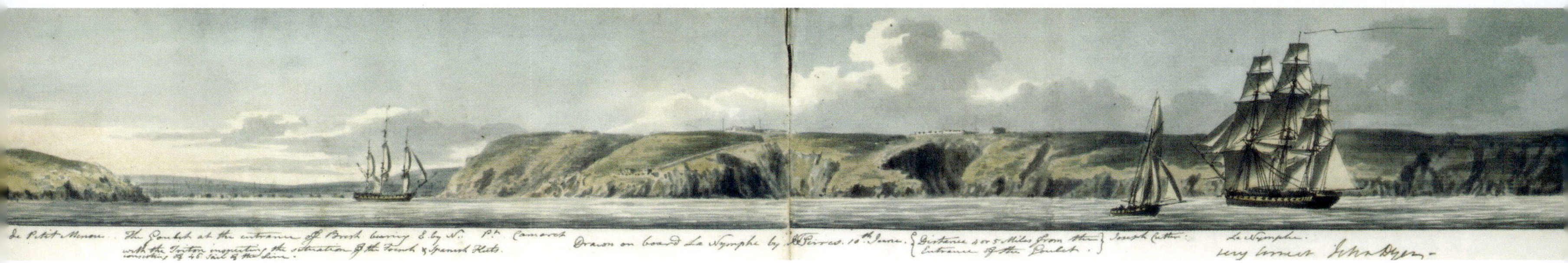

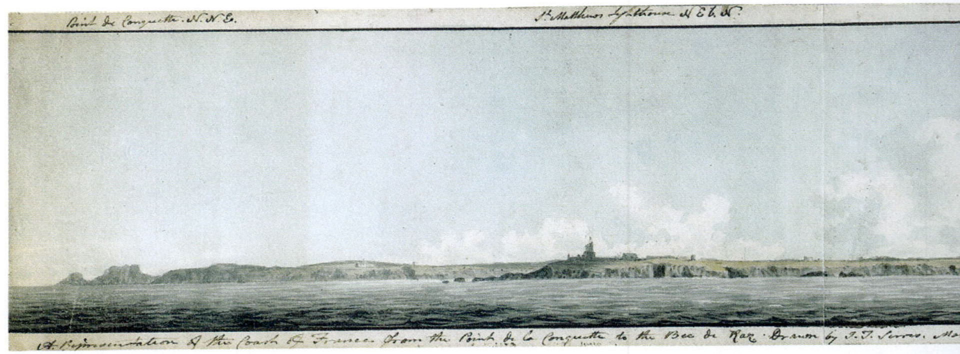

Above **Having completed his views in the immediate environs of Brest, Serres had time to make detailed observations of the ships in company for his magnificent triptych. Here he shows the *Triton* weighing anchor and *La Nymphe* underway in l'Iroise. *La Nymphe* was a classic eighteenth-century frigate captured from the French in a famous action in these very waters in 1780 during the war of American Independence. The *Triton* was a new ship, constructed of fir in 1796 to an experimental design with the aim of economising on timber and improving performance. She had proved to be one of the fastest cruisers in the fleet.**

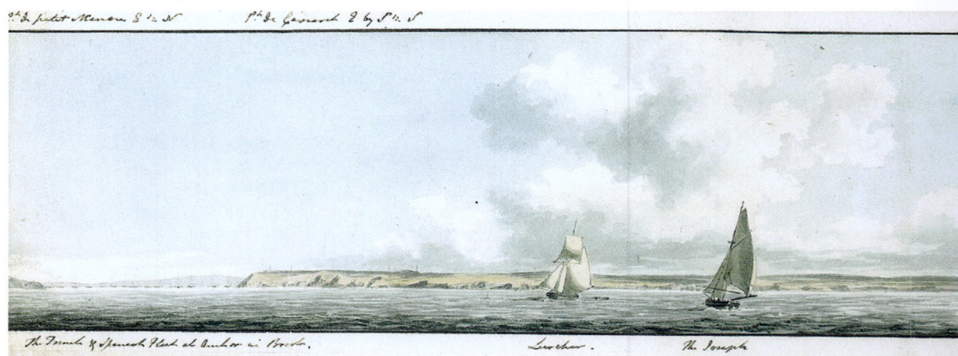

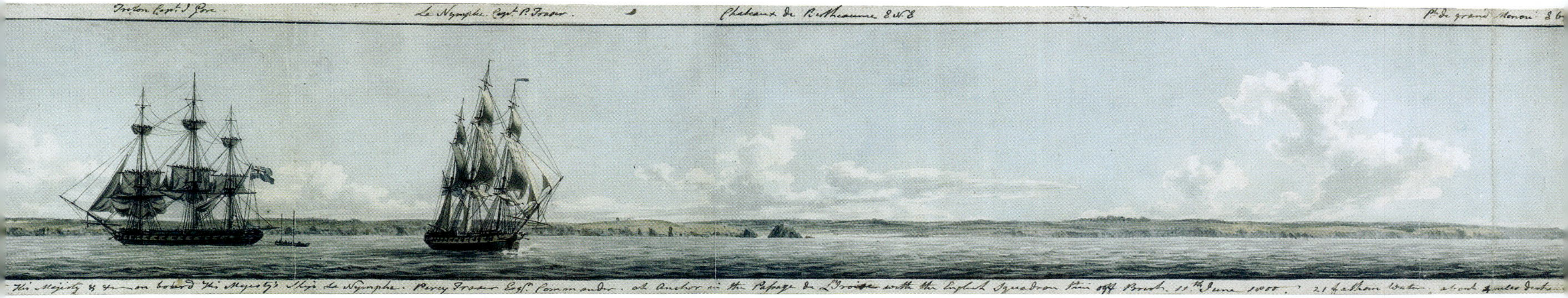

for watching le Goulet during the night. *Joseph* was commanded by Lieutenant John Lapenotiere, who in the next war would bring the news of the Battle of Trafalgar to England in the *Pickle*. His capture of coasting vessels close to the French batteries in Camaret Bay forced the French to deploy a frigate and other small warships outside le Goulet. The *Joseph* was regarded as too slow and in grave danger of being captured by faster and more powerful French vessels. Subsequently St Vincent commented that: 'With 6 more good cutters, well commanded, we would prevent any supplies coming to Brest from Nantes, Rochelle and Bordeaux; at present the chasse marées laugh at us.'[98]

Below **The small vessels of the inshore squadron do not go unrepresented in Serres' picture of the advanced squadron. They are shown against the backdrop of le Goulet, where they would spend the hours of darkness, watching for any movement from the huge Combined Fleet.**

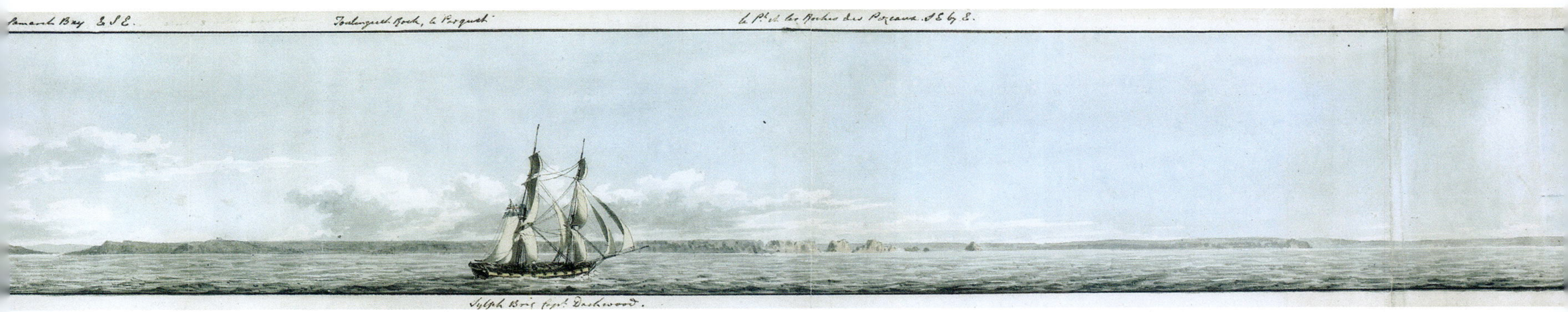

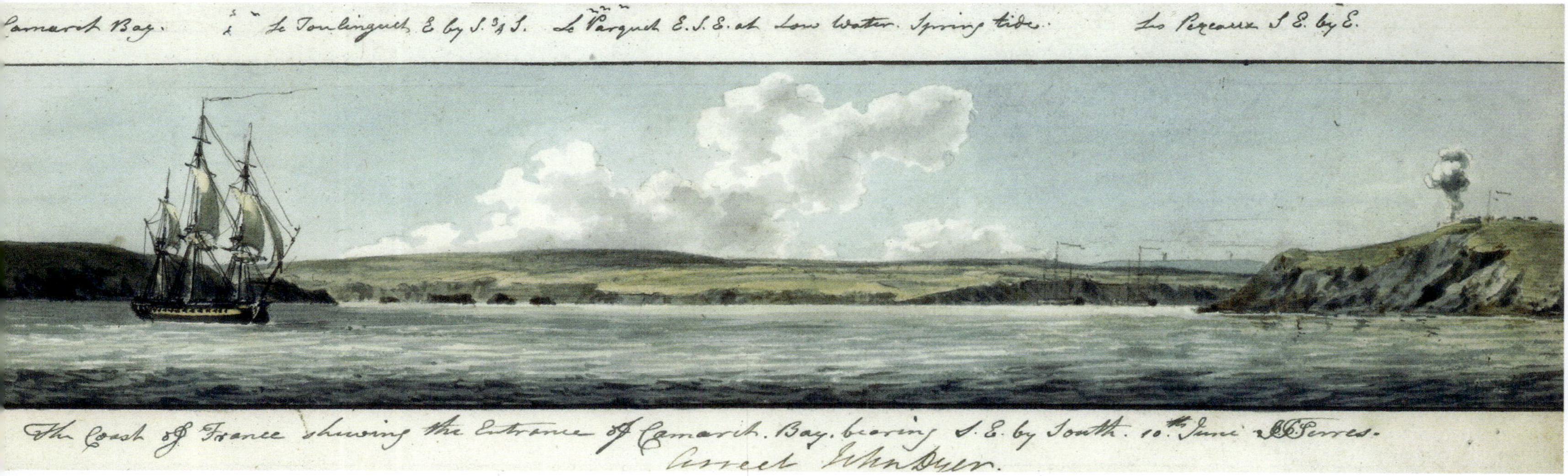

Nonetheless, in June 1800 the frigates and small craft were making such an impact that St Vincent declared that 'the whole coast is petrified'. Large ship tents were visible on the high ground around Brest roads. Fishermen interrogated by the *Sylph* stated that a descent by the British on Camaret heights, depicted in Serres' sketch, was feared by the French and that marines had been landed from the Combined Fleet to protect them. By 20 June the inshore units were intercepting supplies for fortifications, and a force of four large frigates and two corvettes put to sea to chase off *Triton* and *La Nymphe*. Meanwhile, French convoys coming down Channel through the Passage du Four were getting no further than Lochrist Bay near Le Conquet. Here they were protected by batteries. They also profited from the inadequacy of the navigational knowledge of the British fleet, which was only remedied by surveys of these passages conducted by Captain Thomas Hurd in 1804 and 1806.[99] Nevertheless, St Vincent remarked after one large convoy turned back that it 'acted wisely for Captain Gore of the *Triton* would otherwise have carried some of them last night'.[100]

The interception of movement from Normandy is illustrated in a sketch which shows that Captain Percy Fraser was himself an accomplished draughtsman. Serres appears

Above **The British small vessels were said to be vulnerable to attack by two French corvettes which had been stationed in Camaret Bay. On the same day as the foray into le Goulet, *La Nymphe* checked on these enemy units. Smoke can be seen rising from the battery on the heights to the south.**

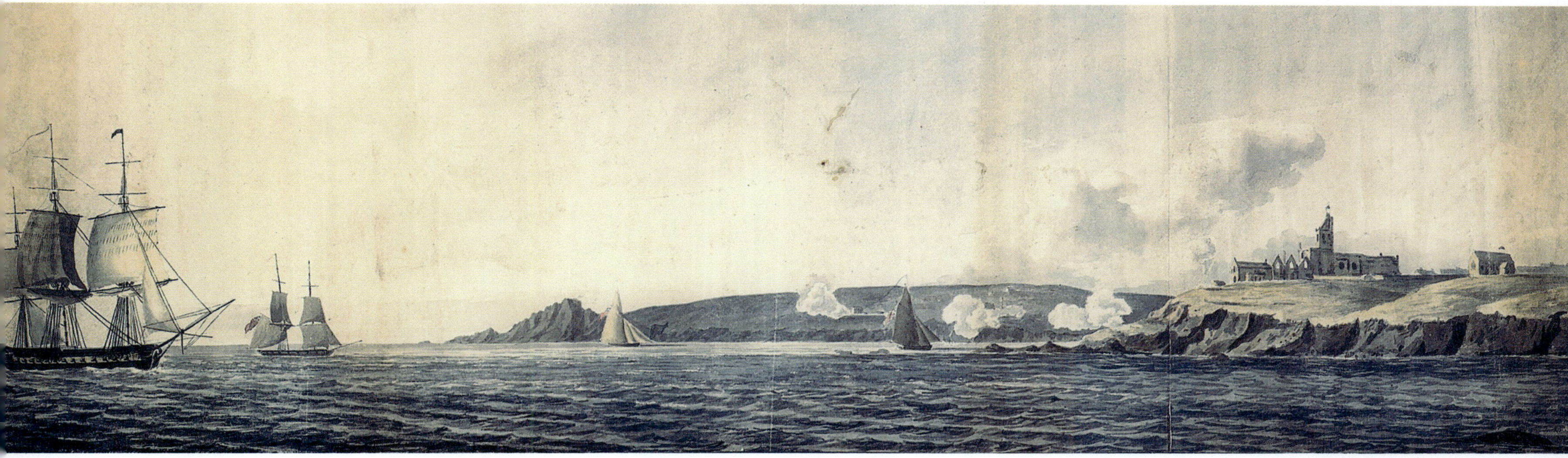

Above Captain Percy Fraser's accomplished sketch of an engagement off Pointe de St Mathieu may reveal one factor in St Vincent's allocation of Serres to *La Nymphe*. At least one other fine navigational view by Fraser has survived, and he and the professional artist must have had much to discuss. In this scene the British vessels may be wearing red ensigns rather than the blue of the advanced squadron under Berkeley's command so that the cutters could be readily distinguished from the enemy they were pursuing.

to have adopted techniques from him for coastal views, including the use of flying seagulls for the descriptive labels.[101] The engagement off Pointe de St Mathieu on 11 June is captured graphically, with the *Lurcher* and *Joseph* in action and *La Nymphe* and *Sylph* lying to. At first light, Gore had spotted a large escorted convoy coming through the Four Channel and anchoring under the French batteries, and had planned an attack by the boats of *Triton* and *La Nymphe* with cover from the *Sylph* and the armed cutters. During the afternoon a cutter had been spotted leaving Brest and heading towards the convoy. The *Lurcher* and *Joseph* were sent to cut her off, and pursued her among the offshore rocks 'under a tremendous fire of round and grape'[102] from several of the heavy batteries at le Conquet. So enthusiastic was the pursuit that no one saw Gore's signal to withdraw, prompted by his concern that the cutters would be too damaged to contribute to the night's task of dealing with the convoy. *Lurcher* was the faster sailer and pursued the French vessel up the creek at le Conquet. Fraser's notes to the sketch concluded, 'Lieutenant Forbes of the Lurcher boarded her very gallantly notwithstanding her situation and would have brought her out had the tide not left her.'[103] Forbes' despatches noted that the French crew took to the boats and jumped from the end of their bowsprit on shore among the rocks as he and five sailors arrived. Four of his company were wounded, two mortally, and *Lurcher* was left with considerable damage.[104] Forbes and his cutter were to face retribution the following February when they fell foul of a French privateer on the enemy coast.[105]

During these same days Serres produced a two-part sketch with annotated sailing directions which illustrates the close liaison between captain, master and artist in their task of amplifying the guidance for the blockading fleet. The images depict the natural transits to be used to clear the Parquette shoal, round which soundings had been taken by one of *La Nymphe's* boats on 7 June under the direction of the master, John Dyer.[106] All Serres' sketches now contained evidence of careful measurement of angles between edges of land and prominent objects, and they are certified by the master. It was now the artist's invariable practice to have each sketch of this type approved in this way. Before he left the *La Nymphe*, Serres made sure of getting a general written approbation from Fraser which he preserved carefully.[107] Fraser wrote: 'I have great satisfaction to assert that all the sketches which were made by Mr Serres on board H.M. Ship Nymphe under my Command are the most correct things possible.' The artist was proving to be an inestimable asset in fulfilling the standing remit in the Admiralty Regulations and Instructions that the master was 'to observe the appearances of coasts'.

Serres was settling happily into the routine of shipboard life, blissfully unaware of events back at home in Wimpole Street. In the wealthy West End of London the season was in full swing, and Olive was determined not to miss out. Critical observers noted that she appeared at the popular masquerades 'in dress which female modesty might shrink at'. At home she embarked on an extravagant round of entertainment, forging her husband's signature on the bills. One at least of these was sent to the Admiralty on 8 June, to be meticulously logged by the clerks in an entry headed ominously 'Mrs Olive Serres' rather than with the name of the Admiralty's artist.[108]

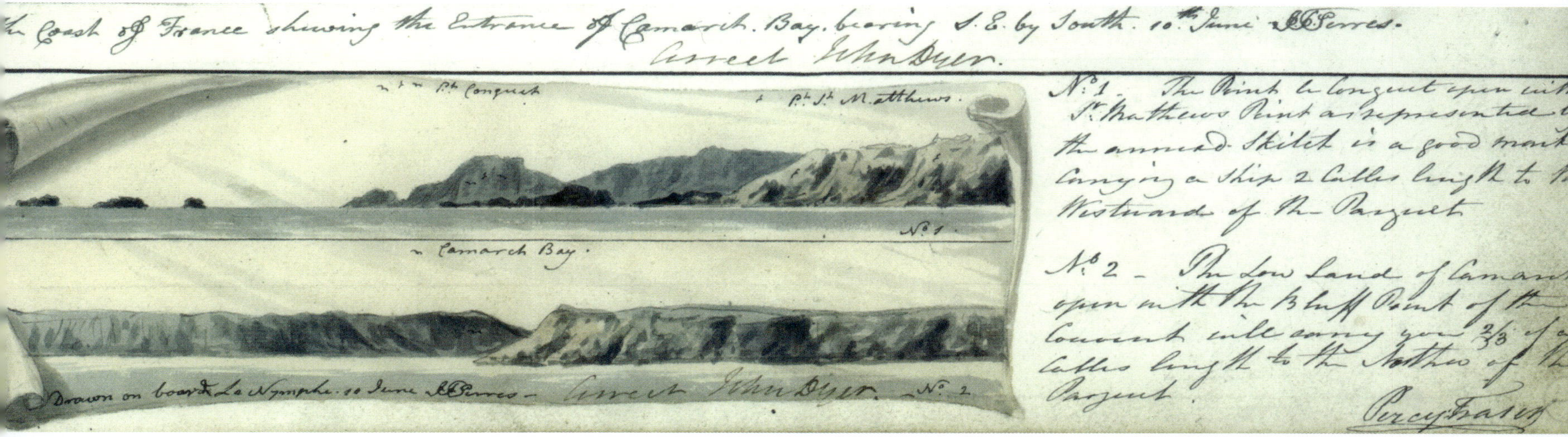

Collaboration between Serres and Fraser could not be better demonstrated than in this composition: a view with artistic flourish on the left and written sailing directions on the right, guiding the mariner clear of La Parquette shoal.

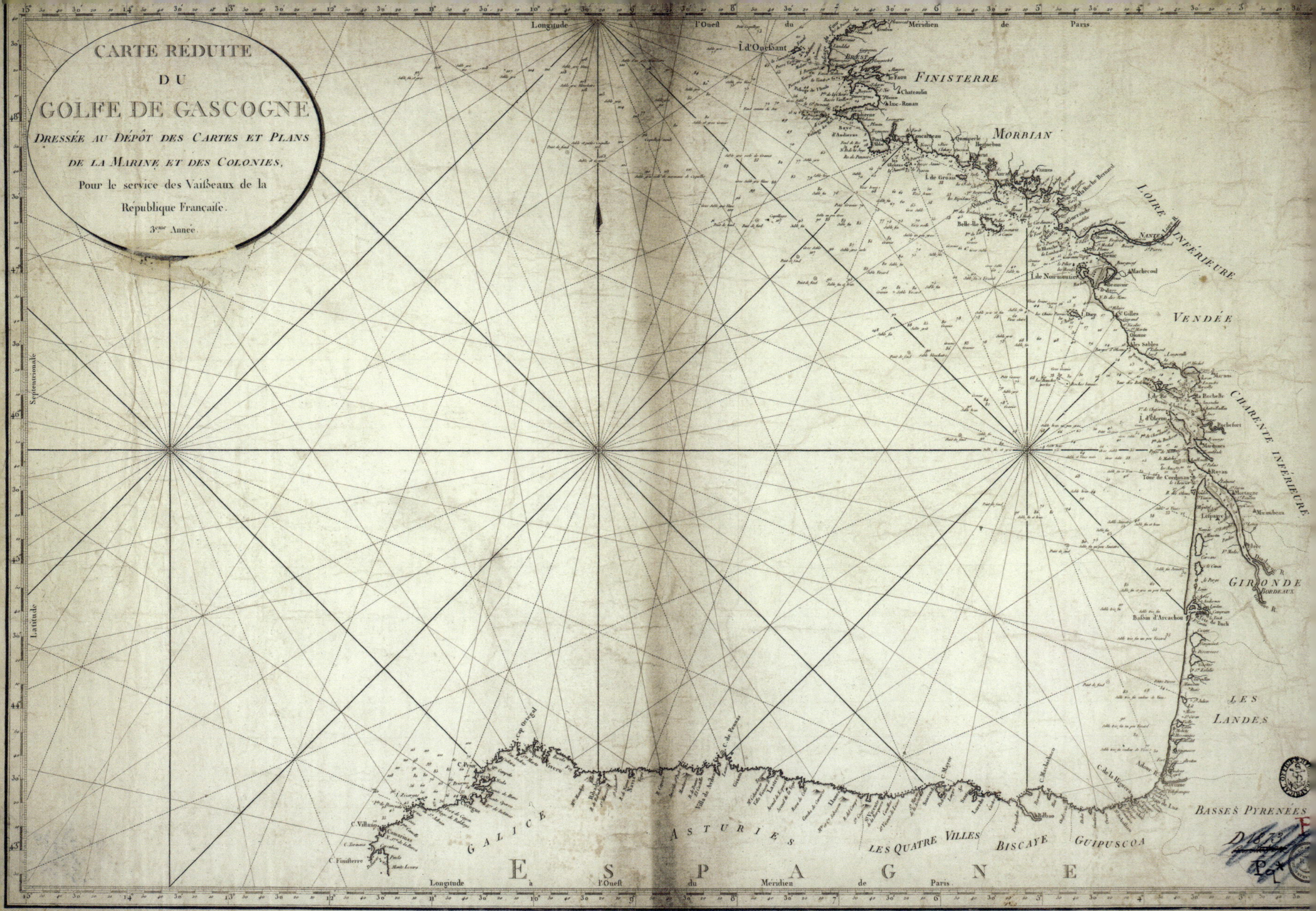

Prix deux Francs et demi

CHAPTER SIX

A fruitful partnership

Opposite This contemporary French government chart shows the coasts round which J.T. Serres was to cruise in HMS *Clyde* with Captain Charles Cunningham.

Serres' contentment was enhanced further when, on 28 June 1800, he transferred from *La Nymphe* and was reunited with Captain Charles Cunningham in the *Clyde*, which had just rejoined the fleet after refitting at Plymouth. Serres made no secret of his admiration for Cunningham. As his portrait (overleaf) suggests, the 45-year-old was an imposing figure with a firm countenance relieved by a sense of humour. Serres' high opinion was shared by the stern disciplinarian in command in the Channel, who thoroughly approved of Cunningham's record. After three distinguished commands in the Mediterranean fleet, he had been appointed to the newly built *Clyde* in home waters in 1796, at a time when severe discontent was brewing in the fleet. When mutiny broke out in the ships anchored at the Nore, Cunningham's taut leadership and authority became evident. He retained control of the *Clyde* and, early one morning, sailed her clear, afterwards sending a boat back to assist another frigate, the *San Fiorenzo*, to make its escape. During the summer of 1799 Cunningham was chosen to attend on the King at Weymouth. By late August, however, he was back in the demanding waters of the French coast where, later in the autumn, he became the senior officer of the inshore squadron, at which time Serres had had his first taste of the blockade.[109] He was another frigate captain with the spirit which St Vincent sought to exploit inshore, and the Commander-in-Chief had just commended his 'vigilance and zeal'.

Now his passenger was to bring the reward of a break from the rigorous routine. On 13 June St Vincent had written to the First Lord of the Admiralty: 'Captain Gore watches the motions of the enemy with a zeal and ability not to be surpassed and conducts these enterprises so ably that I persevere in my intention to send the Boadicea off Ferrol

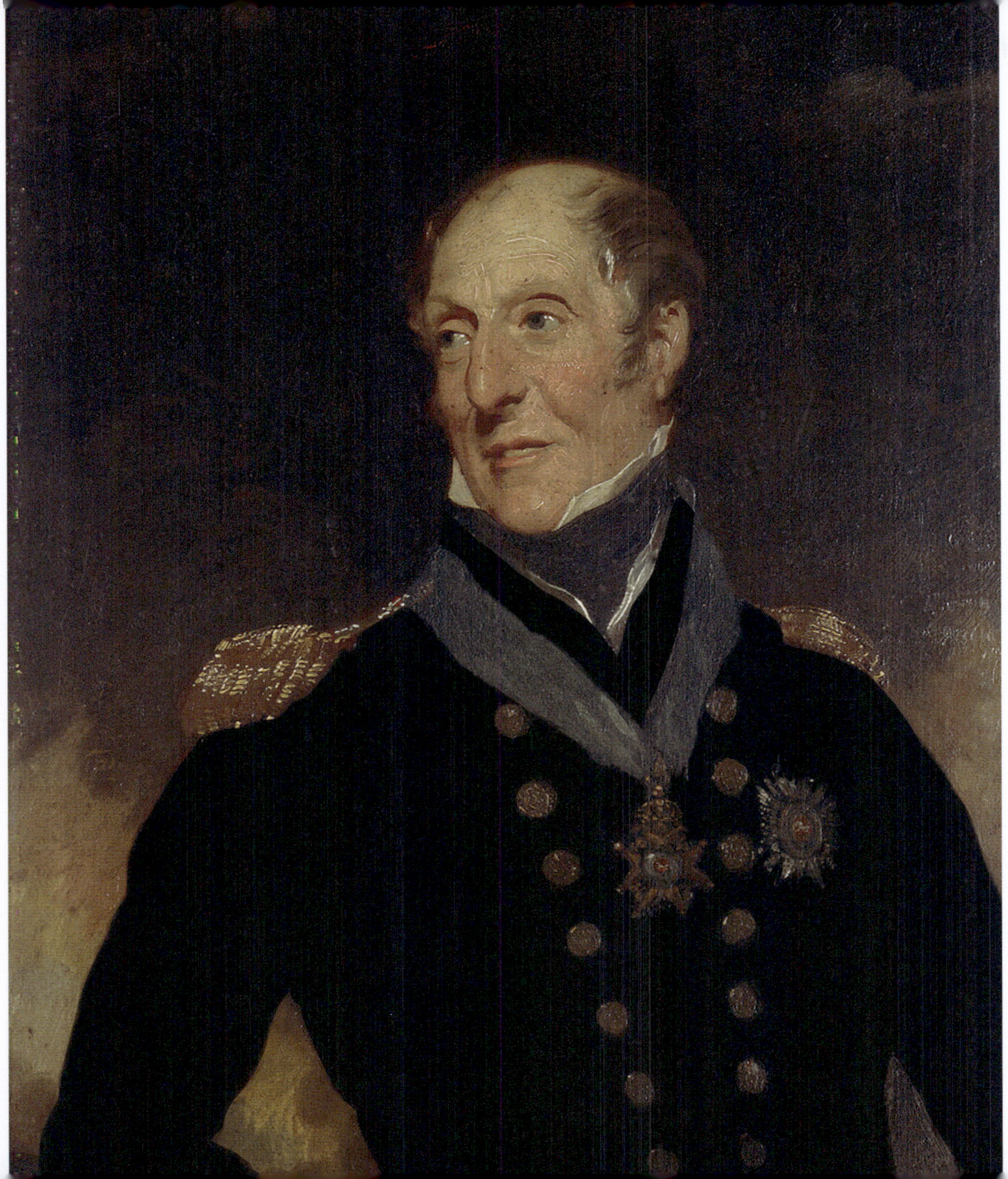

and the Clyde along the coasts of France, Spain and part of Portugal to enable Mr. Serres to complete his views.'[110] Cunningham now took his ship past the cruising stations on the coast of South Brittany, with Serres working with the ship's navigation team. His sketchbook records that he resumed his coastal panoramas 'commencing from the Bec du Raz'. Serres' 'appearances' were once again carefully annotated with information provided by the master, with the captain taking a close interest. Serres had been teamed up with men with a sharp professional approach to navigation and pilotage. The records of the *Clyde* indicate that they held not only the *Neptune François* but also the atlas of charts produced by the great Spanish hydrographer, Don Vicente Tofiño de San Miguel.

The masters of the navy's ships in the eighteenth century were the predecessors of the later specialist Navigation Branch. They had to pass a qualifying examination at Trinity House and they enjoyed a privileged position onboard. The Royal Navy valued and fostered the contribution of these warrant officers far more than was the case in the French navy of the eighteenth century with its rigid social stratification.[111] They were in many respects the captain's 'right-hand man', standing at his elbow directing the working of the ship, and constantly 'upon the lookout' when she was underway. They were specifically charged to provide themselves with 'proper instruments, maps and books of navigation' and to keep 'an exact and perfect journal' in which they were to note 'the appearances of coasts and how they show themselves in different points of view and . . . any new shoals or rocks underwater . . . with their bearings and depth of water'.[112] When Thomas Hurd began to build up a corps of uniformed hydrographic specialists he employed a number of masters.

The skills of observation which they could bring to bear are well illustrated in the Remarks of Mr Thomas Nott, who had received his first warrant in 1799 on joining the *Clyde*. Though the most junior of the masters with whom Serres served, Nott had the sharpest awareness of the artist's mission. Undoubtedly with the encouragement of his captain, Nott kept a comprehensive record of bearings, soundings and observations for every location where the artist 'drew the shape of the land'.[113] During 29 June, Serres' first full day onboard, the ship hove to off the Îles des Glenans to record the cruising ground off the Penmark rocks.

Opposite **Captain Charles Cunningham by H. Wyatt.**

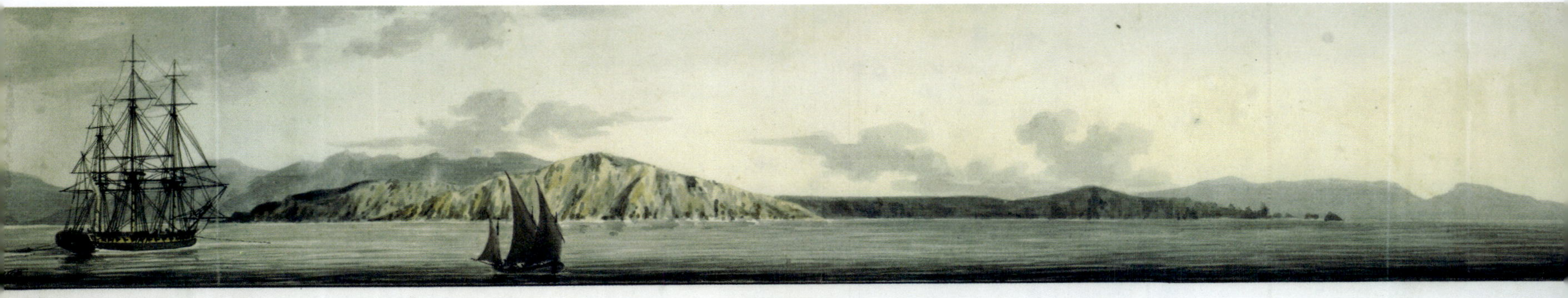

Cape Ortegal – bearing W. ½ N. distant 17 miles — Drawn on board H. M. S. Clyde 22nd July 1800.

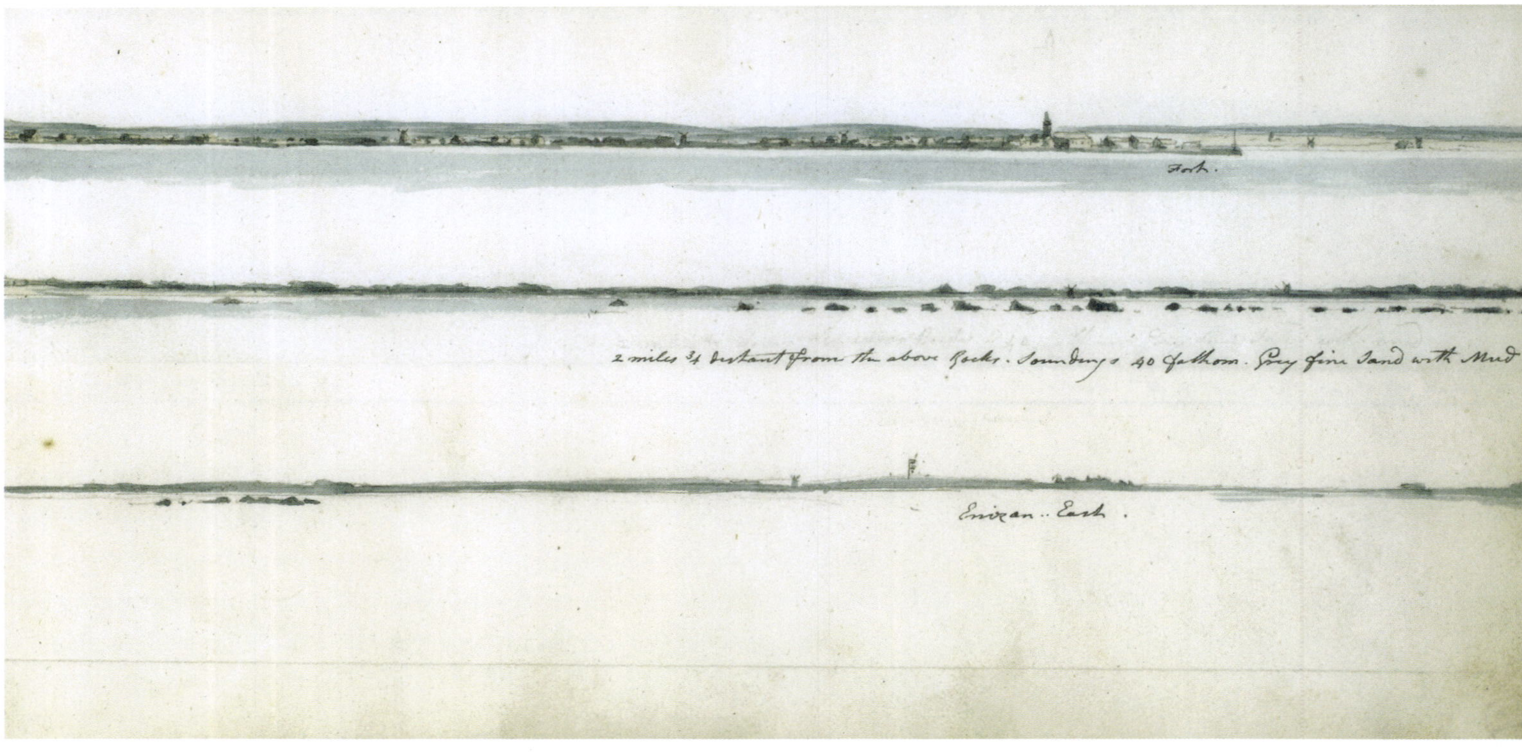

Left This image of HMS *Clyde* off Cabo Ortegal at a later stage of the cruise possibly shows her with a sea anchor streamed ahead 'to try the current'. The master's Remark Book includes several records of the results of this procedure.

Right Close inspection of Serres' sketchbook reveals a number of tantalising images which were never worked up. In most cases, although the faint images appear to have been erased, the page has not been reused, suggesting that the artist preferred to keep his material in clear chronological sequence. If he subsequently found time in his schedule he may have concluded that his memory for detail and colours was insufficient to recapture the scene accurately. From its position in the sketchbook this image is probably part of the town of Les Sables-d'Olonne, off which the *Clyde* hove to for a view.

Left Serres' panorama of the area around Pointe de Penmarc'h indicates his use of the reference material available to him in addition to the guidance of the ship's navigational team. Enizan, the only place name on the sketch, was shown conspicuously in the *Neptune François*.

While Serres sketched this complex inshore area, Thomas Nott took two boats across to the vicinity of the Îles des Glenans to sound for La Jument shoal, on which the *Agamemnon* had grounded. He found it to be much larger than he had expected, and fixed the outer limits with bearings. He was also alert, when tide and weather offered, to measure the current, and this procedure may be shown in the vignette from one of Serres' views off Cabo Ortegal later in the cruise. While his spelling and grammar may not be polished, Nott's skill at description is undoubted. On 2 July he records prominent marks on the coast between Île D'Yeu and Les Sables d'Olonne, noting that 'you see them like vessels, before you see the land'. It so happened that Serres never worked up his pencil sketch for that day, and the faint outline looms from the page of his sketchbook rather as the anxious mariner would see it. On 15 July Nott noted a headland at the entrance to Bilbao with a distinctive profile 'very like the Berry Head'. This was a man well qualified to ensure that the embarked artist did not miss a detail of significance to the mariner. Serres later paid tribute to the efforts of captains and masters to place him in the optimum position to ensure that his drawings provided a panorama of the settings of the exploits of the blockading force. They in turn valued his skill in turning their observations into pictorial form. His portfolio now contained comprehensive coverage of the immediate environs of Brest. It was time to record the refuges and passages along the adjacent coast to the south.

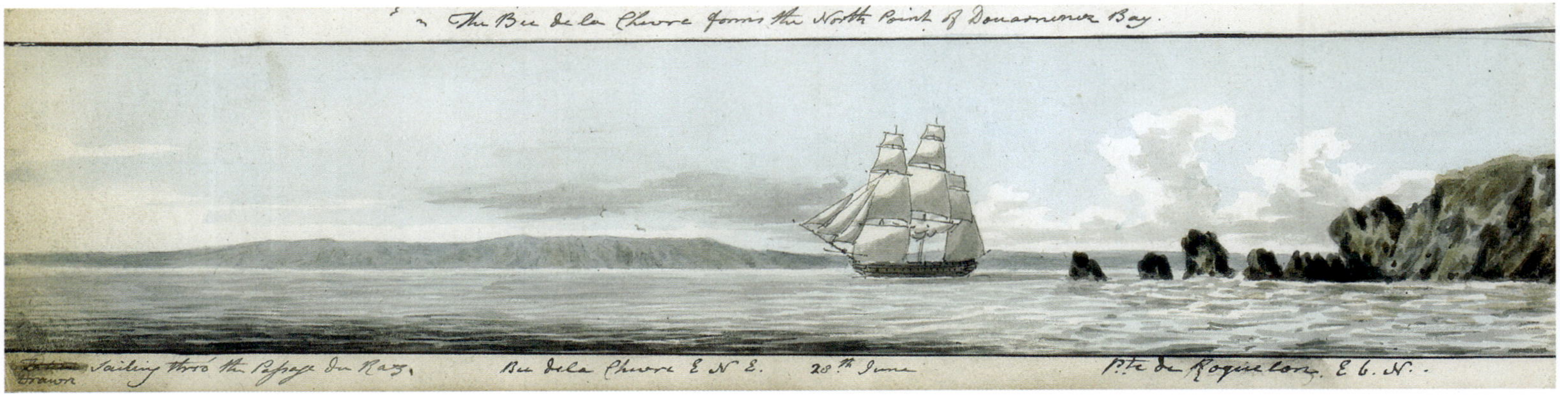

As British fleet commanders agonised over the decision to withdraw the main squadron from the rugged French coast when westerly gales set in, they longed for a refuge which would allow them to be back on guard before French units could slip out of le Goulet. Douarnenez Bay had attracted attention during Hawke's blockade in 1759 as a possible anchorage in such circumstances.[114] Captain Knight, while in command of the advanced squadron, used Douarnenez Bay as an anchorage in westerly winds, and after riding out a north-westerly gale there in September 1800 he suggested to St Vincent that the fleet might do so rather than return to Cawsand Bay or Torbay. His conclusion was that: 'The winds that oblige the Advanced Squadron to quit their Post, will enable them to fetch in 2 hours Douarnenez Bay, where they may lie undisturbed and sheltered from NW winds, and by having a look out ship near to Basse Vieille, every movement of the enemy from Bertheaume or Camaret is seen, and from whence they can work out, when those in Brest with the same wind cannot.'[115] He had armed and sent his boats away to take soundings. He described the clean fine sand which was far less liable to wear the ship's ground tackle than in the home anchorages with consequent 'saving to the crown'! His depiction of the bay in his general chart contains the telling note: 'Clean ground open to the wind at W b S only and out of range of shot and shells'.[116] St Vincent and Spencer debated the use

Serres sketched the southern entrance point to the great Bay of Douarnenez as the *Clyde* approached the challenging waters of the Raz de Sein. The frigate in the bay is probably the *Unicorn* (32) from Rear-Admiral Warren's squadron stationed off the Penmarck rocks.

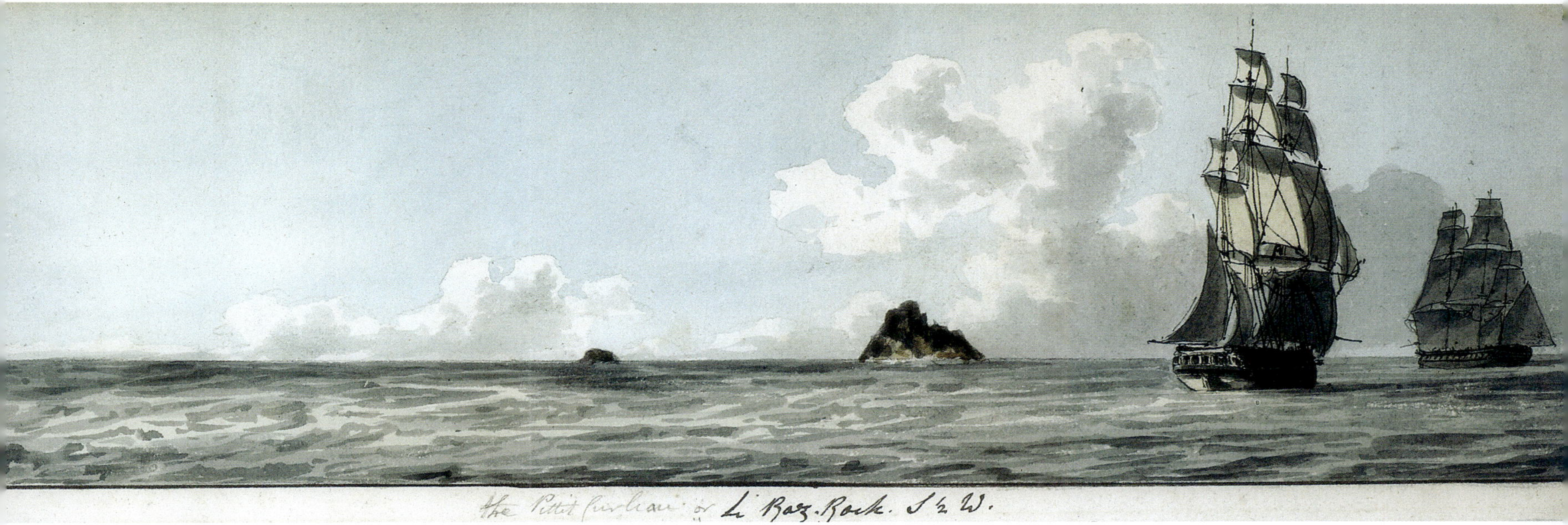

The *Beaulieu*, shown ahead of the *Clyde* during passage through the Passage du Raz in June 1800, had been built as a private venture by Henry Adams at his famous yard at Buckler's Hard, and her hull-form was closer to normal merchant ship practice. Although seaworthy and well-armed, she was not one of the fastest cruisers on the blockade.

of this bay rather than Torbay. A sample of the ground in Douarnenez Bay, taken by Knight, had been submitted to Mr James Sadler, the famous ceramics manufacturer of Stafford, for analysis of its holding properties, and St Vincent noted that 'I am very glad to have my opinion in favour of the anchorage in Douarnenez Bay confirmed by such authority . . .'[117] Later, Hurd would note in his remarks on 'The Grand Bay of Douarnenez' that: 'The present Admirals Knight and Sir James Saumarez have both anchored in this Bay and recommend it as a safe and secure anchorage.' In his published directions he recommended the Bay as an anchorage for the advanced squadron in a westerly wind, pointing out the difficulties of working out of the Iroise in the murk and swell which attended a westerly, with the shoals of Ushant and Chaussée de Sein on either hand.[118] As the winter of 1800 set in, St Vincent put Spencer's fears over the advanced squadron to rest by telling him that they were making use of Douarnenez Bay. However, the views of Knight and Hurd did not find favour with the commanders in the next stage of the French wars, any more than they had with Lord Bridport, and the anchorage was not exploited.[119]

Working under the careful direction of Cunningham and Nott, Serres took particular care to record in some detail the strategic Passage du Raz as the *Clyde* passed through in company with the *Beaulieu* (38), which had detached from the fleet on the same day. The performance of the frigate stationed to watch this channel was critical to the peace of mind of the Commander-in-Chief as he weighed up the intelligence passed to him by the Admiralty. Cunningham himself had issued strict orders for this station during his

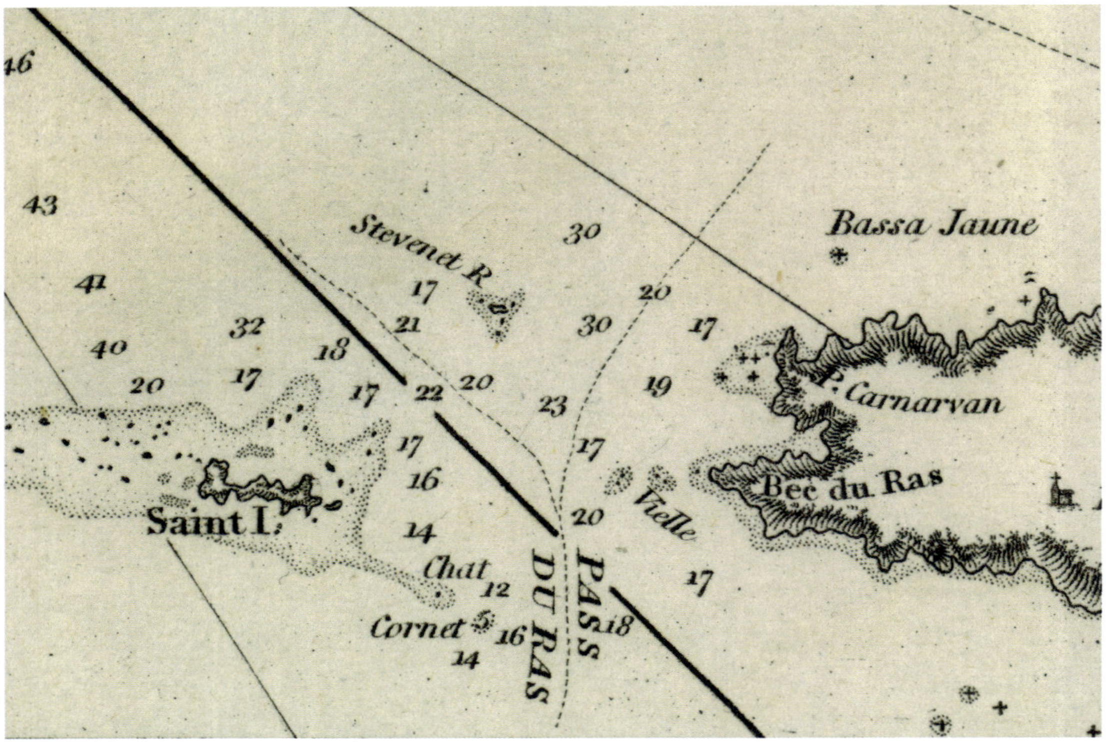

Left The Passage du Raz depicted in Captain John Knight's general chart, with leading and clearing bearings and recommended tracks. The dangerous Basse Jaune is shown with the bearings which marked its position.

time as senior officer.[120] On 18 June St Vincent wrote: 'I believe Admiral la Crosse to be in Brest with his 7 ships of the line and 3 frigates, and that the Prince of Bouillon's[121] intelligence describes what is intended, not what has happened, but this I do not hold myself responsible for: Captain Cunningham of the Clyde, who appears a very well informed man, assured me nothing had passed through the Raz at the time specified.'[122] The passage was a testing one for a large sailing vessel, with fast tidal streams and a complex regime of currents. The Plateau de Tévennec lies athwart the northern approach. Today's sailing directions remark that 'it is never free from danger when conditions are unfavourable'.[123]

The French mostly used the wider eastern channel on their way to and from the inshore passages around Pointe de Toulinguet. During these same fine summer days Captain Knight sounded the area with his boats, and took his ship of the line through the passage between the Tévennec and the Saints. His sailing master claimed that this was the first time that this had been attempted by any ship, and Knight's larger-scale chart of the area shows a pecked track annotated 'by H.M.S. Montague 1800'. Knight considered that this western channel gave the advantage of laying through without tacking and with less effect from the tidal stream. In his later published directions, Hurd supported this claim and commended the leading transit shown on Knight's general chart. He advised navigators to 'borrow' on the side of the Saints with the flood tide running and on the side of the Tévennec with

Below **The coordination of the navigating team in the *Clyde* would have been thoroughly tested during the pilotage through the Passage du Raz. Serres would have had to work fast to capture the images in his sketchbook. In this depiction of the Plateau de Tévennec he has removed the profile of the frigate to avoid obscuring detail of the rocks.**

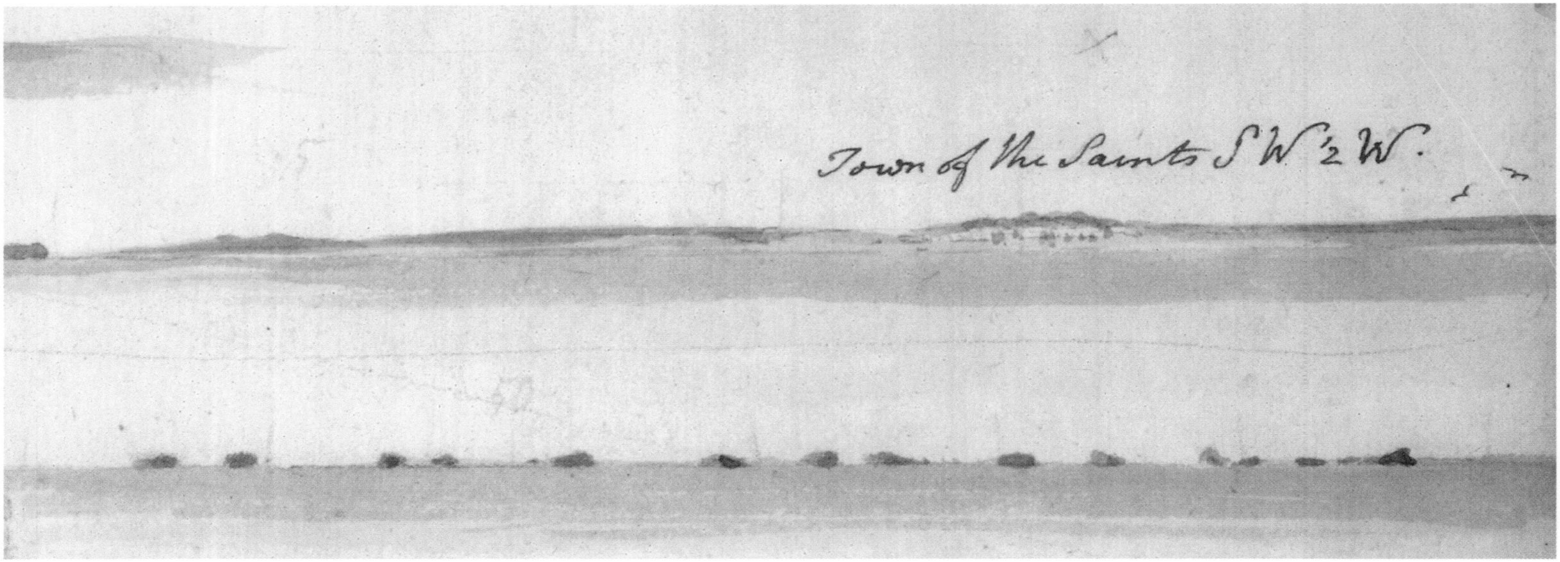

the ebb until the channel was well open. Knight's own remarks contained further advice on the optimum passage and anchoring places around the Saints for a patrolling vessel when the wind failed.[125]

Knight would also receive grudging praise from St Vincent for his investigation of the Saints: 'The weather has been very unfavourable for your exploring the danger of the Saintes and I am very agreeably surprised to learn that you have ascertained so much.' Serres was given firm and expert guidance on the salient features of this significant archipelago, which Captain Robert Stopford had suggested might be seized and fortified. Materials for blockhouses had been prepared in England and the armament identified, and Knight had been instructed to assess the feasibility without arousing the curiosity of his men, or of the French fishermen, 'who are an acute race'.[126]

With the detailed depiction of this taxing pilotage area complete, Serres resumed his general panorama of the coast, sketching in the church belfries and other conspicuous buildings of Cornouaille behind Hodierne (Audierne) Bay. The striking belfry of Plovan

Above Serres' depiction of the Saints shows the town on Île de Sein and the great row of rocks stretching out into the Atlantic.

Right Serres' companions have ensured that he includes the traditional seaman's marks in his sketch. Locronan mountain, above the famous old sail-making town, appears on most charts of the period, such as that on p. 26. Serres provides a detailed sketch of the belfry of Plovan church, and marks the village of Hodierne (Audierne) with a seagull.

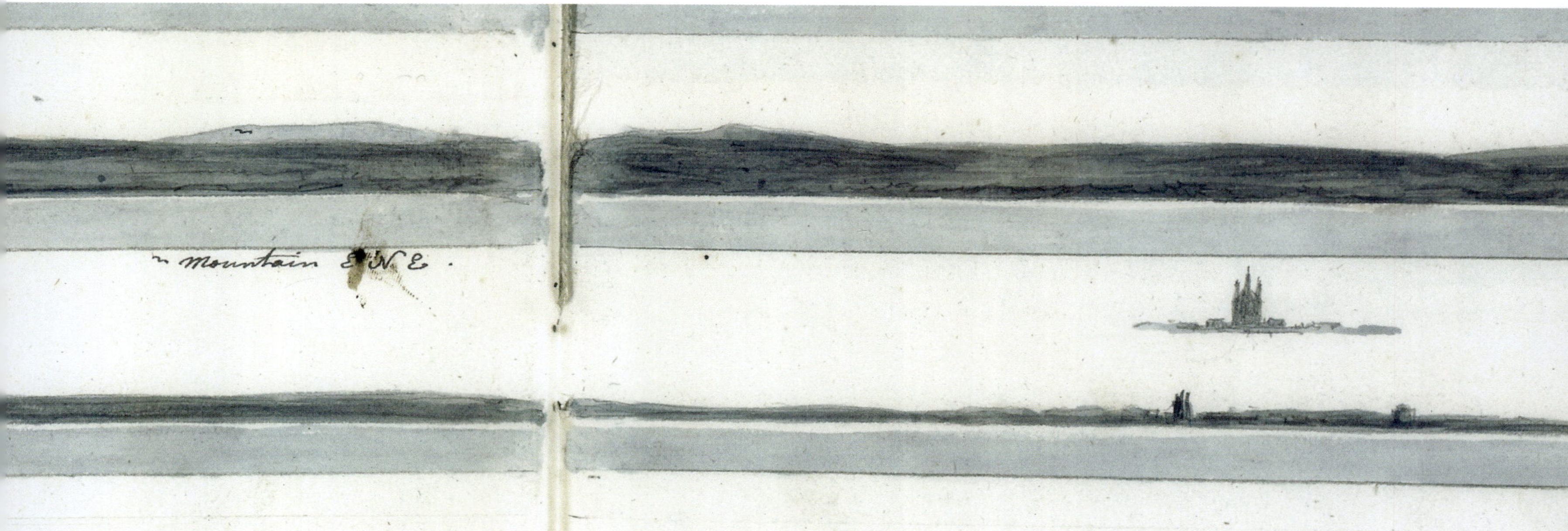

Mountain E N E.

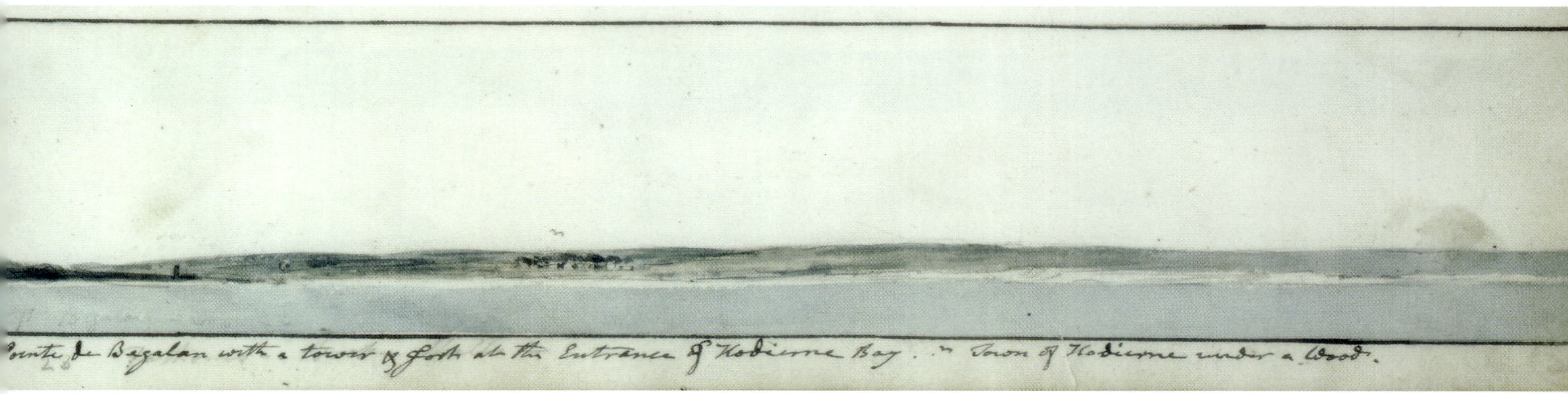

Pointe de Bazalan with a tower & forts at the Entrance of Hodierne Bay. Town of Hodierne under a Wood.

merited a small sketch. He also includes the traditional seaman's mark of Locronan with its 'mountain top', looming in the background. The area was well known to the frigates deployed to the Passage du Raz to watch for approaching convoys bound for Brest with supplies from the south. The *Triton* and *Stag* were employed on this task on 6 April when they entered the bay and found the wreck of the *Repulse* (64) which had been run ashore there during the previous month after grounding on the Saints.[127] Nott considered Hodierne Bay to be as safe as it was shown to be on the French charts, although he warned against anchoring for any length of time 'as the bottom is of such a substance as to put it out of the power of any purchase to save the anchor and cable'.[128] By the middle of 1800 it was normal for the bay to be used as an anchorage during an easterly wind by the substantial squadron which St Vincent put in place to watch for an excursion of French forces which might threaten the amphibious preparations off the south coast of Brittany.

French convoys coming in the opposite direction from Bordeaux or Nantes would wait in the complex inshore waters around Pointe de Penmarc'h until the coast was clear, and then make a dash towards Brest. William Cathcart recorded that during a five-week cruise in Hodierne Bay in March 1801 the *Triton* chased a French cutter ashore in Trecoutré Bay in the Penmarks. 'We . . . laid our ship as close to the signal house as possible and opened a tremendous fire from our larboard guns, double-shotted upon the cutter and signal-house. The tide drifting us out, we made sail, made a tack in-shore, and brought to, to open our starboard guns.'[129] The eleventh gun burst, killing two and wounding eighteen, and devastating the area of the quarter-deck. One of the dead was the second lieutenant who had left the captain's dining table to check the fall of shot. Gore himself narrowly escaped injury from flying splinters.[130] Nott's Remark Book shows that the *Clyde* was stationed off the Penmarks from 24 April to 8 June 1800, and this area will have been well known to them. Now they encountered Rear-Admiral Warren, who had been given three ships of the line and two frigates for this important station. Just after *Clyde's* departure, the boats of the squadron attacked and took part of a convoy and escort within the Penmarks. On this occasion Warren wrote: 'I hear of another convoy unloading within the Glenans,

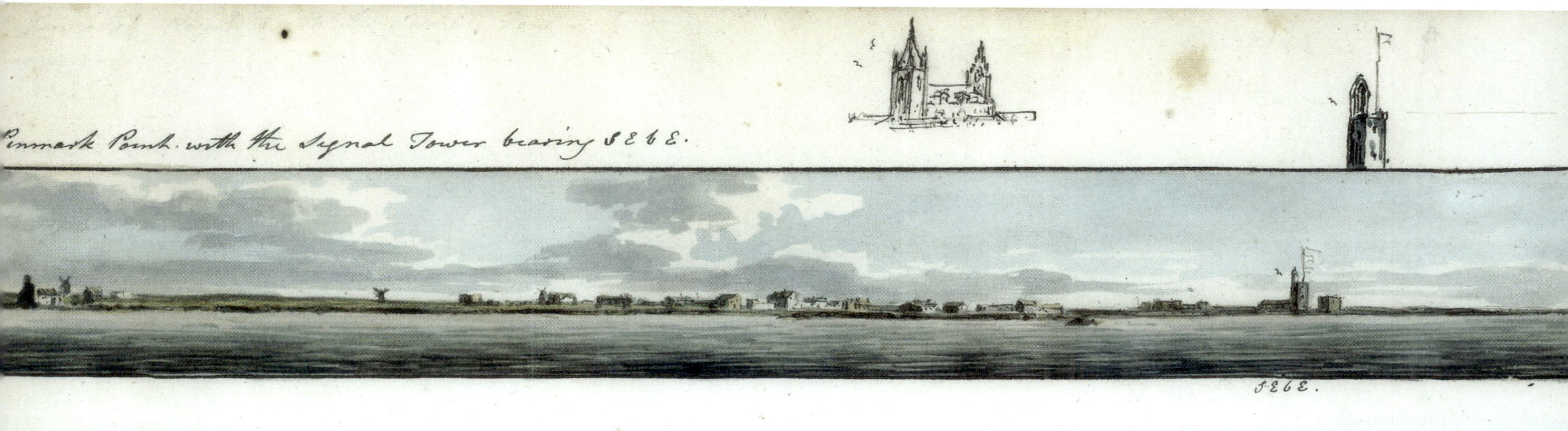

More detailed sketches are matched to Serres' view of the environs of Pointe de Penmarc'h, including the Signal Station where a chase was to cost *Triton* dear in the following year (see p. 74).

I suppose transporting their cargoes overland to Brest.'[131] The disruption caused by St Vincent's inshore dispositions was beginning to tell. It was to be sustained throughout the Napoleonic wars, leading to the development of the Nantes–Brest canal as an expedient to maintain the supply of the arsenal.

The captain and master in *Clyde* were making the most of a period in which their primary operational task was hydrography. As Mr Nott and his weary boat's crew returned to the ship from their work of surveying the offshore hazards to the blockading squadrons, Serres completed his panorama of the Breton coast and stowed away his sketchbook. The *Clyde* was now passing from the immediate theatre of the Brest blockade into a complex sea area where many of the Admiralty's plans were being put into execution.

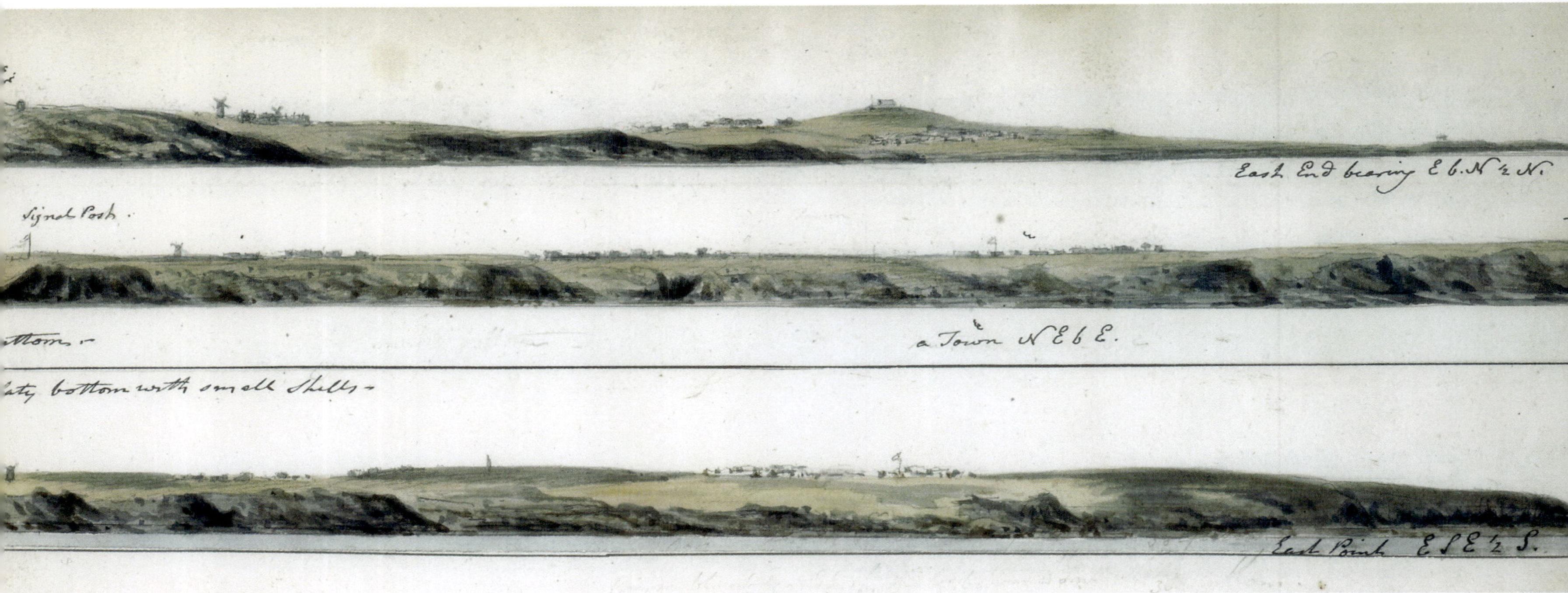
East End bearing E b N ½ N
Signal Post
ttom –
a Town N E b E
aty bottom with small Shells –
East Point E S E ½ S

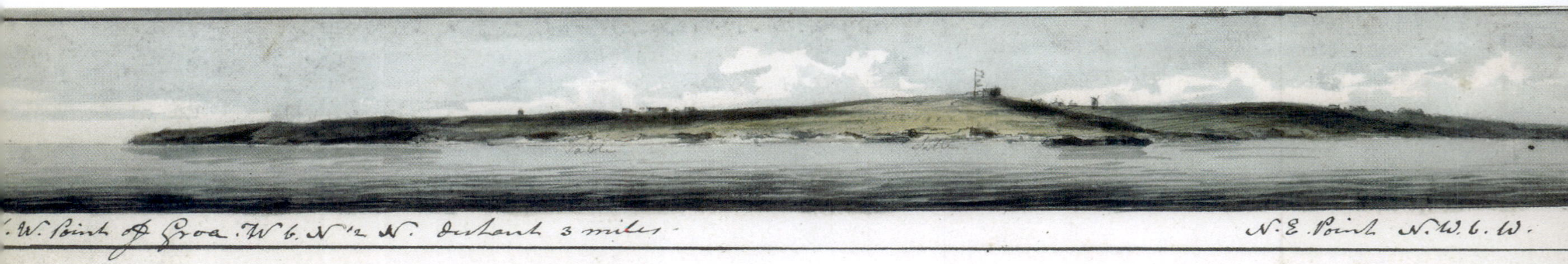
W. Point of Groa W b N ½ N distant 3 miles –
N. E. Point N. W. b. W.

CHAPTER SEVEN

The Biscay coast

The *Clyde* now began a sweep round the Biscay coast, passing through waters where St Vincent had to balance several tasks as he juggled the stations of his cruising ships. The top priorities were undoubtedly the blockade of naval ports to contain squadrons that were ready for sea and to deny inbound supplies. However, he was also expected to counter the operations against British merchant shipping waged by privateers from French and Spanish ports, and to support amphibious operations and associated attempts to raise the countryside against the Revolutionary government. The navigation of the blockading ships required an intimate knowledge of the offshore islands and seamarks. Cunningham and Nott had extensive experience of the waters and they now made sure that their artist built up a comprehensive visual record.

Isle de Groix, athwart the approaches to the naval base of Lorient, was the first important station to be depicted during a full day of sketching on 30 June. During a patrol a month earlier Captain Cunningham had reported *L'Argonaut* (74) and frigates to be ready for sea in Lorient, and Rear-Admiral Warren had stationed a 74-gun ship between the Îles des Glenans and Île de Groix ready to intercept them. Now the *Clyde* found a frigate squadron at anchor off the island. This was protecting the British amphibious forces off the south coast of Brittany, but it also provided a deterrent to the movement of supplies through the area. Once such a deterrent was removed, St Vincent expected the French to resume their attempts to pass convoys of provisions through the Îles des Glenans and Penmarks. In August, intelligence sources reported that the authorities in Brest were energised by expectations of a visit by General Napoléon, now the First Consul, freshly returned from his

Opposite **Thomas Nott's Remark Book records the position for each of these views by Serres of Île de Groix, with the bearings amplified with details of depths and the nature of the seabed.**

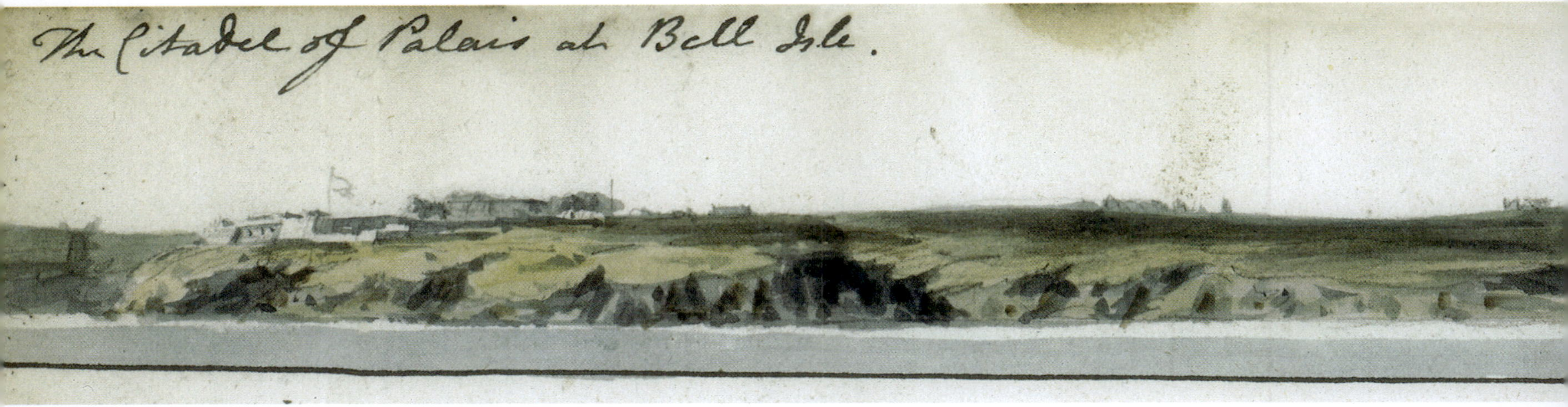

victory over the coalition forces at Marengo. The abundant harvest was expected to supply the extra troops being concentrated there. However, Morlaix, on the north coast of Brittany, afforded the only entry point for these supplies because of the tight blockade of Audierne and l'Iroise. In September the 74-gun ships *Magnificent* and *Marlborough* were ordered to cruise between the Îles des Glenans and Point Quiberon to intercept supplies being gathered at Noirmoutier to be pushed into the Quimper river and from there by land to Brest.[132] It was a testing patrol area, and on the night of 3 November the *Marlborough* was wrecked on the Plateau des Birvideaux, an extensive shoal 10 nautical miles south-east by south of Île de Groix during a severe south-westerly gale.[133]

The large island of Belle-Île was the most strategic landfall on the French Atlantic coast, one that homebound warships and merchantmen would raise before laying a course for their home ports. It also lies south of the peninsula and bay of Quiberon, on the doorstep of the most tempting avenue for support to the Breton Royalists, somewhere along the complex coastline of the Gulf of Morbihan and the rivers which lie between Lorient and the mouth of the Loire. Belle-Île loomed large in the correspondence and thoughts of the

Pages 78–80 **Serres' panorama of the north coast of Belle-Île, including the great citadel built by Vauban at Palais, is shown on the next three pages. Unfinished views in his sketch book reveal how he worked, starting from a rapid pencil outline. Occasionally, as shown in this view, he has to stifle his artist's impulses. The pencil outline of a frigate has not been worked up, thus avoiding any loss of detail from the panorama of the coast.**

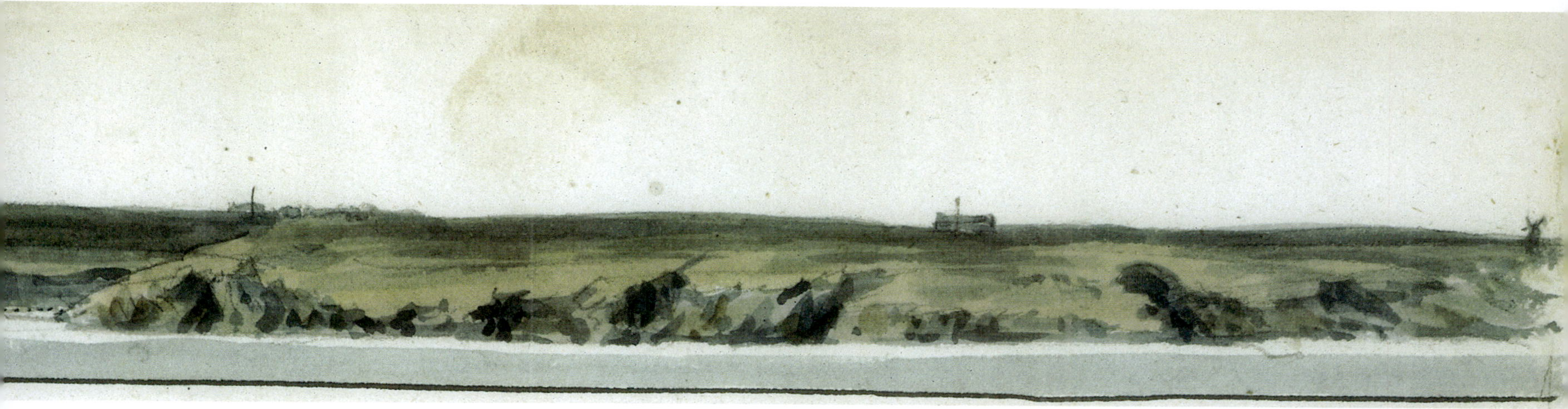

First Lord of the Admiralty and the Commander-in-Chief in the summer of 1800. The war cabinet placed great weight on a successful amphibious operation there. The expedition to Holland had failed and the Russian forces that had taken part had wintered in the Channel Islands, but returned home in the spring as a result of reluctance to serve again under British command. In Italy, the Austrian command was also unwilling to combine with an expeditionary force. At the War Office, Dundas declared a preference for British diversionary operations on the Atlantic coast of France. With the help of Nepean's agents Lord Spencer had conducted a detailed study of the prospects of an attack on Brest,[134] but the Cabinet had concluded that they had too little information on the shore defences or landward approaches to the city. Several members of the Cabinet continued to believe that pressure could be exerted by supporting the Chouans, counter-revolutionaries in the Atlantic regions of France. Their revolt had been suppressed during the previous winter, but only after all unprotected land communication with Brest had been disrupted. The Royal Navy's ships were frequently engaged in clandestine activity, landing arms and agents. On 19 May 1800, the *Cynthia* sloop was ordered by the Admiralty to land a M. Magon in the Morbihan.

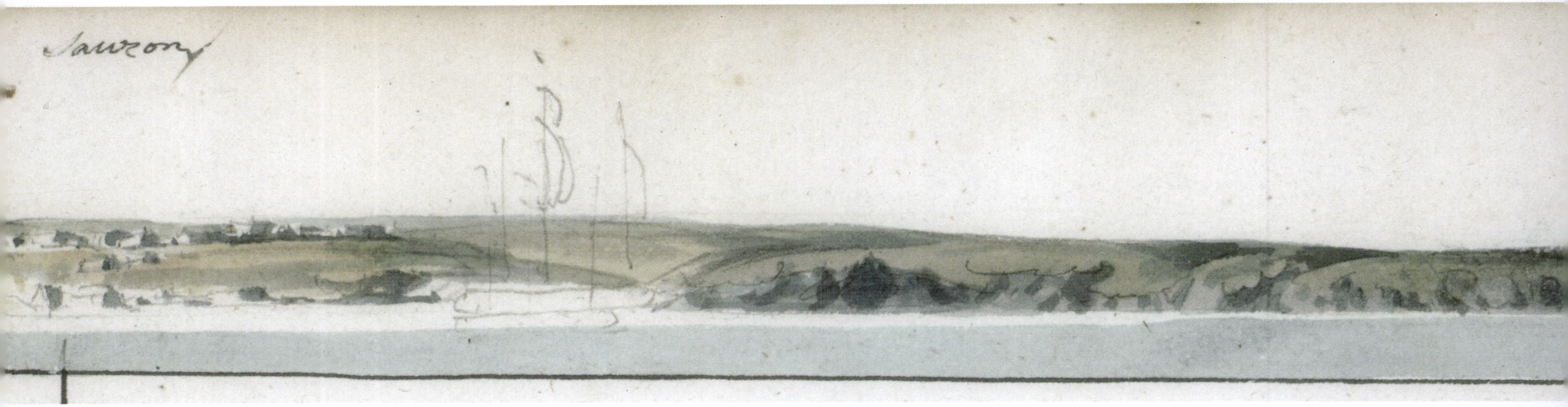

He arrived with a sum of £20,000.[135] The naval units in the substantial British amphibious force which was finally despatched to Breton waters were under the command of Sir Edward Pellew, who knew the area well. On 25 May he asked the First Sea Lord to send him six French Royalists in a cutter. 'There are at Falmouth, on board some chassemarées, several Royalists, who are good pilots, and were messengers and spies with me at Quiberon.'[136] St Vincent was constantly aware of the need to allocate sufficient assets, especially frigates, to protect the vulnerable troop transports and support the attack.

Serres' father had produced an extensive series of oil paintings based on sketches arising from an assault on Belle-Île during the Seven Years' War.[137] The son's watercolours show him at full stretch during 1 July, sketching and inserting the bearings provided by the master. A month before he undertook this work, part of Pellew's squadron had attacked the south-west end of Quiberon, and a landing had been effected in the Morbihan.[138] However, a secure beachhead was not available on the mainland, and attention switched back to Belle-Île. The allied plan of attack involved a bombardment of Palais and deployment of a diversionary force off Saumezon Bay in the north-east of the island while troops were landed in Havre

Vieux Fort to march on Sauzon, shown in Serres' view (see p. 80).[139] In early August, before the plans for the attack on Belle-Île could be put into effect, the decision was made to move Pellew's force, with reinforcements, to attack Ferrol.

Later on the same day, Mr Nott carefully recorded the position where the *Clyde* hove to off Île d'Yeu for another set of sketches (see p. 82), commenting that 'this island will be known by the Tower. The boddy of it white with a black top . . . it appears with a windmill at each side of it . . . on the West end there is a village with two windmills a small sails length asunder.' Serres uses Fraser's seagulls in association with more detailed sketches to highlight the conspicuous buildings which the master identified. This island was again very familiar to the British fleet. Rear-Admiral Warren had commanded the ships supporting amphibious landings on the Quiberon peninsula and in the Morbihan in the summer of 1795. He had occupied Hoedic, Houat and Île d'Yeu. As in the Seven Years' War, the islands were immensely valuable as sources of water and livestock to supplement the supplies brought and transferred, at some hazard, by the fleets of victuallers. Shortly after the *Clyde*'s visit, Warren partly justified an excursion rather further from the Brest blockade than St Vincent approved, by endeavouring to supply his ships with cattle from the island. He even sent back 'two nice calves and a young bull' for Lady Spencer! Rear-Admiral Berkeley had recommended the occupation of Île d'Yeu as a base for operations to interrupt the coastal convoys. It was occupied for a short time in summer 1800 by a small force from Pellew and Maitland's amphibious task force, as a stepping stone for the assault on Belle-Île.[140]

In several detailed larger sketches, Serres depicted the distinctive seamarks of Les Baleines and Pointe de Chassiron (see p. 84), pointed out to him by Mr Nott in a particularly exposed and dangerous blockading station in the approaches to the naval base at Rochefort. It was, however, one which would have brought back happy memories to his companions. A year earlier, on 20 August, following reconnaissance of the French forces in Rochefort, the *Clyde* had sighted and given chase to the *Vestale* (36) and the *Sagesse* (28). Concentrating on the larger frigate, Cunningham compelled her to strike after an engagement lasting an hour and 50 minutes. The *Sagesse* crept away into the Gironde. Cunningham's 'modestly-written'

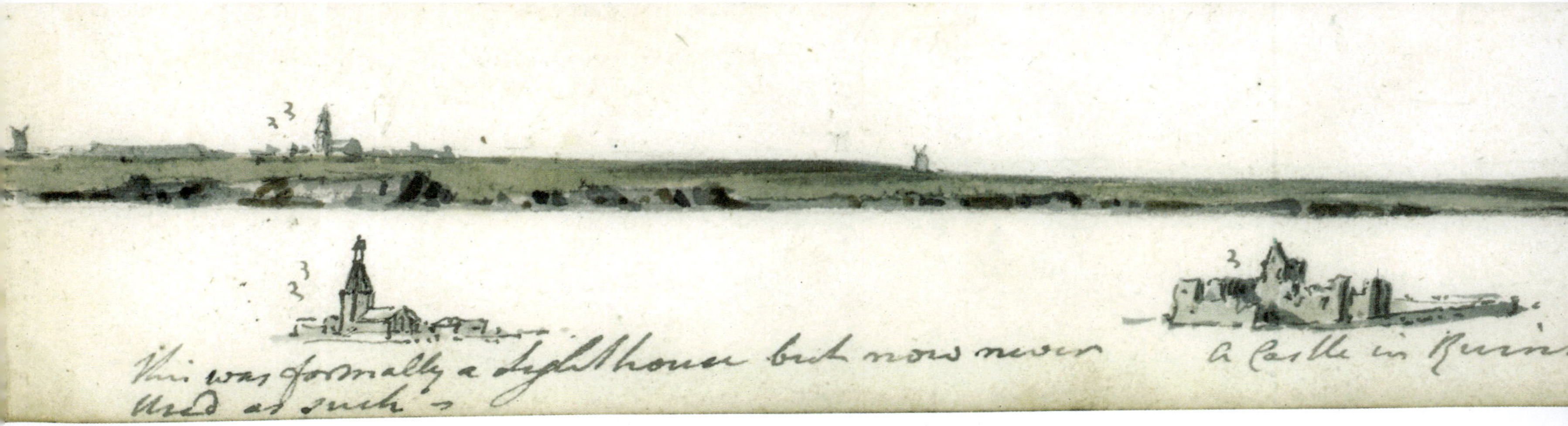

official despatch, followed by valuable intelligence from the captured ship, was forwarded to the Admiralty by Vice-Admiral Lord Keith, with a glowing covering letter. The news reached the King during a theatre performance in Weymouth. 'His Majesty, pleased at the good fortune of a ship so lately attending upon him, immediately stood up in his box, and commanded the news to be communicated to the audience: when '*Rule Britannia*' was loudly called for from every part of the house, and performed with reiterated applause.'[141]

Serres' shipmates were also familiar with the blockading station for Bordeaux. The *Clyde* had been among the frigates which Lord Bridport had detached to cruise 'from the latitude of Belle Isle to that of the Garonne'. The Commander-in-Chief allowed the frigates some latitude, but directed them to avoid being near the land. He specifically disapproved of them making the Cordouan Light.[142] Serres' page of sketches of the three great lighthouses of this coast (see p. 85) undoubtedly reflects the awareness of Cunningham and Nott that they were the key to safe navigation in the area. Now, while the artist sketched, ships and boats were employed in bringing to and interrogating inbound and outbound shipping.[143] On 7 July three sail were chased in fresh breezes. They turned out to be Guernsey

Île d'Yeu sketched by Serres on 1 July 1800 with some information which was not replicated in the master's Remark Book.

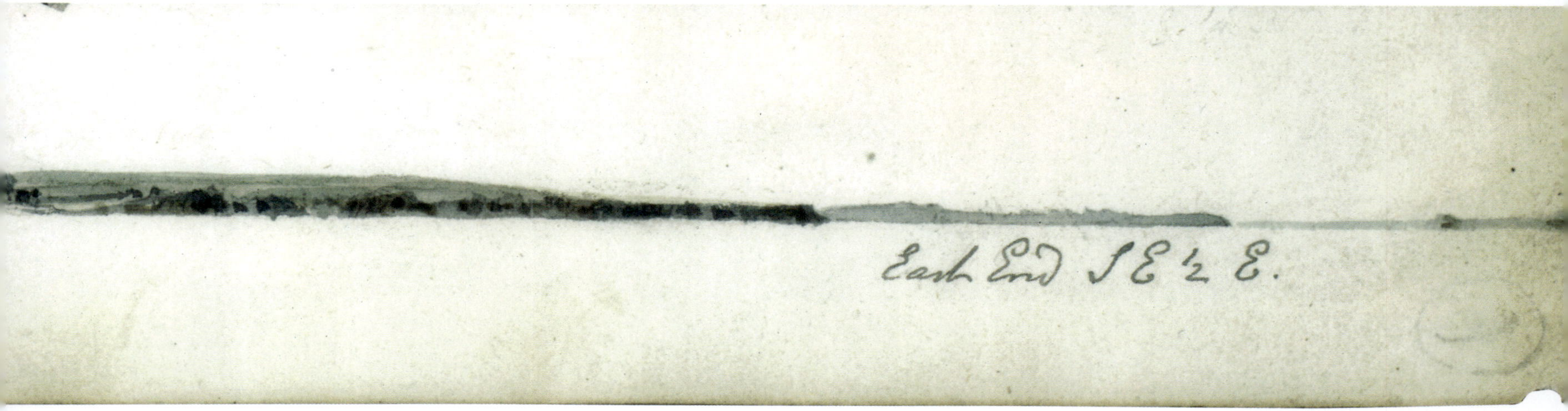

privateers. The following day, some 50 nautical miles south-west of the Cordouan Light, the *Clyde* was in company with Rear-Admiral Warren's squadron, and 'exercised great guns and small arms firing at a butt with the great guns'. In a light westerly breeze the frigate kept well clear of the low coast of Aquitaine, much of which, Nott noted, has 'not the smallest mark on the land to know it by'. Landfall was made in hazy conditions west of San Sebastian on the north Spanish coast. Cunningham now altered course and coasted close inshore towards Bayonne, hoping the weather would clear for his artist.

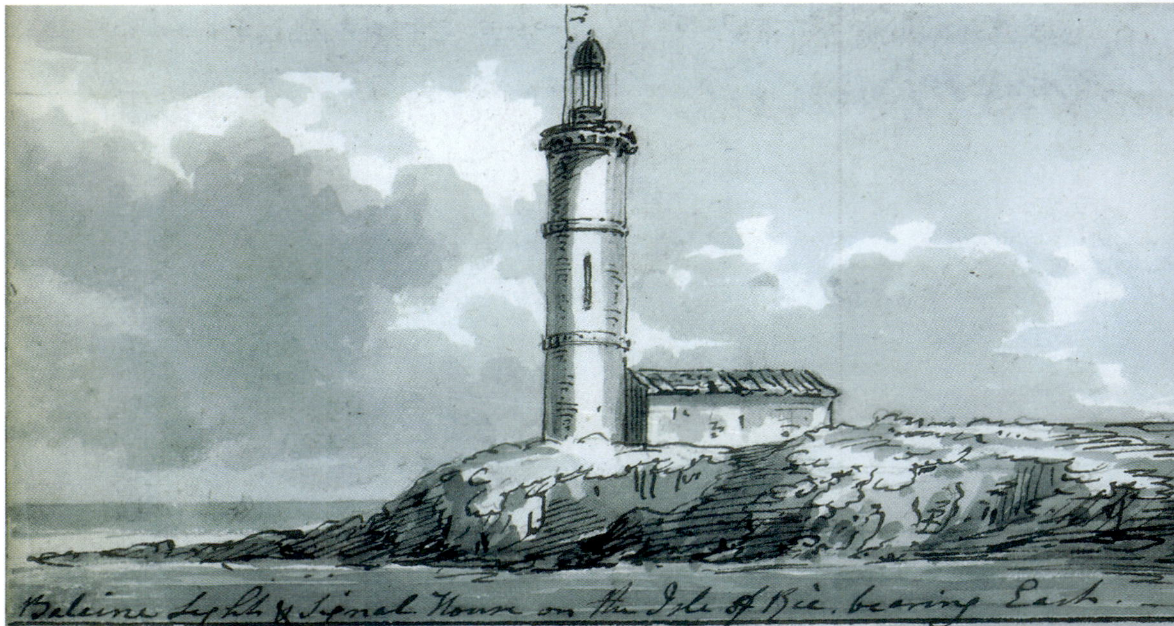
Baleine Light & Signal House on the Isle of Rhé, bearing East. –

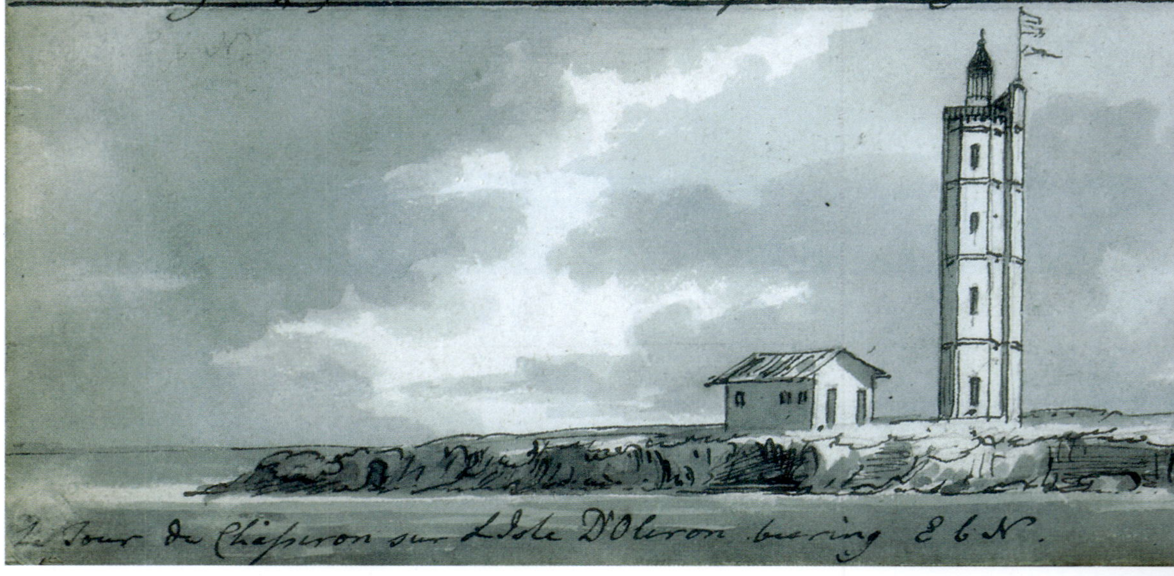
La Tour de Chasseron sur L'Isle D'Oleron bearing E b N.

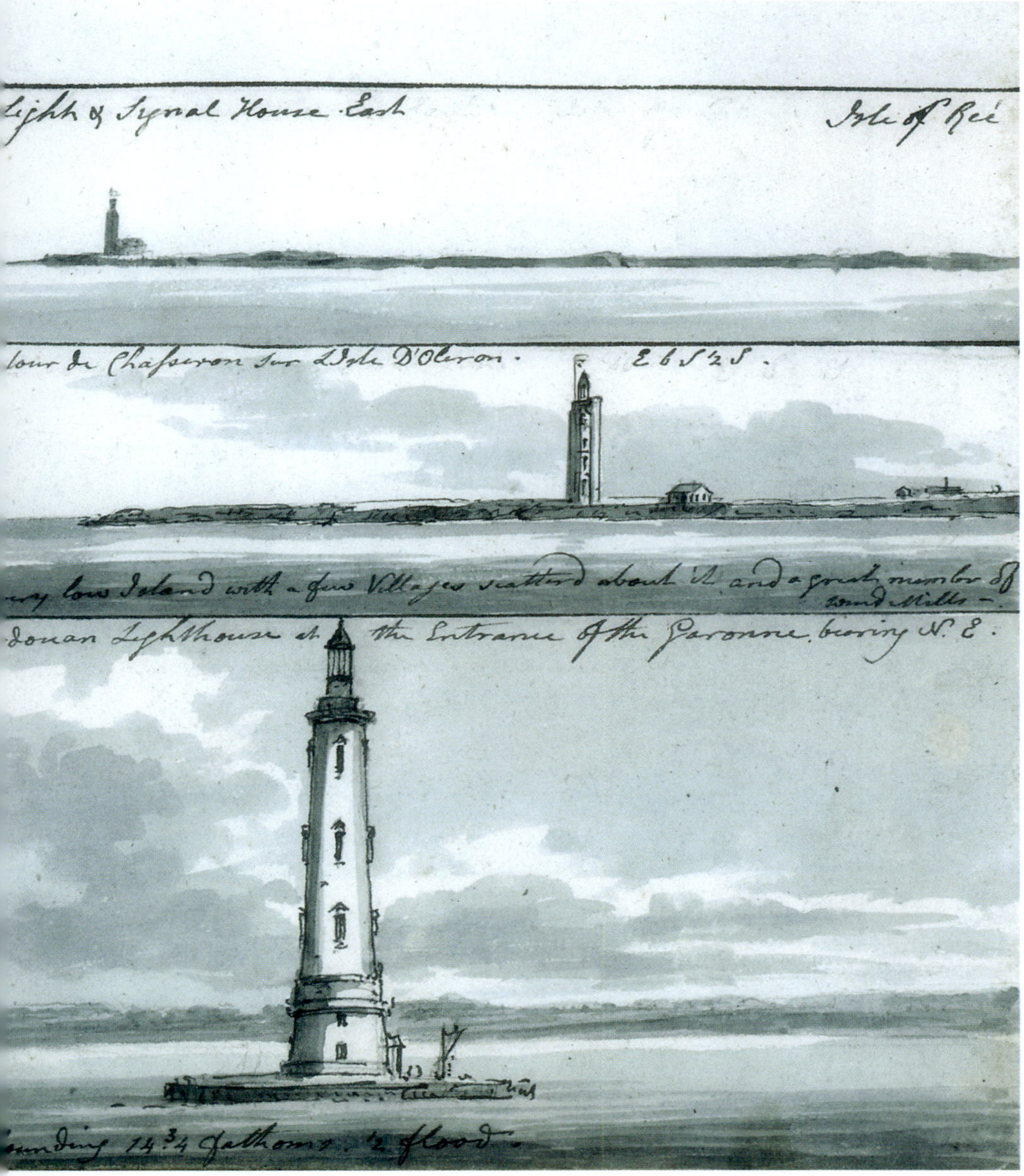

Serres' views of the great lighthouses of the French Biscay coast (Les Baleines on Île de Ré, Pointe de Chassiron, and Cordouan).

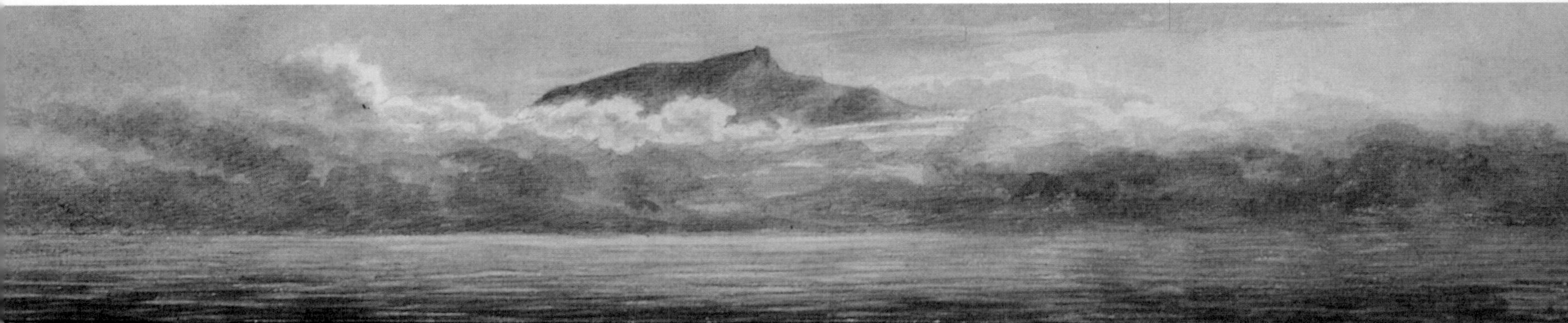

ppearance of the Mountain de la Run at St. Sebastion on the Coast of Spain. bearing by Compass. S½ W. when the risi
Clouds of Evening had enveloped the whole coast, except its Summit. 9 July 1800.

CHAPTER EIGHT

A rewarding cruise

Opposite **Modern charts still depict the Montagne de la Rhune on the French–Spanish border. When he saw it, did Serres think of his father, setting off on the life of adventure which would eventually take him to England?**

Rear-Admiral Berkeley had been a loyal witness to the efforts of the hardworking inshore frigates,[144] and on 8 July St Vincent wrote to Captain Keats of the *Boadicea*: 'Being extremely solicitous to mark my approbation of your meritorious services and those of Captain Cunningham of the Clyde, I hereby authorize you to water at Oporto . . . and to direct Captain Cunningham should he fall in with you to do the same and to cruise as long as your and his provisions will last . . .'[145] Correspondence with the Admiralty indicates that such cruises, with their opportunity for action and prize money, were generally given to ships which were reaching the end of a stint on inshore blockade. However, it is clear that much lobbying for the opportunity went on, and that the admirals were at pains to maintain fairness and good practice. St Vincent had declared in his waspish style: 'Serres I have long known to be a loose and tricking character, nevertheless I shall give the Clyde orders to receive him and to profit of a good cruise which he & Capt Keats are greatly intitled to, and neither Birthly Patronage or intrigue, in favour of others, shall deprive them of.'[146] Despite the Commander-in-Chief's indictment, there is ample evidence that relationships between Serres and his hosts were good. His anonymous biographer describes him as 'a pleasant companion, though not an intellectual one' . . . 'sensible and thoughtful', and dedicated to his profession with a deep interest in and enjoyment of the maritime scene.[147] All these qualities would have commended him in a naval wardroom, and assured him of support as the cruise continued in waters which his seafaring father would have known well.

Off Bayonne, on 11 July, despite a persistent haze which Cunningham feared would defeat their object, Serres began a series of magnificent appearances of the Biscay coast[148]

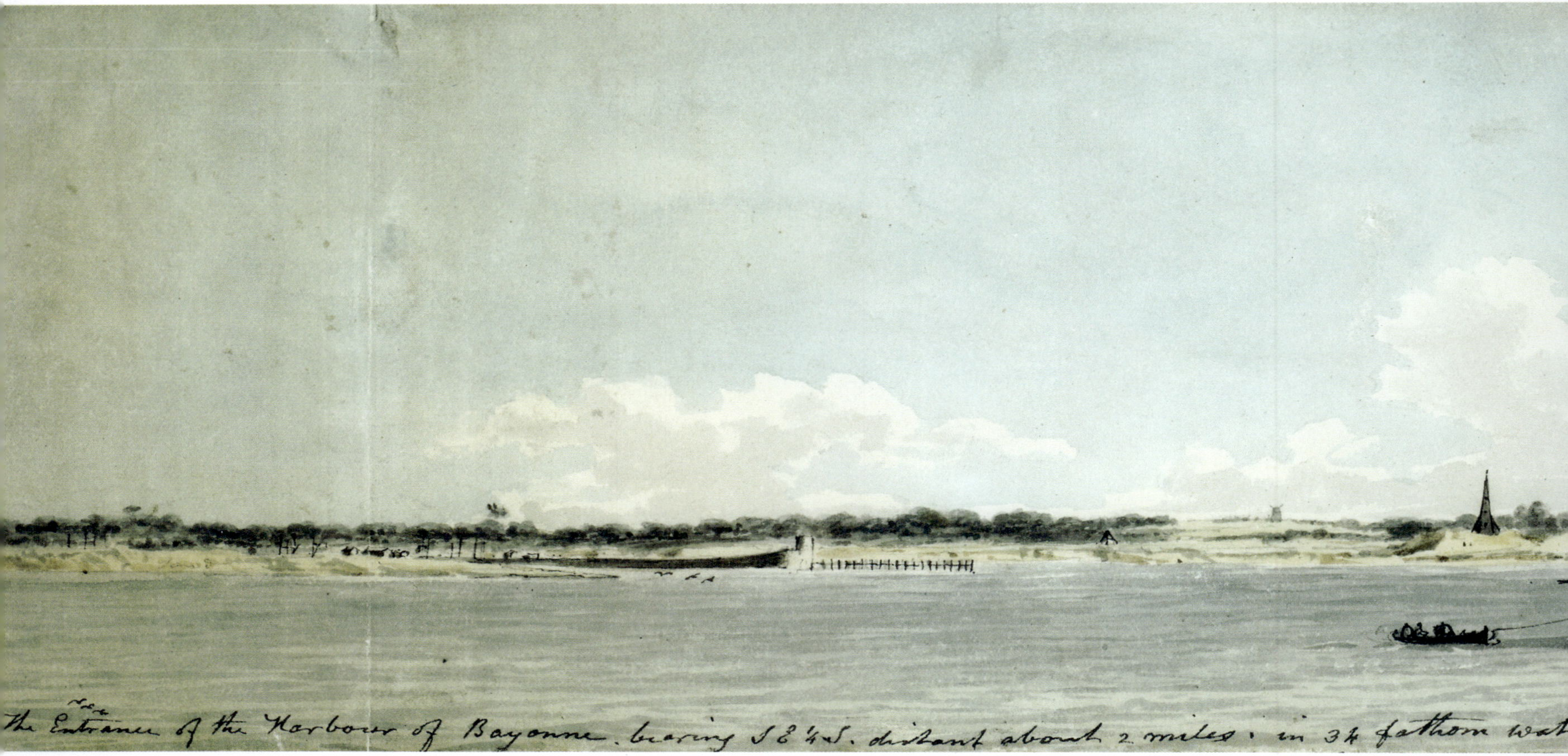

The first of Serres' magnificent views along the southern shores of the Bay of Biscay also includes his finest image of HMS *Clyde*. She was one of the 'heavy frigates' of the war-time building programme designed with the demands of blockade duty in the North Sea and English Channel very much in mind. For speed of construction six of these frigates were built out of fir. The two ships of the 38-gun *Artois* class, *Clyde* and *Tarter*, were very highly regarded. Their lighter hulls gave them a shallower draught for inshore operations. If ballasted more heavily in the more exposed Channel waters they could carry more sail than their heavier sisters and tended to outsail them. The *Clyde* was so esteemed that at the end of her life in 1806 many of the main members of the hull were reused in the construction of a new ship of the same name. Full details are in Robert Gardiner's classic studies of the frigates of these wars. Here *Clyde* is depicted off the entrance to Bayonne on the 11 July 1800. As in other views, the position of the ship is carefully judged so as not to mask any important feature. The inclusion of the ship also lifts the whole image and gives it enhanced perspective and impact.

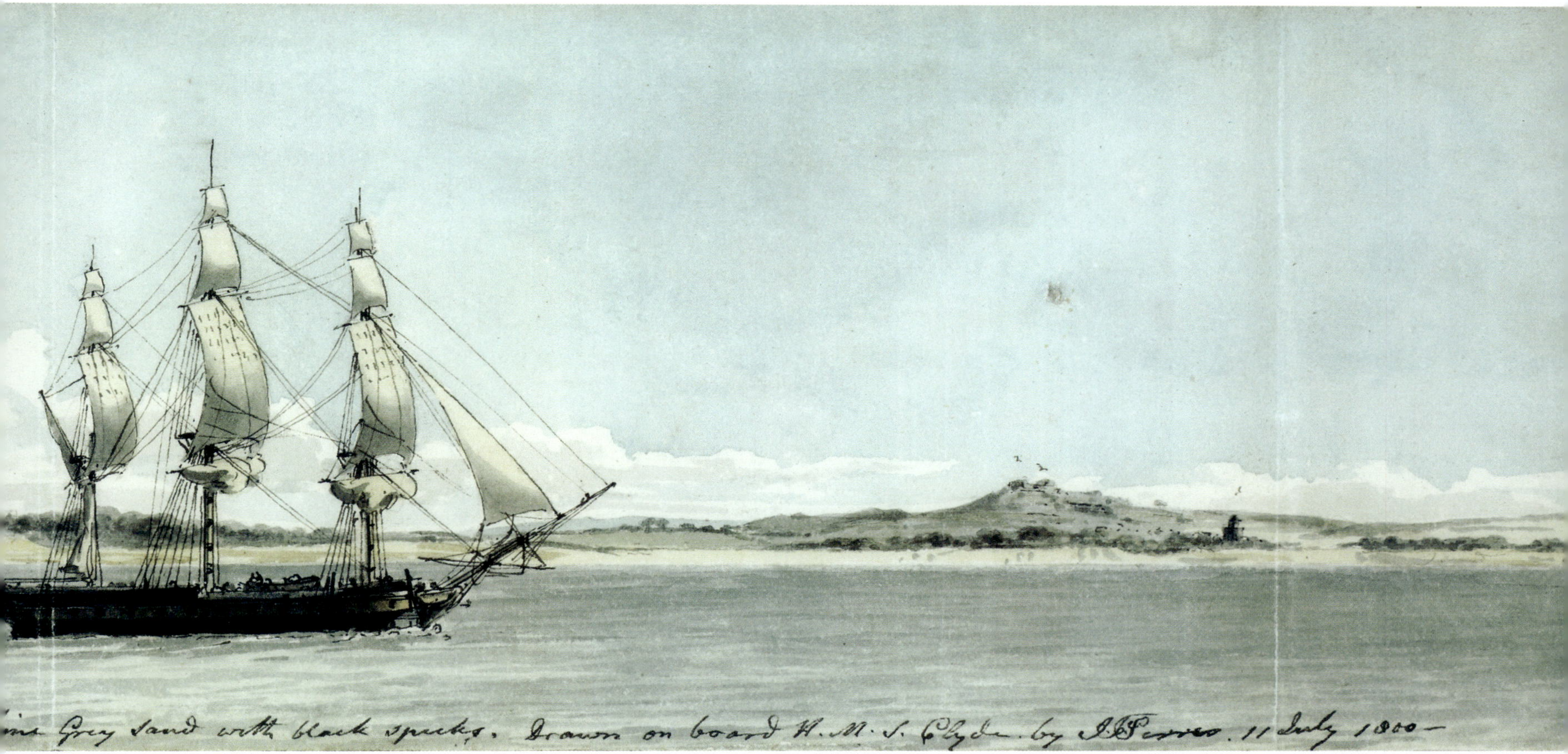
ine Grey sand with black specks. Drawn on board H.M.S. Clyde. by J.T. Serres. 11 July 1800–

in which his mastery of the techniques of the navigational view is best displayed. Until now he had worked in his sketchbook, which by this time he had all but filled. Now, with the vessel 'backing and filling occasionally for Mr Serris',[149] he appears to have had time to work in a larger format. The sketch of Bayonne ties in closely with Mr Nott's remarks, showing the church spire and windmill, 'the only ones to be seen along the coast', which make Bayonne known to a vessel approaching from the north. When a ship saw the windmill in transit with the 'little white signal tower . . . on the end of a long pier' the harbour entrance would still be 'blind' because its sandy entrance points overlap. Serres also uses Percy Fraser's seagull convention to tag the conspicuous citadel and cathedral, towering above the low land of the Adour, and Pointe Saint-Martin lighthouse at Biarritz to the south. Familiarity with this coast was to become of the utmost importance ten years later towards the end of the Peninsular campaign, as the fleet supported Wellington's advance into France. In February 1814 units crossed the entrance bar of the Adour in treacherous conditions with materials to bridge the river and complete the investment of the city.[150] The final shots of the war were fired during the last sortie of the garrison of Bayonne.[151]

Serres filled the last half page of his sketchbook with an appearance which again shows master and artist working closely together (see p. 86). This coast was not regularly frequented by the Channel fleet and the *Clyde* was experiencing these waters in benign conditions.[152] Even in summer months onshore winds made the bottom of the Bay a testing area for square-rigged ships, and the stretch east of Cabo Machichaco was avoided by frigates and larger vessels in winter, when easterly currents driven by the prevailing westerly gales could reach a rate of 4–5 knots and carry vessels to destruction on the banks of Cape Breton and Arcachon.[153] Nott remarked that while there were no off-lying dangers, and the Spanish charts published in 1788 from Tofiño's surveys of the previous year were thoroughly adequate,[154] it was difficult for those unfamiliar with the coast between Bayonne and San Sebastian to get their bearings, since the high mountains looked so alike. 'The most remarkable one is Montane de Larune.' It is the starting point for Tofiño's fine plate of views of the Cantabrian coast, which Nott particularly praised, and it is still listed amongst the principal landmarks in the British Admiralty Sailing Directions.[155] Tofiño showed it prominently on his charts with the boundary between France and Spain running right through the summit.

Nott noted that bearings of Montagne de la Rhune helped to find the narrow opening of the harbour of Pasajes. Serres' views overleaf convey clearly the depth of the cleft in which the twin towns of Pasajes de San Juan and Pasajes de San Pedro are hidden. Cunningham took the frigate in for a close inspection, recording that he 'saw a French frigate and several other vessels, apparently merchantmen'. In fact for Serres to sketch the detail in his inshore view, with the Castillo de Santa Isabel to port, the Torre de San Sebastian to starboard, and the road in the background, winding away into the mountainous interior, the *Clyde* must have penetrated some distance within the channel. Cunningham's late prize, *La Vestale*, had dropped off many passengers from San Domingo here before the fatal encounter off her home port. Lord Bridport had pressed the Admiralty to allow him to detach two or three frigates to the north coast of Spain between Cabo de Peñas and 'Port Passage', 'that place being a rendezvous of a number of the enemy's privateers and as one of the best stations to intercept captures they may make'.[156] In fact most privateers from east Biscayan ports operated from Vigo and other havens which were closer to the main trade routes.[157] Their home ports were constrained by weather. Both Pasajes and San Sebastian were subject to heavy swell in the winter months.[158] Another hazard at San Sebastian was error in identification of the harbour entrance. Such navigational difficulties were also reported during the Napoleonic wars.[159]

The ship's daily routine went forward as they passed Cabo Machichaco in fine summer weather, as depicted on the title page of this book, and their artist gathered the material for another fine diptych, from which portions are illustrated on pp. 94–5. A Spanish fishing vessel was stopped. The ship's company purchased its catch. They would pay half-a-crown apiece for 'bonetta', the bonito that is highly prized in the cuisine of northern Spain. An American brig was examined. Samuel Brown (seaman) passed

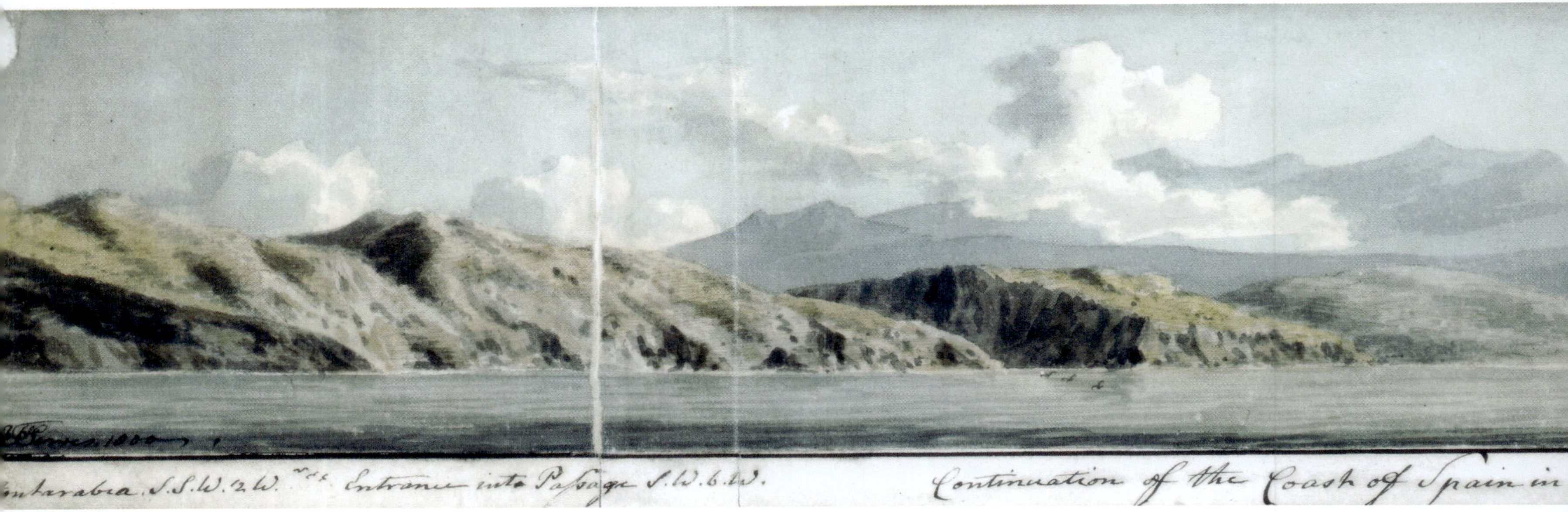

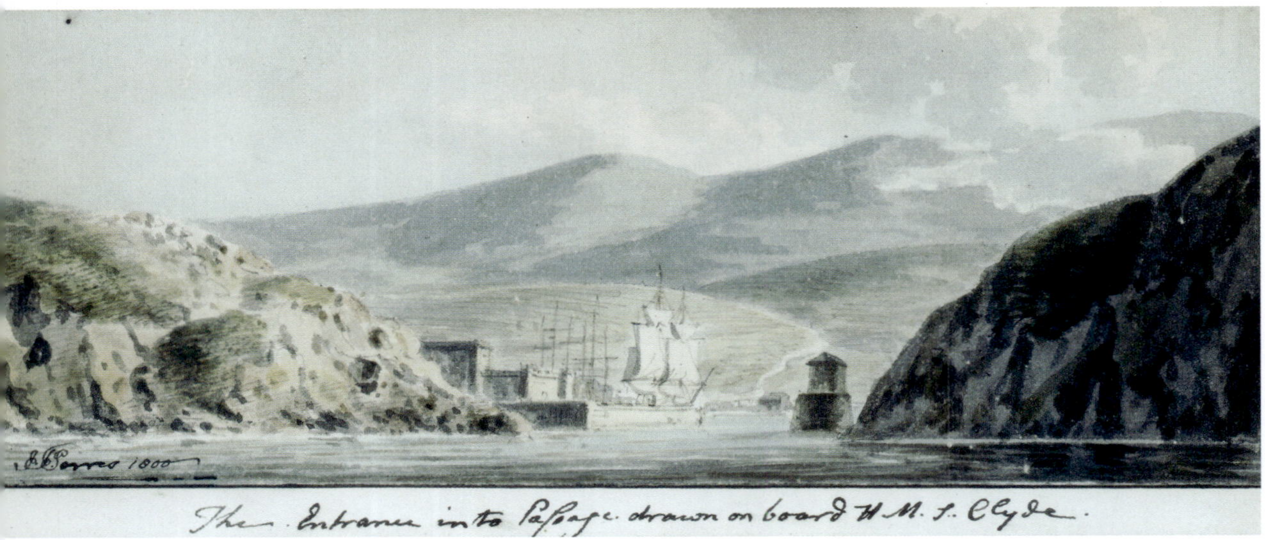

Left **The narrow entrance to Pasajes, the first north Spanish port to be inspected by the *Clyde*, is well illustrated by Serres, although the perspective of the view made within the entrance is not quite correct. The tower on the starboard side of the channel would have been further away than the castle, suggesting that the artist had to work swiftly on his sketch.**

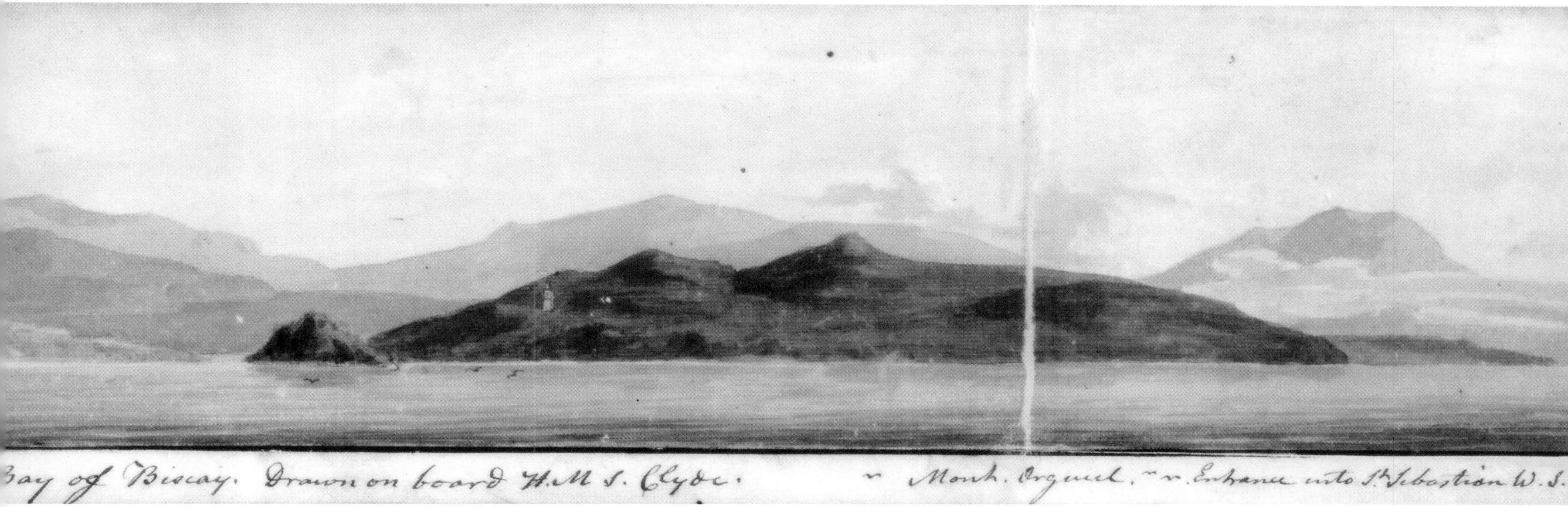

Above **Describing the entrance to San Sebastian, Mr Nott remarked that the white tower of a lighthouse on a sugar-loaf hill is conspicuous from at least 7 to 8 leagues distance against the black mountain chain behind. All this is captured by Serres. This old lighthouse is still listed in the British Admiralty Sailing Directions, which note that the profusion of modern lights along the coast has led to fatal errors by visiting mariners. The town of San Sebastian lay on an isthmus behind Mount Urgell, which Serres marks with a single seagull.**

away.[160] Light breezes and fine weather persisted throughout the period, and the illustrations of the *Clyde* in the views suggest that all sail was furled while the artist sketched the coast and approaches to the key ports such as Bilbao, where the captured fishing vessel was 'liberated'.

Nott noted of the next port that: 'Mount de Santona lies at the West side of a deep Bay, where convoys stop, and are protected by a small Battery . . .'[161] Cunningham sent a boat in to reconnoitre Santona (see p. 95). This port was later held by the French as their main base throughout the Peninsular campaign, despite attacks by the Royal Navy and Spanish guerrillas. Supplies were run in by fishing vessels. The seamen of the Biscayan villages such as Castro Urdiales and Laredo were experienced voyagers who had enjoyed close links with the other Atlantic countries since the Middle Ages.[162] As Cunningham closed the coast Serres was able to make a more detailed study of some of these small ports. The back end-paper depicts the *Clyde* off the bluff of Quezo. The smaller vessel inshore may be an instance of artistic licence, since the log does not mention an encounter with any other warships.[163]

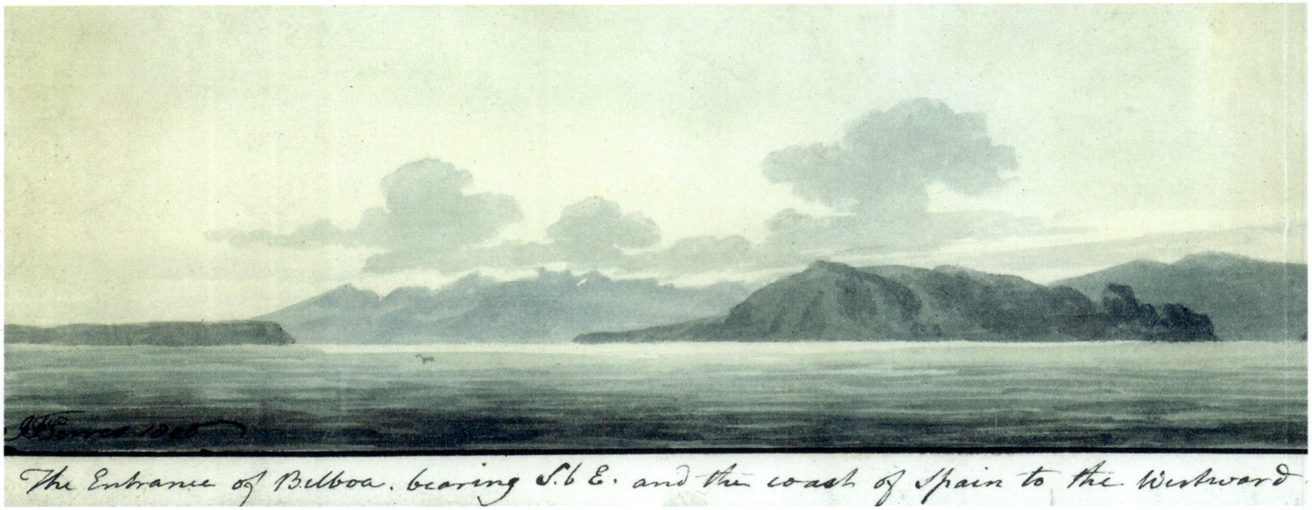

Serres' depiction of the entrance to Bilbao shows Punta Galea, the headland which Nott considered '. . . to stop short perpendicular, and very like the Berry Head'.

However, Mr Nott's log makes mention of a Spanish *chasse-marée*, and this may well be the small vessel at the right hand of the view. The current British Admiralty Sailing Directions[164] note that the church in the village of Noja is prominent, as depicted by Serres. Quezo village, to westwards, is now 'clearly visible from seaward due to its several hotels and apartment blocks'!

The next port to be examined for activity was Santander. Improvements in internal communications during the latter part of the eighteenth century had increased the importance of this port for the export of wool, and of flour to the colonies. Santander was the only commodious base between Ferrol and San Sebastian, and it would be occupied by both the French and the British during the Peninsular campaign. As a forward victualling port it was crucial to Wellington's final advance to the French border.[165] In this earlier war it merited close watch by the Channel fleet when ships could be spared. The task was often allocated to brig sloops such as the *Sylph*, which Serres had seen off Brest. Captain

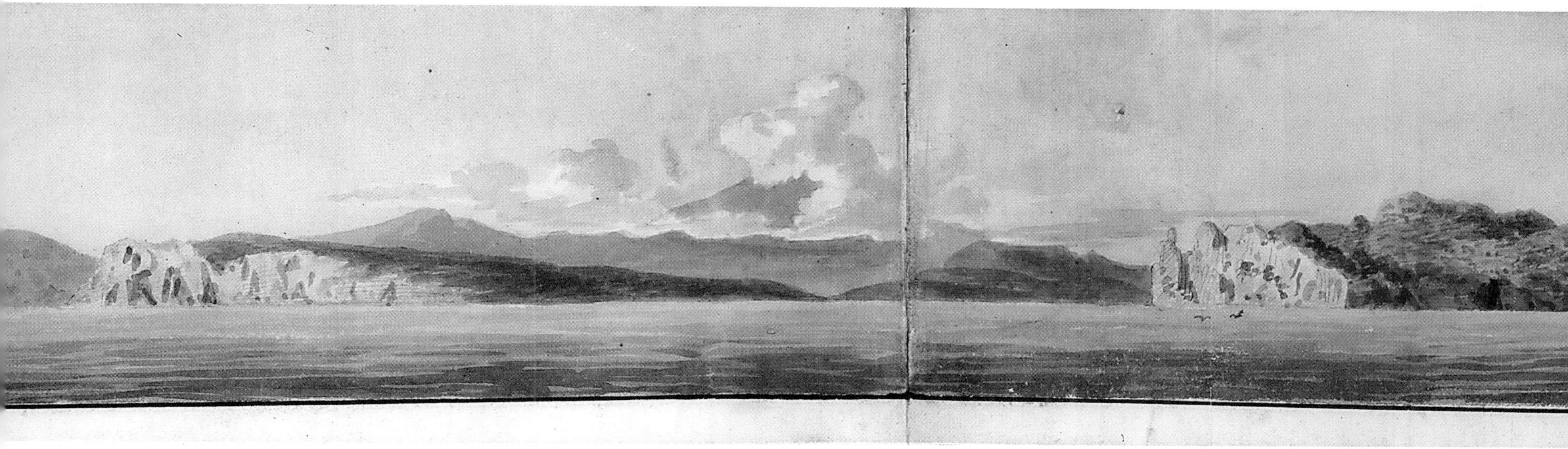

Above In his view of the entrance to Santona, Serres carefully delineates what the master described as '. . . a slender tall rock like the figure of a man – and is called by the Spannish Mariners the Fryer – which is a good Mark to know it by'. Nott's Remark Book illustrates the verdict of Captain W. Smyth, one of the first officers to be recruited into Hurd's new hydrographic specialisation, that much had been expected of the masters, given their limited education and demanding general ship duties. Smyth did acknowledge, however, their sharp eyes and diligence in collecting remarks. Punta del Fraile (Friar Point) is marked on today's chart, and the anchorage in the approaches to Santona is called Fraile. In the background looms the peak of Serantes which is nearly always topped with a distinctive plume of orographic cloud which Tofiño had also recorded in his coastal view.

Dashwood of that vessel would earn promotion to post rank in 1801 after twice driving off a large French frigate in the approaches to Santander.

The coastal panorama was now dominated by the great Cantabrian mountain chain, below which were several more small ports, two of which can just be seen in Serres' interpretation (see p. 97). Nott notes that 'the Havens of St Vincent, and Riba de Sella, have batteries to defend their trade'.[166] On 18 July the *Clyde* chased a Spanish letter of marque, the *Deux Amis* (4) from Vera Cruz, into St Vincent de Barquera. This enterprise was not without hazard. In his sailing directions Tofiño advised that, because of the shallow bar and fringing reefs and shoals, a vessel should only enter this harbour 'in a case of absolute despair'![167] Cunningham called away the frigate's boats and sent them into the attack. Soon they came under fire from the enemy vessel and a battery beneath which it had taken refuge. Cunningham took his ship even closer and 'brought our broadside to the battery and partly silenced their fire'. Now the boat parties succeeded in burning the Spanish vessel, which was

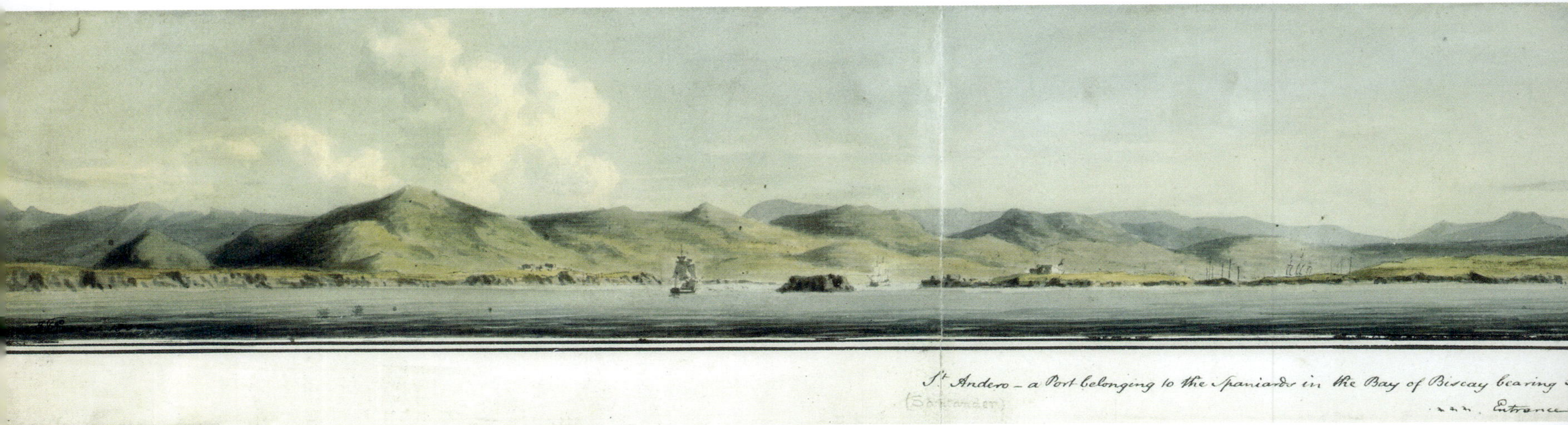

found to be bound for Santander with logwood and sugar. The exploit was not without cost. Two of the boarding party were blown up by loose powder.[168] The same view shows Cabo Peñas, which Nott declares 'is much lower than any of the Head Lands before mentioned, and will be easily known by the drawing of it'. This headland marked the western end of Lord Bridport's frigate line. The *Clyde* was approaching what was arguably the key landfall on the Atlantic coast.

Both Admiralty and Commander-in-Chief maintained a close interest in dispositions off the north-west of Spain. In summer 1800, Captain Keats in the *Boadicea* was on patrol in this area with the *Indefatigable* and the *Sirius*. *Uranie* joined him on 17 July and *Fisgard* on the 20th. St Vincent also promised *Beaulieu* and *Cambrian* as soon as they could be relieved in their current stations, 'which I think will enable you to spread from latitude 46.00 to Cape Finisterre so as to intercept the frigates and numerous privateers of the enemy which are now at sea'.[169] A set of five views illustrate the coast around the southern end of this patrol line and British warships are illustrated in all of them. The magnetic attraction of this cruising ground undoubtedly drove the

Above Both Nott and the *Neptune François* stressed that Santander can be picked out easily, because the surrounding land is flatter than the rest of the rugged coast. This is clear from Serres' view. Serres picks out two prominent marks – a fort (Castillo Ano) and a Signal Tower on Cabo Mayor – which would become apparent as the mariner closed the port. As usual, they are marked by seagulls. Merchantmen are entering and leaving harbour round Isla de Mouro.

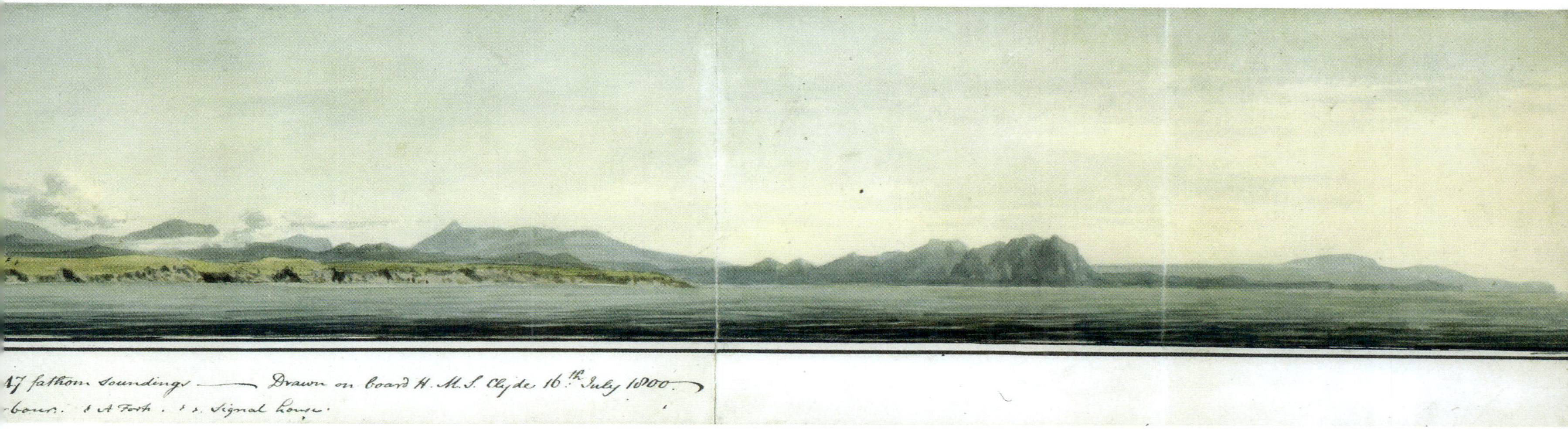

Below **Nott's directions draw attention to the Urricles (Zurricles in Tofiño), or Cantabrian, mountains to the west. 'The tops of them are in notches like a saw'. Today's Sailing Directions note that these Picos de Europa are visible from a considerable distance out to sea in clear weather.**

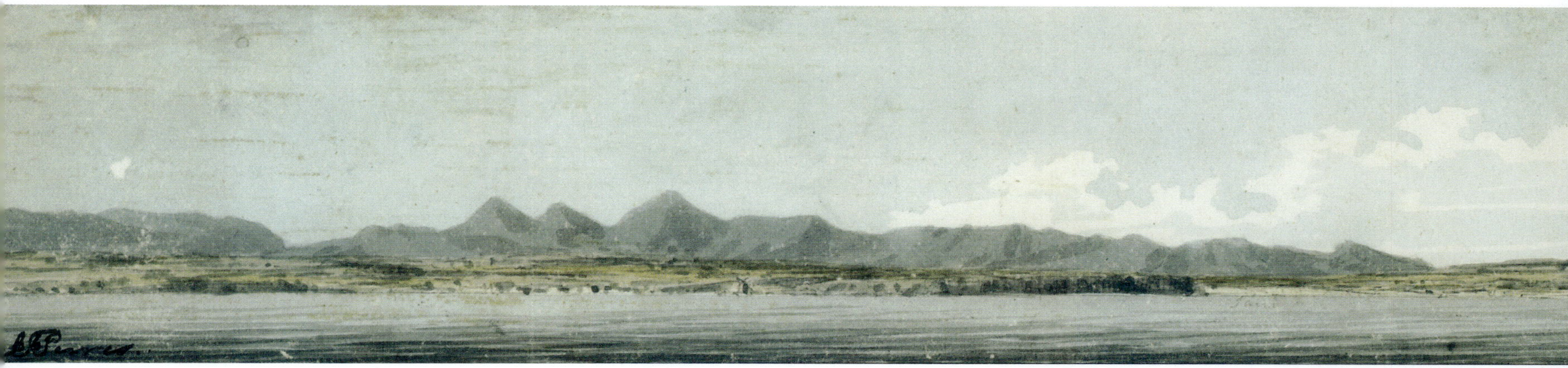

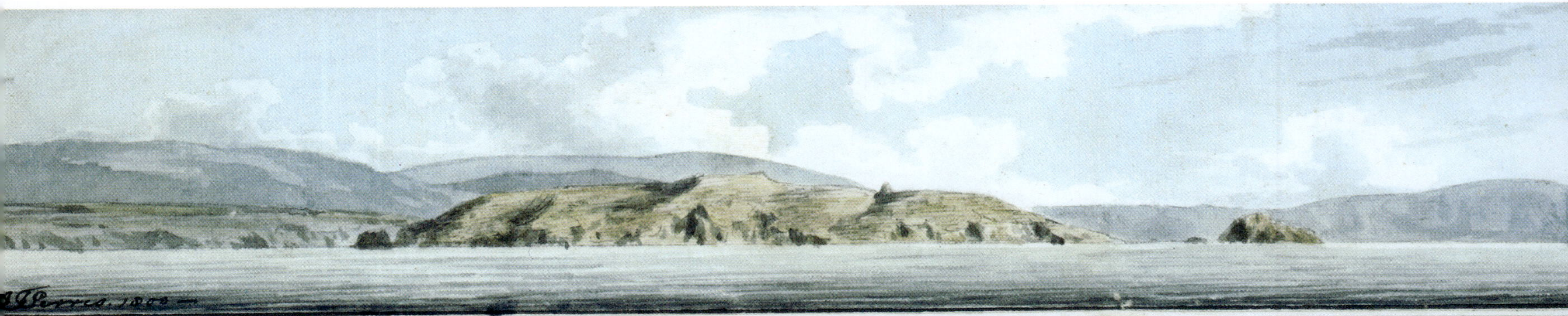

Cape Torinana - bearing S. by W. —— Drawn on board H. M. S. Clyde 14th August

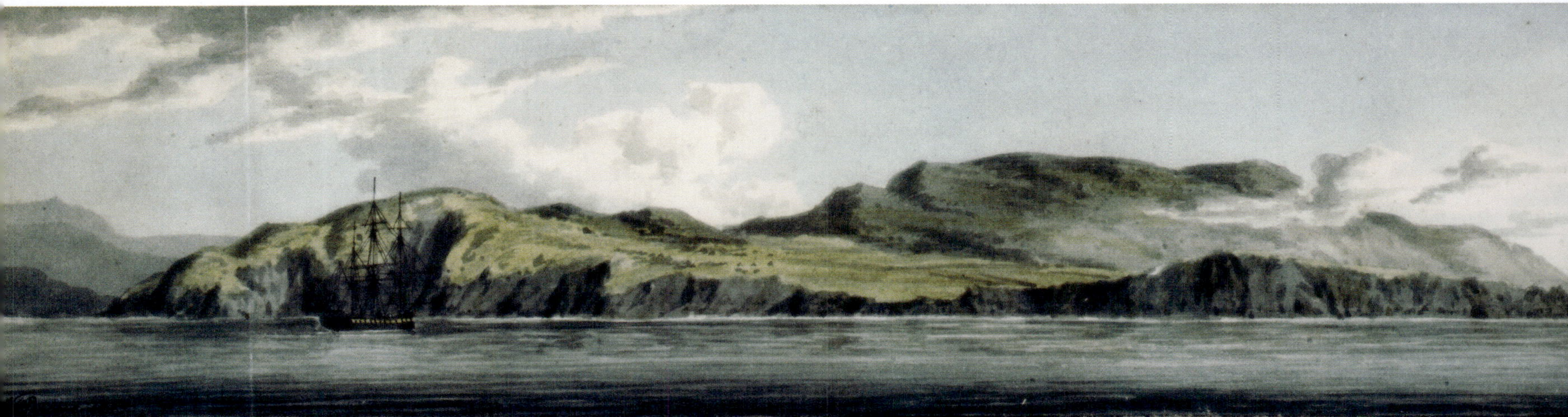

Cape Ortegal - bearing W. by S. ½ S. about 3 leagues distant —— Drawn on board H. M. S. Clyde 22nd July 1

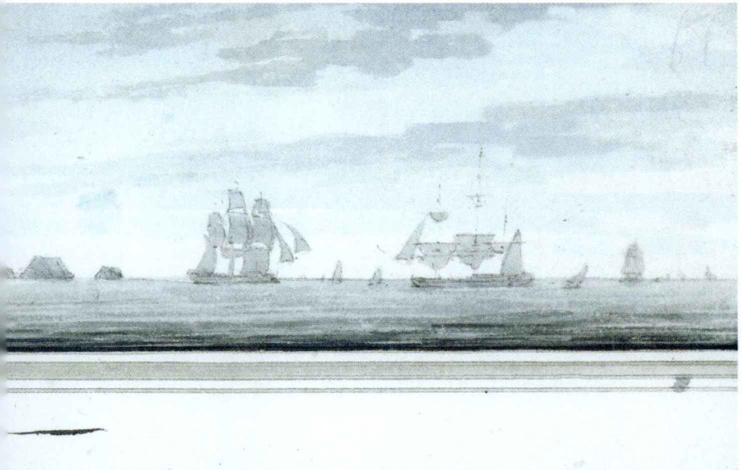

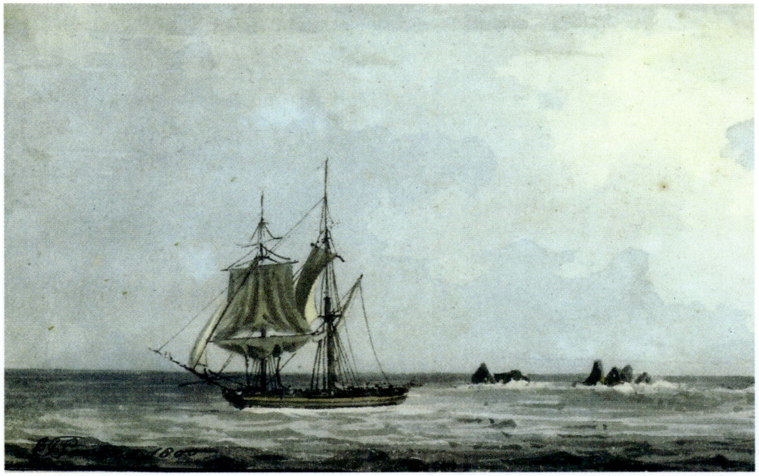

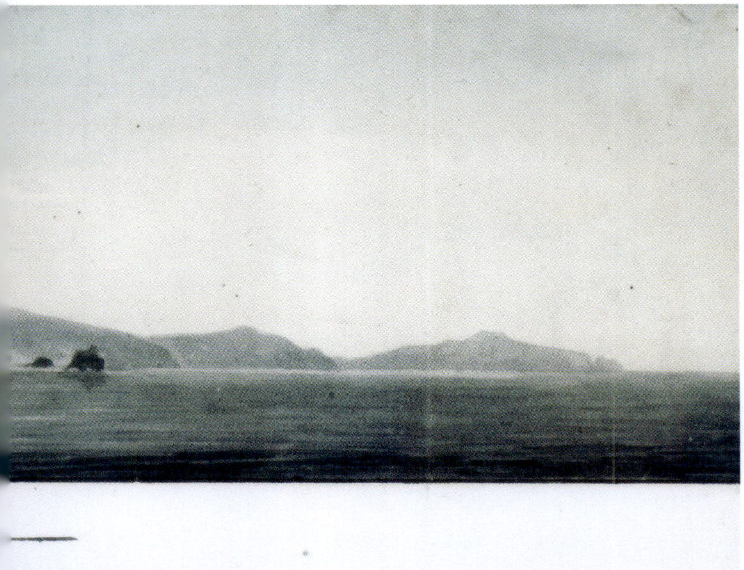

Serres' views of the Galician coast show how frigates and sloops of the Channel Fleet clustered at the extremity of their approved cruising area around the headlands between Cabo Ortegal and Cabo Finisterre at the southern entrance to the Bay of Biscay.

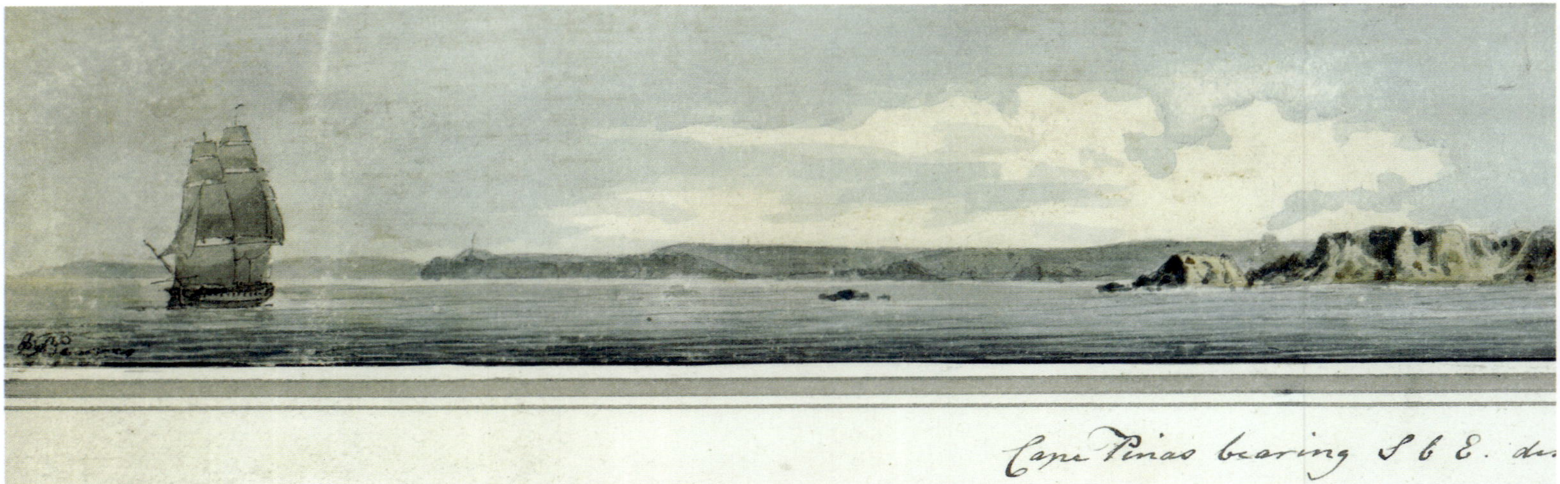

efforts of the Board to control the allocation and tasking of frigates. Lord Bridport, who chafed at this central direction, had himself noted 'What think you of 7 frigates cruising off Corunna under the orders of 3 Commanders-in-Chief?', when ships from the Channel, Mediterranean and Irish stations were reported in the vicinity.[170] The *Clyde's* log mentions an encounter with the *Boadicea* and *Sirius* during 23–4 July, and these are almost certainly amongst the vessels which Serres uses to give depth and interest to his views.

The other task for Keats was to watch the Spanish bases on this exposed coastline where it was virtually impossible to sustain a rigorous blockade. The *Boadicea* was engaged in a reconnaissance of Corunna and Ferrol, recording six or seven enemy warships in the latter.[171] The British amphibious force in the Channel landed on 25 August, on the flat coast north of Cape Prior (see opposite page), achieving complete surprise. The heights above Ferrol were quickly secured by the army, assisted by a detachment of seamen who dragged sixteen field pieces to the summit. Then, to the dismay of Rear-Admiral Warren, who was planning an attack on the warships in the harbour, the army commanders decided they must withdraw.

Above **One of the frigates which St Vincent placed under Captain Keats' orders for a patrol to intercept enemy cruisers and privateers as they entered the Bay of Biscay is shown here off Cabo Peñas.**

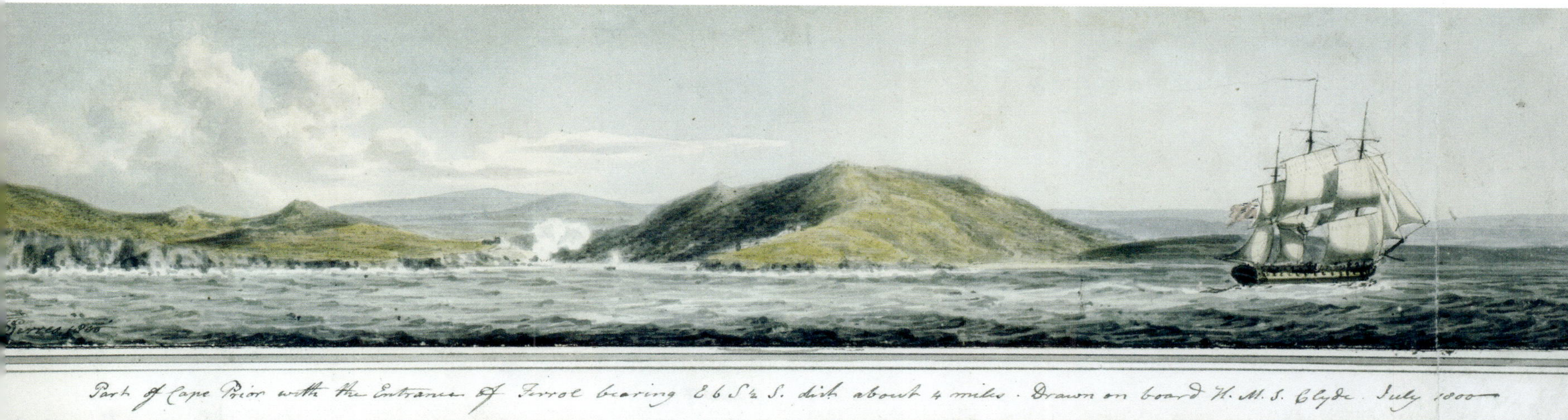

Nott mentions four views made by Serres of the area of Ferrol and Corunna, but only this one remains in the hydrographic archive. Nott notes that 'the Harbour of Ferrol is quite blind until it is brought to bear E by S half S or East'. The fine modern dockyard of Ferrol lay deep within the ria, protected by a boom just beyond the castle at San Carlos on the promontory, one of four fortifications which protected the narrows. Another fort is visible on the south shore at Punta del Segano. The drifting puffs of smoke may indicate that the small craft in the entrance is from the British squadron conducting a reconnaissance, and that it has come under fire. The day after Serres made this view, the War Cabinet, fearful that French victories on the eastern front would be followed by a renewed effort to build up European naval power for an assault on the British coast, authorised an attack on Ferrol. The frigate in the view is the *Sirius* (36).

Finisterre marked the division between the Channel and Mediterranean fleet commands, and trespass across the limits was frowned upon. Keats had been directed to give his captains 'the most precise orders to return to the northward of Cape Finisterre the moment the object of anchoring off the Bar of Oporto (i.e. watering ship) is accomplished, for I wish that the utmost degree of delicacy may be observed in avoiding a trespass on the limits of Admiral Lord Keith's command'.[172] In his note to Nepean, St Vincent had remarked that to extend Serres' work to Cape St Vincent would go 'several degrees beyond my district'. Cunningham's directions were to range the coasts as far as Finisterre.[173] So Serres concluded his intense period of work with an illustration of the twin peaks of the capes Nave and Finisterre (see above). He would now have ample time to work up his sketches, for on 25 July Cunningham began his cruise athwart the approaches to the enemy's Channel and Bay of Biscay ports. They ranged over 250 nautical miles to westwards, and then northwards until the reckoning put them 440 nautical miles from Cabo Ortegal. For over a fortnight they encountered only neutrals and other British frigates. On the 31 July two men were punished for drunkenness. Finally, on 11 August, they reaped the rewards of the cruise which

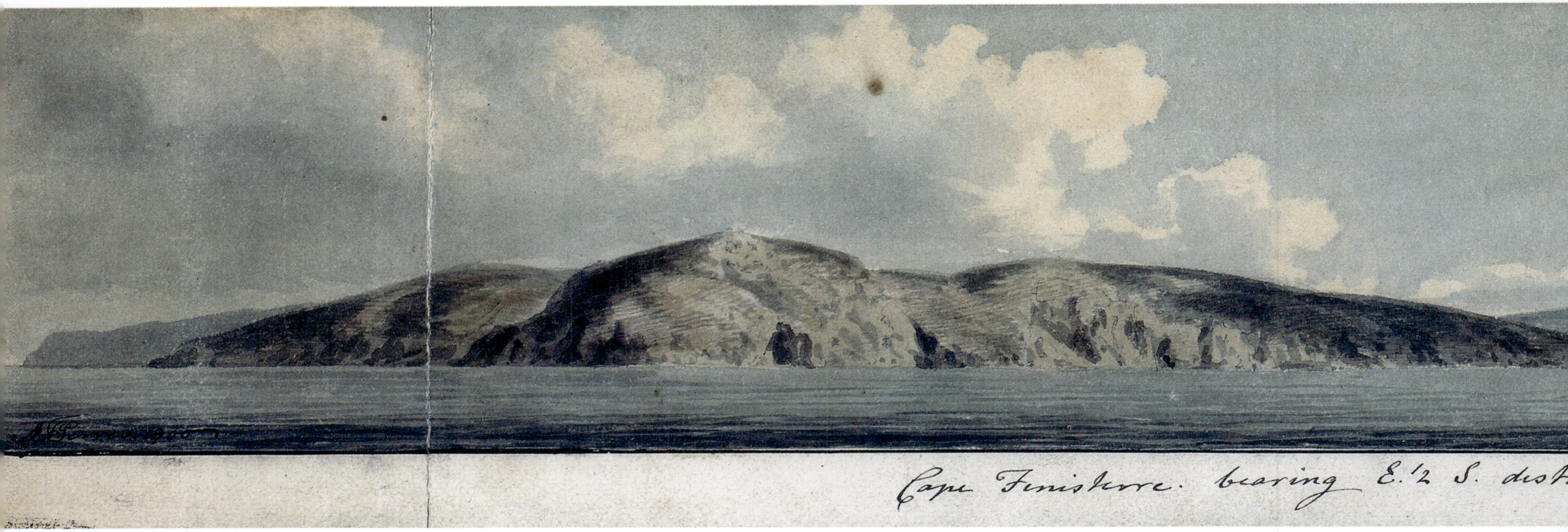

St Vincent had allowed them. They intercepted a packet from Havana, the Spanish brig *El Beloz* (4), laden with sugar, cotton and cochineal, bound for Corunna. The brig managed to drop its mail overboard with an anchor, but 3000 dollars were brought onboard the *Clyde* before the brig, manned with a prize crew, parted company for Plymouth.

Captain Cunningham and Mr Nott both remark that Serres resumed his work as the frigate closed the Spanish coast off Cabo Villano and the prisoners were transferred to an American vessel bound for Bilbao. *Clyde* coasted south until 17 August when she came to anchor off the bar of the Haven of Viana (between Vigo and Oporto) on the coast of Portugal, where there is 'a remarkable Hill which lies on the Sea Shore, which Mr Serris drew the shape of . . .'[174] Sadly, none of these later views appear to have survived. The ship's company, encouraged by the distribution of the dollars from *El Beloz*, set about the onerous work of watering ship. They also embarked a welcome stock of 1000 lbs of fresh beef.

Serres' depiction of the twin capes Nave and Finisterre earned professional approbation. Tofiño had noted that the bight between the capes, with its sandy 'Atlantic shore' (Area del mar de faera), was particularly conspicuous. Nott declared that with benefit of this view noone could mistake Finisterre, which was unlike any other prominent point on the coast.

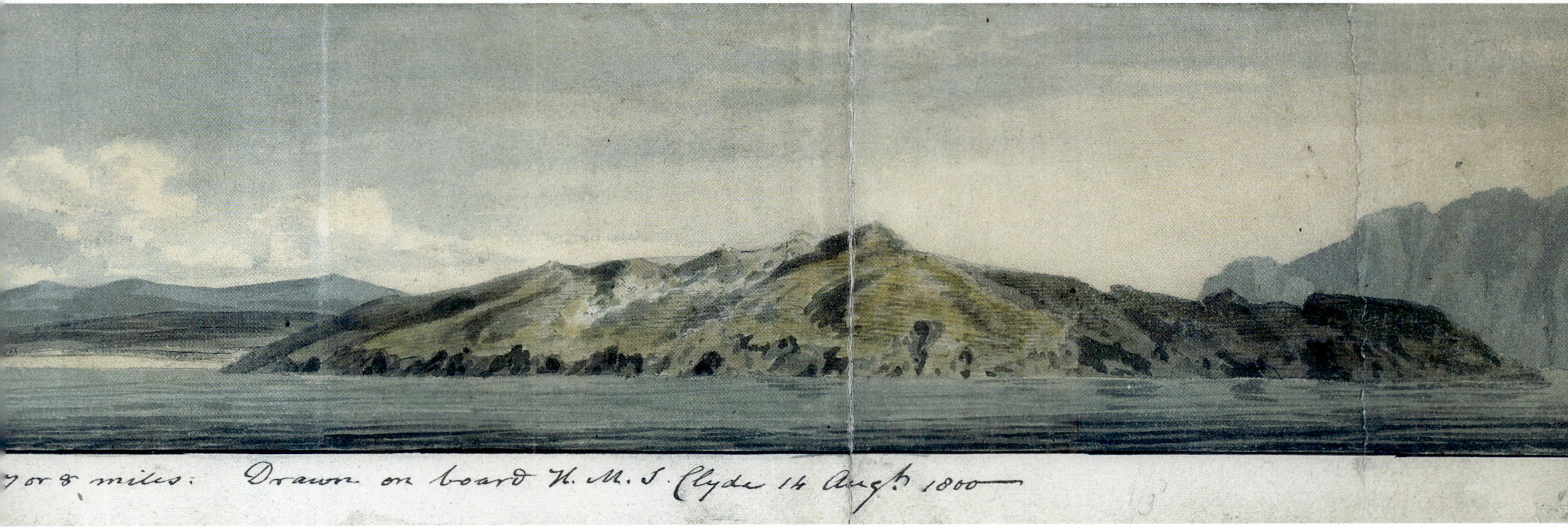

At the end they had time to wash their clothes before the ship weighed and resumed her cruise on 21 August.[175] The *Clyde* took no part in the amphibious operations at Ferrol.

On 5 October St Vincent forwarded a letter to Secretary Nepean.[176] It read:

> Portsmouth, 11 Sep 1800
>
> My Lord,
>
> Having made Views along the Coasts of France and Spain to Vianna, the first Port, on the coast of Portugal, where the Clyde water'd, I expressed my wish to Capt Cunningham that he would permit me to imbrace the first opportunity that offerd me a Conveyance to England, as the ship under his command was to continue his Cruize much longer. Being desirous not to encrease the Expence to Government any more than I could help, thereby induce the Lords Commrs of the Admiralty to continue a work which will be Interesting, Useful, and ultimately I hope reflect no discredit on themselves.
>
> It would ill become me, my Lord to comment on my own productions, therefore trust your Lordship will hear of them from those gentlemen of the Navy the Clyde has fallen

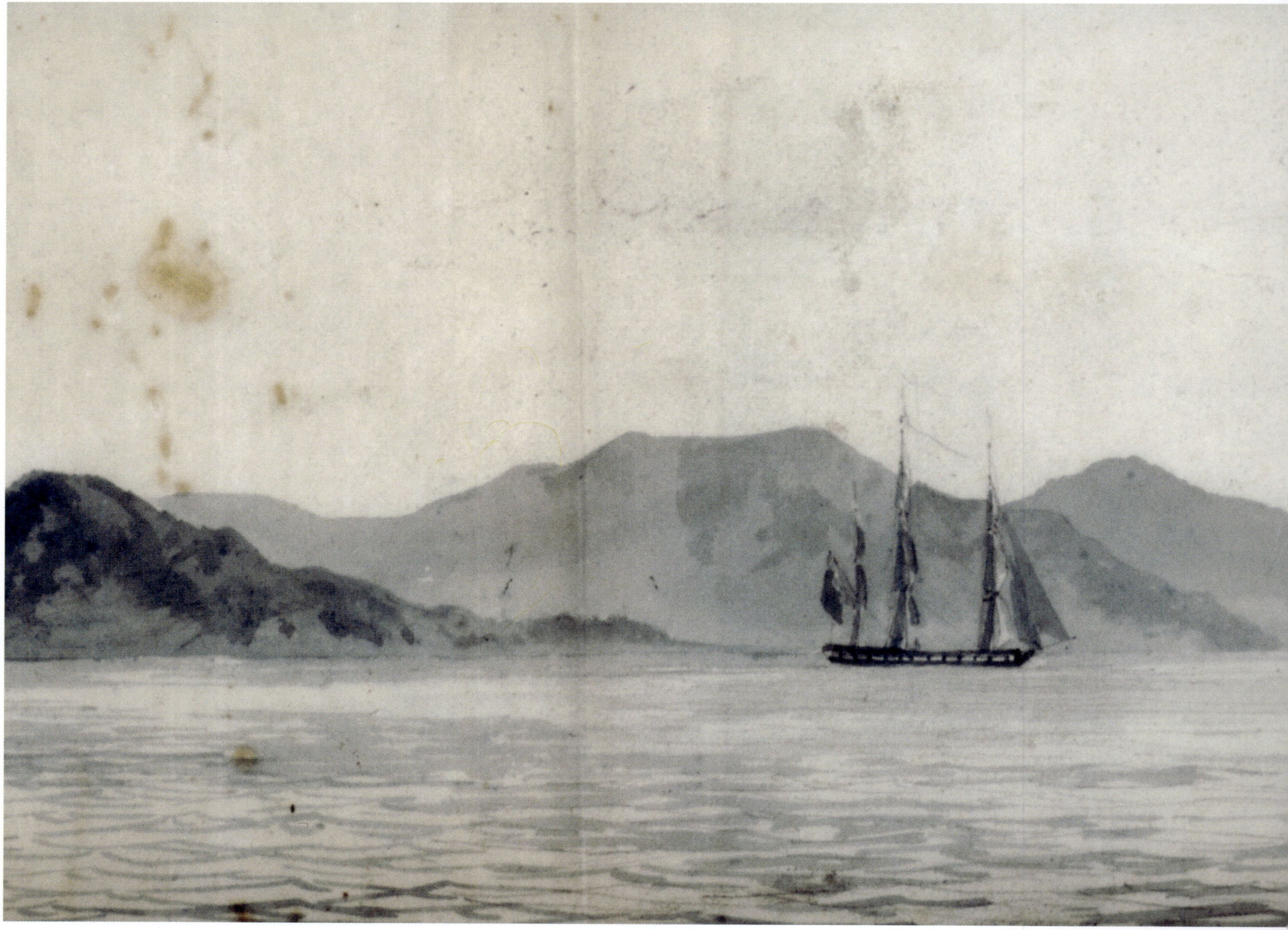

in with at sea, who flatter me much by their encomiums as to the correctness of the drawings. – Were they otherwise, indeed it would be unpardonable, as Captain Cunningham exerted himself on every occasion to render them so – by placing his Ship advantageously, and keeing [sic.] her stationary till my sketch was finished.

I shall not further intrude on your Lordship's time to inform you that on the 29th August we fell in with HM Ship Endymion in Latt 44°=0 Long 11°-0 on her way to England and on the request of Captain Cunningham, Sir Thomas Williams honor'd me with a passage home and arrived at Spithead on the 8th inst but unfortunately for me the Endymion was oblig'd to perform quarantine therefore am just landed.

I remain, My Lord, Your Lordships most respectful Humble Servant, JTS.
The Right Honourable Admiral Earl St Vincent

It was on 29 August that Thomas Nott had scribbled his note for Serres: 'I cannot but approve of the Drawings representing the Coast of France, Spain and Portugal done by Mr Serres while on board H.M.S. Clyde they being Exquisitely Correct.' Serres had also made the most of his time with Captain Sir Thomas Williams, who added a postscript to his lively report of proceedings noting the transfer of 'His Majesty's Marine Painter' from the *Clyde* and commenting that 'I have seen also his drawings of the coast of France and Spain and those parts that I am acquainted with are most accurately taken.'[177]

An entry in the Admiralty Digest for 19 September 1800 notes the arrival of 33 drawings accompanied by a letter from Mr Serres, requesting to be appointed 'Draughtsman to the Board'.[178] A manuscript annotation by Dalrymple on Serres' sketchbook records that he received it from Nepean on the 18 November. The appearances

A frigate and smaller vessel off the Spanish coast in a view which became separated from the main body of Serres' work in the Hydrographic Office archives.

took their place in Dalrymple's painstaking assessment process but there is no evidence of their long-term display or use by the Board. Isolated in their floating worlds, Serres and his shipmates were unaware that the decisive events of 1800 were taking place on land and far away from the Atlantic seaboard. On 14 June, while *La Nymphe* lay at anchor off Brest, Napoleon had won his devastating victory at Marengo in the north of Italy. The winter saw another French victory on their eastern front at Hohenlinden, and by the spring of 1801 the Second Coalition had collapsed leaving Britain once more confronted with a hostile continent. While the importance of the work of the Channel fleet was undiminished, the attention of the War Cabinet was now elsewhere, in strategic debate which would lead to victories on land in Egypt and at sea off Copenhagen. The artist himself would also soon be too preoccupied by a family crisis to champion his work.

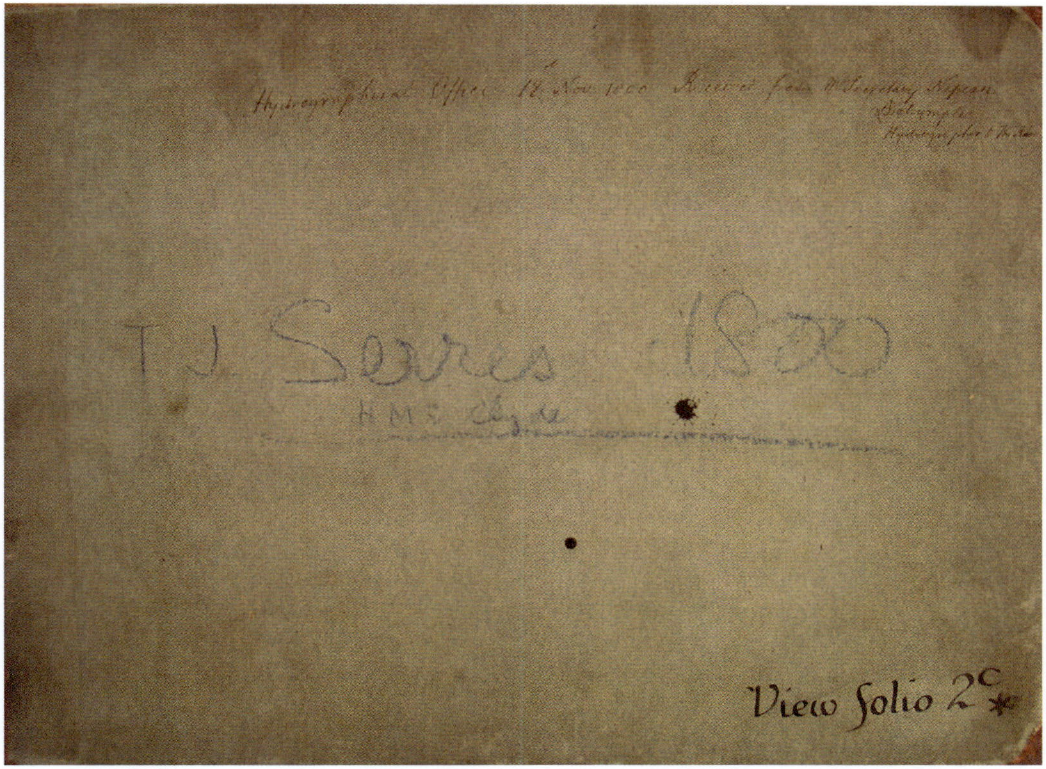

The cover of J. T. Serres' sketchbook annotated by the Hydrographer to record its receipt from the Secretary of the Admiralty Board.

Ars Church ESE ½ S.

CHAPTER NINE

The Little Sea Torch

Serres had made arrangements for a friend to pay Olive an allowance for household expenses during his absence. These payments had proved quite unequal to the round of entertainment which she launched herself into, let alone her expenditure on costumes for the season's masquerades. Serres recorded sadly: 'She accepted bills with my signature for £20, £30, and £70; and not satisfied with that, to complete my ruin, executed a bond, forging my signature, for £150.' He endorsed one promissory note: 'This bill is a forgery: my wife, O. Serres, having drawn it and signed my name to it, when I was on the coast of Spain, on government service, and without my knowledge. – J T Serres.' Arriving home in London he found himself declared a bankrupt, with a bond against him. If he revealed the truth, Olive was liable to transportation for her offence. He kept quiet and bore the stigma.[179] In what was to become a characteristic reaction to the misfortune arising from his wife's actions, he buried himself in work which he hoped would sustain his reputation and retain the favour of his contacts.

Less than a year after Serres' return to England, a handsome large folio book was published in London entitled *The Little Sea Torch, or the Guide for Coasting Pilots*. The unusual title and the main text derive from a much earlier work, *Le Petit Flambeau de la Mer* (1684) and the title page states that it had been translated with corrections and additions by J.T. Serres, Marine Painter to His Majesty, and to His Royal Highness the Duke of Clarence, and Marine Draughtsman to the Right Honourable the Board of Admiralty. The artist had secured his appointment. The book was 'enriched with upwards of one hundred appearances of headlands and light-houses . . . ' The appearances were from drawings by Serres, engraved

Opposite The bell-tower of Ars church was a landmark which Bougard had highlighted in his directions, yet this view is not used in *The Little Sea Torch*, perhaps suggesting that Serres may not have had access to his sketchbook while compiling his publication.

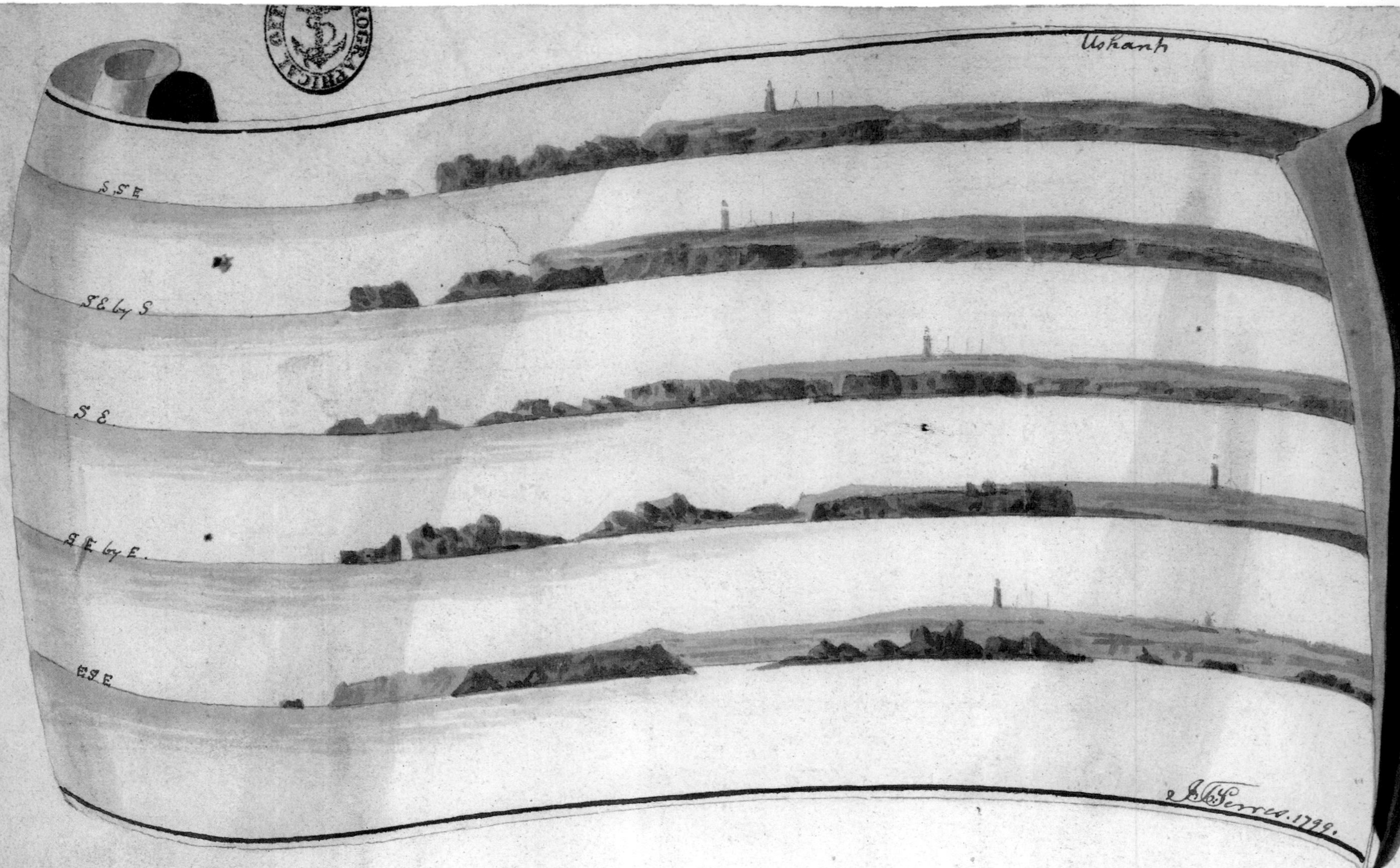

Ushant
S.S.E
S.E. by S
S.E.
S.E. by E.
E.S.E.
J. W. Ferres. 1799.

Opposite **This set of profiles of Ushant is dated 1799, and was probably drawn while onboard Lord Bridport's flagship *Royal George*. It became separated from Serres' other drawings and was not catalogued in the 'coffin'. It was reproduced in *The Little Sea Torch*.**

by J. Stadler, but the provenance of the chartlets also included is unclear. Serres declared that his purpose was 'to produce a work that might be of utility to my countrymen, who might not understand the French language'. The volume was available from shops in Portsmouth and Devonport as well as from five booksellers in London. A list of subscribers includes the Board of Admiralty (two copies),[180] Earl St Vincent (two copies), Evan Nepean, and a long list of serving officers including Admiral Nelson and Captains Cunningham, Gore and Keats.

The dedication to Earl Spencer rewards the First Lord's support in securing the sanction of the Board of Admiralty for the project. Serres also singled out Captain Cunningham, 'with whom I had the honor of making two cruises', as one the 'most able judges of Maritime Affairs [who] have long ago pronounced '*Le Petit Flambeau de la Mer*' a work of the highest value and authenticity'. Cunningham is credited with steering Serres' approach to the English version. '[He] put it into my hands with the warmest commendation of its contents, declaring that if I were to give a version of it, I should be doing an essential service to my country, and that if the appearances of the Headlands and Charts, were equally well executed as the descriptive parts were just and accurate, it would be one of the most valuable books ever published.' Serres hoped that the result was worthy of the friendship of Cunningham, 'who animated me to engage in the task'. Two letters from Serres to the Admiralty, which have sadly not survived, related to 'his publication'.[181] They date from September 1800 and may have been drafted onboard the *Clyde* with advice from Cunningham.

Le Petit Flambeau de la Mer, by Le Sieur Raulin Bougard, Master Mariner of Havre de Grace, had been a late product of the north-west European tradition that had preferred textual sailing directions, supplemented with views, for coastal navigation, rather than a chart.[182] Unlike Serres' grand production, it was a small pocket book, as the title suggests. Most copies quickly became dog-eared. It was hugely popular, despite savage criticism. One savant, appalled that it survived in the age of the *Neptune François*, nicknamed it maliciously '*Le Petit Bougard*'. The 1789 edition which Serres used, though described as 'revue, corrigée et augmentée', had very few changes from the first edition. It was still illustrated with crude woodblock prints of views and chartlets. One of the views had been printed upside down in the later editions![183]

Serres implies that Cunningham pressed him to translate and illustrate, but that there was no intention to produce an updated edition. It was quick work to produce the book so soon after the cruise in the *Clyde*, and he may have begun the task during the winter months of 1799–1800. The engraved views are annotated with a publication date of 1801. His English version is a strange, unstructured amalgamation, and it does not give the impression that Serres took advantage of the advice of his naval contacts during its production. Certainly Cunningham spent the best part of 1801 on active duty in command of a squadron watching the French coast between Le Havre de Grace and the Île de Batz, from where a descent on the Channel Islands was threatened.[184] Although a view[185] by Serres of Castle Cornet in Guernsey, showing the *Clyde* and other vessels of the squadron, dates from this period, there is no evidence that he had rejoined. Indeed available space onboard was clearly needed for the local pilots who were essential for Cunningham's task in a most demanding theatre which claimed one frigate shortly after he assumed command.[186]

Bougard's text is translated without amendment, augmentation or commentary.[187] His illustrations are omitted, and indeed are not directly replicated by the 20 plates of views and twelve plates of chartlets in *The Little Sea Torch*. Presumably the information on the French and other coasts of Europe was of more interest to Cunningham and other naval men. Yet, in this context, the chosen appearances are particularly haphazard. There seem to be a disproportionate number of the south coast of England. This is especially true of the environs of Plymouth and the coast of Cornwall to westwards, even though many of these would be welcomed by a mariner without local knowledge who was faced with a landfall in murky weather. The first three plates contain a reasonably logical progression of some of the great landfalls of a voyage up Channel, but other associated images are scattered somewhat randomly because of the size at which Serres has chosen to render them.

Although the title page credits J.T. Serres for the views, and they are certainly all in his style, it is not clear that all the original sketches are his.[188] Some can be matched to his earlier travels in Ireland and in the Mediterranean. However, when Serres made a late insertion of some new information of a bank off Beachy Head, he may have also taken the opportunity to salve his conscience. He wrote: 'At the same time [Mr Serres] takes the opportunity of offering his sincere acknowledgments to Captains Keats and Lewis for the honor of their communications, and use of their drawings.' Keats had substantial experience of the Channel coasts of England in addition to the blockading stations off Brest, Ferrol and Corunna. Lewis had commanded a sloop in home waters. They may therefore have supplemented sketches by Serres which have not survived.

Some of the appearances are drawn from the normal perspective of a coastal view, but many others are shown as close-ups. This includes most of the images taken from the 1799–1800 cruising ground. Indeed the material passed to the Admiralty seems to have had limited use in *The Little Sea Torch*. The views in the immediate environs of Brest could have been worked up from the sketchbook, though none are direct copies of the images therein. The appearances of Cabo San Antonio and Cabo Ortegal on the Spanish coast are clearly derived from the views, although, in both, the background land has been altered and heightened. Three appearances of lighthouses (Les Baleines, Pointe de Chassiron, and Cordouan) are engravings of the originals in the sketchbook (see pp. 84–5).

By omitting Bougard's views, Serres had discarded a significant element of the original work, and there is some evidence that he was aware of this. Bougard's most detailed panorama is of the Pertuis d'Antioche in the approaches to La Rochelle, and Serres ensured that he captured the marks therein in his sketches during the cruise of the *Clyde*. However, these sketches are not reproduced in *The Little Sea Torch*. Bougard had included blocks of no fewer than twelve profiles of the island of Ushant from different points of the compass. Serres chose his scroll with five panoramic views of Ushant from 1799 for inclusion in *The Little Sea Torch*. Bougard had also included many profiles of the north coast of Spain. Serres had seen Cunningham and Nott employing the eminently superior atlas of Tofiño, and this may have influenced his choice of subjects for his plates. Overall, however, there is some evidence that his access to his material from the cruises with the Channel Fleet may have been limited. While Dalrymple is likely to have been amongst those with little regard for Bougard's work, there is no evidence that he obstructed Serres, who could probably have used influence to gain sight of his drawings had he chosen to do so.

There is no doubt that the support of eminent naval men for Serres' book reflected the infancy of the organisation of hydrographic support for the fleet. However, their limited constructive impact on its content reflected an abiding complacency with respect to navigational information. John Knight's commendable passion for information-gathering was by no means widespread in the Royal Navy, as the author of the foreword to the account of Anson's circumnavigation had lamented half a century earlier.[189] The collection of Remark Books in the UK Hydrographic Office suggests, for example, that no views of the French and Spanish coasts were rendered from the fleet between the Seven Years' War and the later years of the Napoleonic wars.[190] Dalrymple issued more comprehensive directions for the completion of Remark Books in 1804, but complained two years later that only one response had been received and that '. . . of a well known part of the coast of England, in a very exceptionable stile [*sic*]'. The first report of the Admiralty's Chart Committee, which had been set up to assist with the selection of material for the fleet, noted that '. . . unfortunately

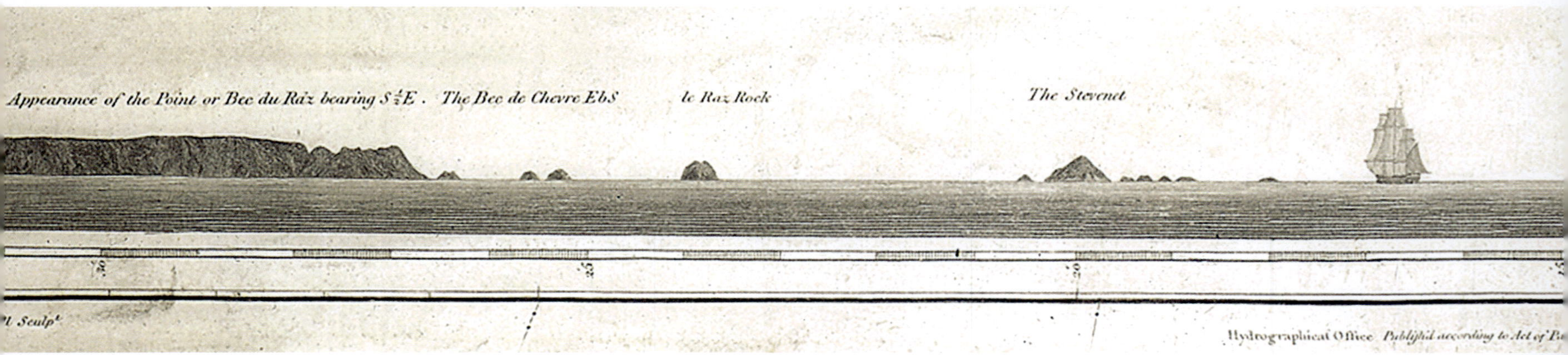

for the benefit of the country hydrography and astronomy are so little encouraged or cultivated in the British Navy, that . . . we are indebted to the spontaneous exertions of a very small number of individuals by whom either of those sciences has been advantageously practised . . .'[191]

Another decade was to elapse before Captain Thomas Hurd, Dalrymple's successor as Hydrographer to the Admiralty, established a system which drilled the navigation teams to expect and exploit the best possible cartographic products. Ultimately, views of the type produced by Serres, directions updated by the remarks of John Nott and other masters, and the chart folios launched by Thomas Hurd, were to be the tools of the Royal Navy and a burgeoning commercial marine market in the nineteenth century. The Hydrographic Office began to produce and extend a world-wide series of official Sailing Directions from the 1820s onwards, but these did not contain views until 1908.[192] Instead the mariner was cross-referenced to the chart, now the unchallenged primary document, where the views could be found in the margins, just as in the productions of John Knight and Thomas Hurd.

The efforts of Knight and others in the approaches to Brest had also revealed the inherent challenge of what is today called 'rapid environmental assessment': that is, the

Serres' sketchbook was the source for this engraved view of the Passage du Raz. By retaining the profile of the frigate from the original drawing, illustrated on p. 71, it emphasises that the recommended track would take a vessel to the westward of the Stevenet.

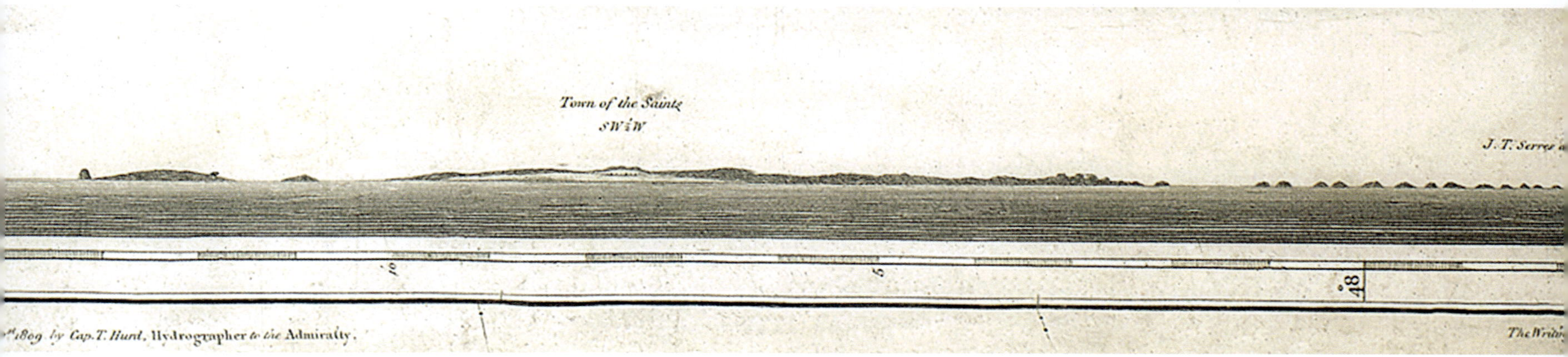

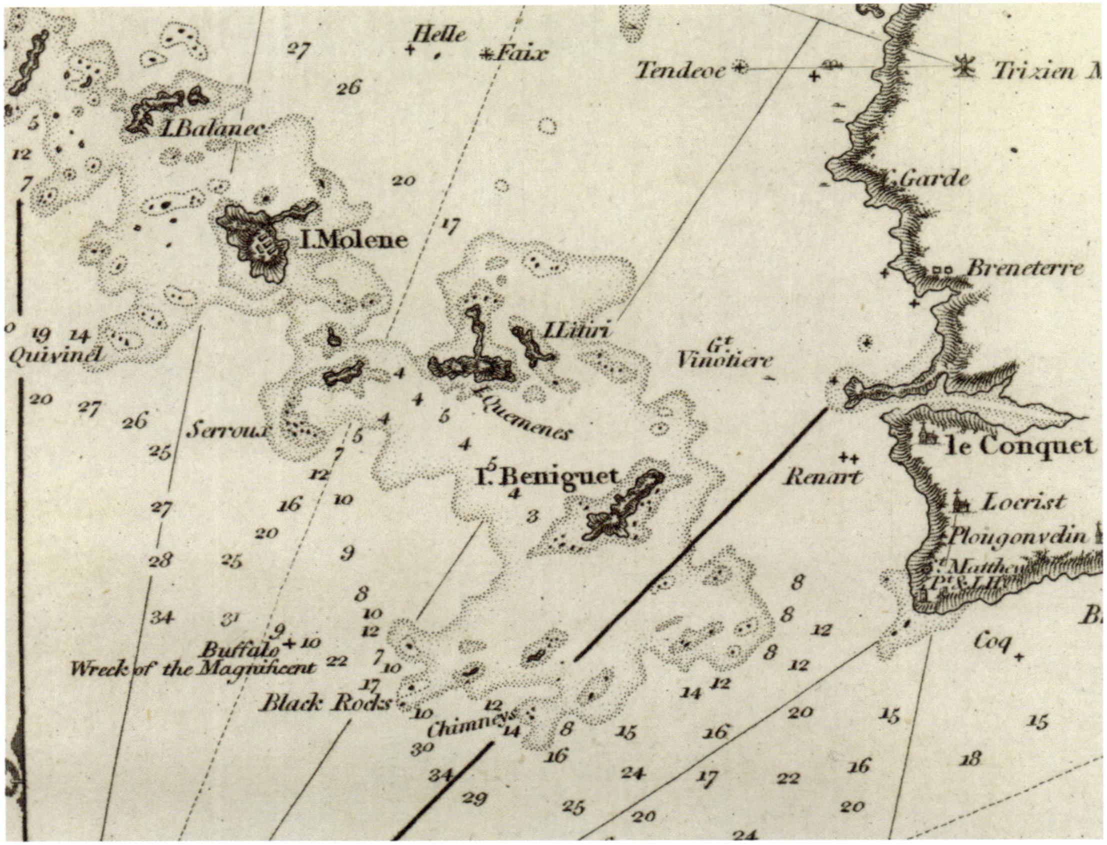

The area of Le Boufoloc from the revised edition of Captain Knight's General Chart. As well as the annotation recording the loss of the *Magnificent* in 1804, the chart also shows the area of sandy bottom where the advanced squadron anchored during Knight's command in 1800.[195]

preservation of accuracy during the rapid and focused acquisition of data for immediate military exploitation. Knight's charts were to come under criticism following the loss of the *Magnificent* (74) on the Buffalo rock (Le Boufoloc) in 1804. In his directions for vessels heading south-east from Ushant to the anchorage of the Advanced Squadron off the Black Rocks, Knight had advised giving 'a full League Birth [*sic*]' to all the lesser islands with their fringing shoals. His charts show where he ran lines of soundings inside this recommended track, and major isolated dangers are clearly marked with their bearings from conspicuous marks. However, although he sounded across the submarine ridge on which it lies, noting the existence of rocky ground, Knight did not detect the outlying Boufoloc which has a charted depth of only a decimetre. While the *Neptune François* showed the rock unambiguously as one that never uncovers, other French charts depicted it as visible at half tide.[193] Not finding such a drying feature, Knight attached the name Buffalo to a larger rock, the Placen ar Béniguet, which lies to the north and inside of the Black Rocks. What is remarkable during the subsequent court martial, however, is that experienced commanding officers and pilots in the squadron were vocal in their witness that they would have anticipated no danger in the location of the grounding. The *Magnificent*'s pilot, Renée Hengait, declared, 'I knew nothing of it, and if there is any pilot knows it, after having passed the Black Rocks a mile and a half I'll suffer condemnation.'[194]

As a result of the disaster, Captain Thomas Hurd, who had made his reputation with a major survey of the Bermuda Islands, was despatched to the scene to conduct as systematic a survey as possible on the enemy's doorstep, employing triangulation and horizontal sextant angle resection.[196] As a result the Boufoloc is shown in its correct position on a later printing of Knight's chart. Hurd's survey of the Bay of Brest led Dalrymple to conclude that '. . . there is great reason to suspect these [French] surveys have not been made with that exactness which might be wished for . . .' Indeed, the successive revisions of the *Neptune*, which was so esteemed by St Vincent and others, included no updates to the seventeenth-century material. Large-scale geometric surveys of the Breton coast conducted between 1771 and 1785 were classified and not released, even to the French Navy, until after the Bourbon restoration.[197] It would only be after the end of conflict and the British blockade that the great French hydrographer Charles François Beautemps-Beaupré would set new standards around the French coast. His supremacy, however, marked a firm decision that responsibility for hydrographic surveying would lie with an establishment of engineers and not with the French navy. By contrast, as Serres observed at first hand, British sea officers had steadily increased their confidence in pilotage in inshore waters. In due course this would enable Hurd to form a cadre of Royal Naval military hydrographic specialists.[198]

Meanwhile, although Serres' magnificent book was destined to be a sought-after item for a collector's library rather than a true leading light for the seagoer, his work in the fleet was to contribute to improved navigational guidance for the Channel. A plate containing nine views based on material from his sketchbook was engraved in the Hydrographical Office.[199] Three panoramas from this plate were incorporated in the 1809

Part of the beautiful view of Cabo Troinana reproduced on the front end-paper in this book was also engraved for use on the published British Admiralty chart.

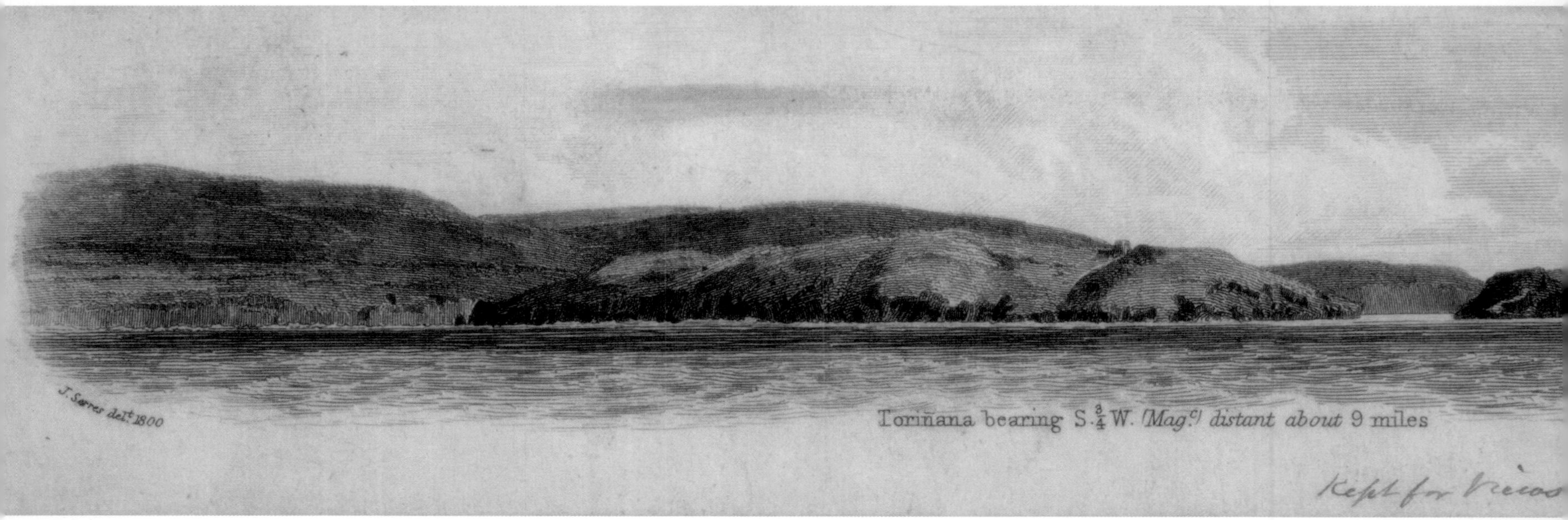

chart of the Bay of Brest based on Captain Hurd's surveys of 1804 and 1806. This chart was also published as part of Hurd's *A Nautical Description of the Bay of Brest with instructions for its navigation; also for A NEW CHANNEL into the FOUR.*[200] The view of Ushant retains the note that it was made from the *Indefatigable*, though wrongly dated as 4 rather than 2 June 1800. That of the approaches to Camaret Bay includes an extract from Percy Fraser's directions which had been preserved in the sketch book. The construction of both this view and that of the Passage du Raz was assisted by the annotations in the sketchbook, including the sea gulls. The engraving of the Passage du Raz retains the profile of the frigate standing through (see p. 114).

Eventually, views of capes Ortegal, Finisterre and Torinana were selected from Serres' sketches and engraved in the Hydrographic Office with his bearings corrected for magnetic change and his distances converted from leagues to miles.[201] These views were used on Chart 2728, *Spain, North and West Coasts, Bayonne to Oporto. From Charts published by the Hydrographical Office at Madrid*, which first appeared in 1846. This chart was not superseded until 1887. The new chart also had new views, possibly made by the officers of HMS *Sylvia* during the preceding year.[202] Serres' work had dropped out of sight. However, in teamwork with his naval colleagues, he had played his part in developing the techniques and standards that were to be applied to such effect by the Royal Naval Hydrographic Service in all quarters of the world in the next two centuries.

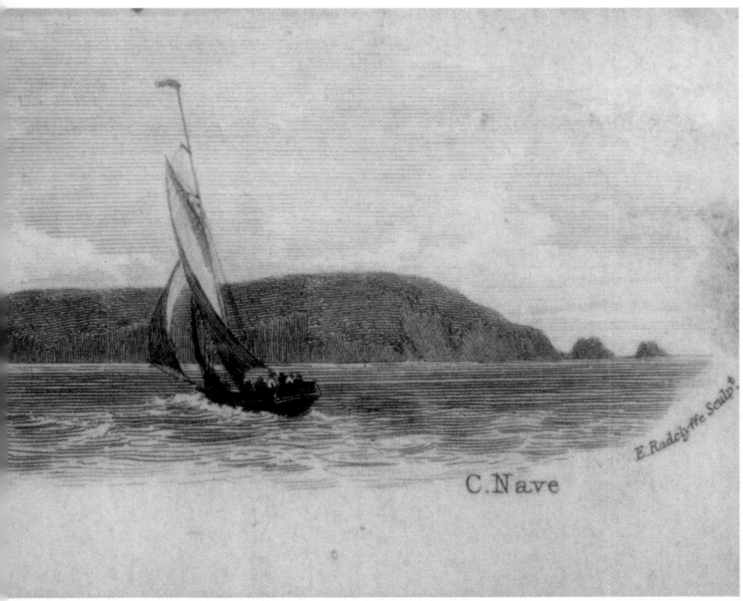

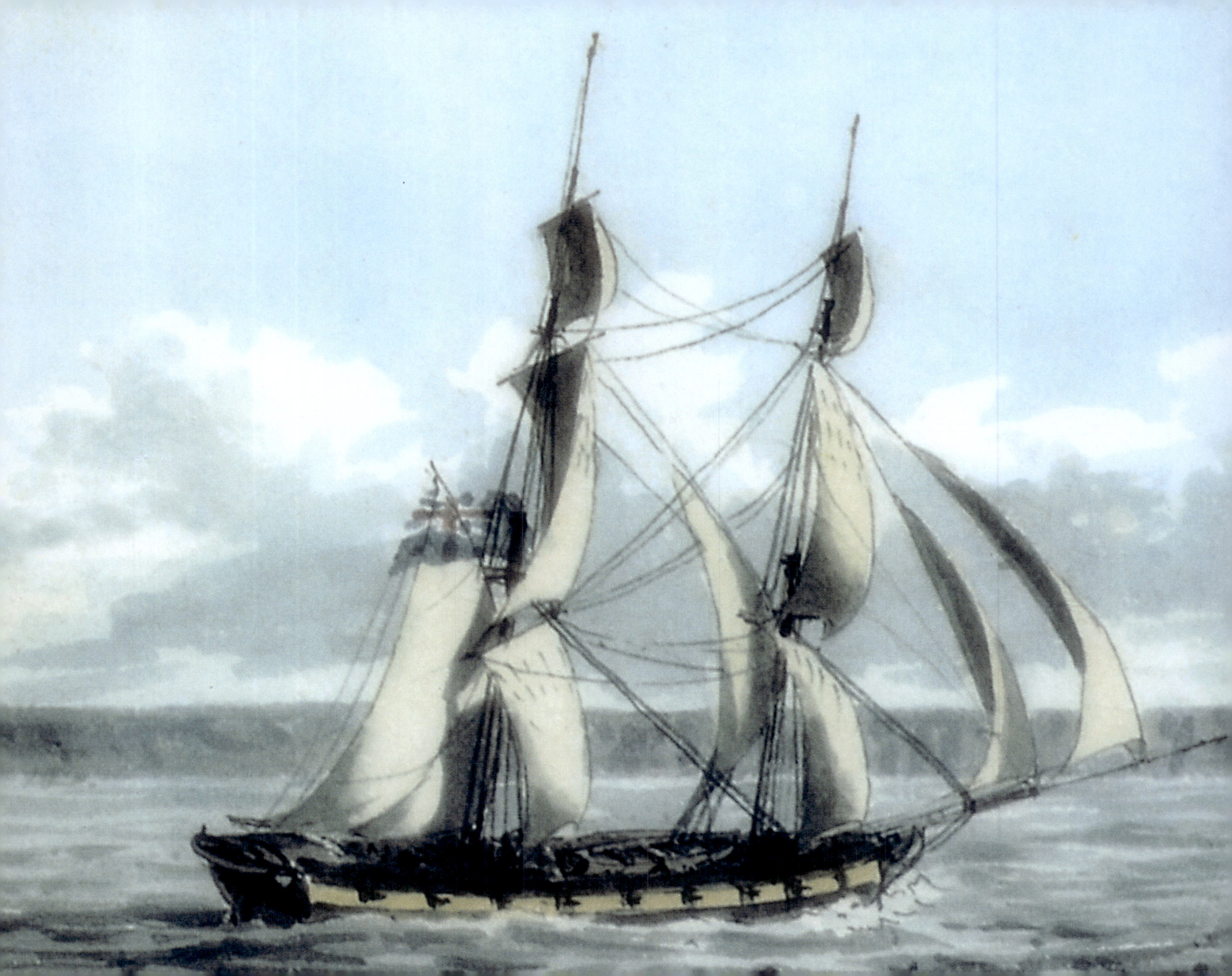

CHAPTER TEN

Postscript

On 25 March 1802 the Peace of Amiens was signed ending the French Revolutionary War that had begun in February 1793. Few expected it to be more than a short-lived truce and the Napoleonic Wars indeed commenced in May 1803. By that time St Vincent was established in a characteristically turbulent tenure as First Lord of the Admiralty. Charles Cunningham had earned St Vincent's firm approbation, and they were to remain life-long correspondents. However, the old admiral's interest was now to have unexpected implications for the active frigate captain. Cunningham had paid off the *Clyde* in June 1802 after over six years in command. He had been instantly re-employed at the resumption of war in larger vessels and in command of a squadron in the North Sea. But in 1803, perhaps as part of efforts to bend the civil administration to his will, the First Lord pressed him to accept an appointment as a Commissioner of the Victualling Board. Cunningham wrote later that the offer was made in a way that 'was so flattering that it was impossible I could act otherwise than I did in accepting of it'.[203] He was to go on to become Commissioner successively at the Thames yards at Deptford and Woolwich, and finally the great yard at Chatham. But as he neared the end of his career he faced a dilemma. Retirement would mean the end of considerable emoluments, including his fine residence. Yet the longer he postponed his transfer to the Flag List, the more seniority he forfeited by contrast to his contemporaries who had remained on the active military list. He petitioned in vain in 1829 to be retired as a Vice-Admiral. In the same year he published a narrative of the events of the mutiny at the Nore, in an attempt to revive awareness of his moment of fame in 1797. He particularly resented the award of KCB to other officers who had gone on to serve afloat in the Napoleonic

HMS Sylph as shown in Serres' great three-panel panorama of the inshore squadron off Brest.

Wars, but who had seen less action than himself. In 1832 King William IV created him a Knight Commander of the Royal Hanoverian Guelphic Order. Two years later Charles Cunningham died.[204]

Thomas Nott vanishes from among the masters in *Steel's Original and Correct List of the Royal Navy* after the issue of June 1806. However, on 23 January 1801 he had been joined onboard the *Clyde* by his son, John, who was entered on the books as a First Class Volunteer. With Cunningham's patronage he had the prospect of crossing the social divide and obtaining a commission. He was finally promoted lieutenant in 1810 after varied service including four years in the *Malta* (84) during which he was present at Admiral Calder's clash with the combined enemy fleet during the Trafalgar campaign in 1805. In the next two years he had an active career in the Mediterranean in a succession of frigates and sloops. But the peace came too soon for him. He eventually reached the rank of commander in 1846 having commanded the *Partridge* (10) in South American waters and the brigantine *Lynx* 'on particular service'.[205] By contrast the well-connected William Cathcart took command of the *Renard* (18) on 28 September 1802, barely a year after his examination for lieutenant. Her operations took him to the Irish coast, the West Indies, and back to the excitement of the Channel blockade. On the 14 April 1804 he was appointed acting Captain of *La Clorinde* (38), which had been captured at St Domingo the previous November. Less than a month later he died at Port Royal, Jamaica, of yellow fever.[206] He was 22 years old.

John Serres' misery intensified. He now knew that Olive had formed a liaison with his business partner in the British Institution, a school for drawing and painting. She responded violently to his attempts to control their family finances. He desperately wished to preserve their marriage. But less than a year after the birth of another daughter, Britannia, a deed of separation was signed in March 1803. Reflecting some legal bargaining, it cited the cause as 'difference in tempers and dispositions and not from any conjugal infidelity on the part of the said Olive'. Serres was committed to paying £200 per annum for the maintenance of his ex-wife and his beloved daughters, of whom she had custody. Olive was to complain bitterly that she saw little of this. Serres was said to have stopped the allowance following evidence of infidelity and an illegitimate birth. In the years that followed, Olive's creditors harried Serres mercilessly, and he was committed for substantial periods to debtors' prison. There are also suggestions that, racked by anxiety over the treatment of his daughters by Olive and her new partner, he had broken the conditions of custody and again been imprisoned. He continued to exhibit at the Royal Academy and to publish prints and one more book, the *Liber Nauticus* of 1805, containing instructions in the art of marine drawing which he had worked on with his father. But his correspondence was increasingly dominated with detailed lists of expenses. One pencil note states plaintively that he had 'completely come to a standstill – not having one penny or the means of promising any'. There seems little likelihood that he made income through further government work during this period. However, in the earlier years he clearly retained friends in the fleet who provided him with sketches which enabled him to tap into the contemporary craze for panoramas, of which he produced two: of the operations against the French invasion forces at Boulogne (1804) and the battle of Trafalgar. By 1808 he was writing from debtors' prison in Edinburgh. He had tried to keep his predicament from his sisters, but brother Dominic had let the cat out of the bag. Now he sought their help in finding commissions and in mollifying creditors, if necessary by selling drawings in their possession. By 1810 his brother was offering him some teaching work 'which will quite set you up'.[207] Meanwhile, a controversy was brewing which would put paid to prospects from patronage.

In the same year that the *Liber Nauticus* appeared, Olive published the first of two romantic novels which have earned her minor celebrity in the field of feminist literary studies. Other manuscripts survive of highly imaginative plots. In 1809 Olive began to translate the fiction into real life. She had obtained the post of landscape painter to the Prince of Wales in 1806. She now began to write to him with allusions to certain 'papers' bearing on the affairs of the Royal Family. The Prince's Private Secretary judged that her histrionic letters showed 'symptoms of insanity'.[208] During the turbulent periods when the Prince ruled as Regent they could not, however, be dismissed too lightly. In 1817 she published a claim to recognition as the natural daughter of Prince Henry, Duke of Cumberland, the younger brother of George III, and in 1821 she followed this up with assertions that she held information relating to the hidden marriage of King George III to Hannah Lightfoot. It seems that J.T. Serres himself was consulted about his wife's version of her birth, which prompted a riposte from Olive: 'What could such a person know of my birth . . . a man who basely falsified his solemn vows – and never paid one shilling for the support of his children during 19 years.'[209]

Serres was in an immensely vulnerable position. Though there is no evidence of further lucrative employment as a war artist, he certainly had enough funds to venture in 1816 as a partner in the construction of a theatre in a new residential area of Lambeth being opened up to the south of Waterloo bridge. His appointment was as Director of Internal Decorations and principal artist and scene painter, following the example of his old hero, de Loutherbourg. In this capacity he launched an ambitious plan, including the decoration of a grand Marine Saloon. A handbill described its ornaments, including some Channel and Mediterranean views and a panorama of the attack on Algiers in 1816 by Edward Pellew, now Admiral Lord Exmouth. However, Serres' main contribution to the enterprise was to secure the permission of Prince Leopold and Princess Charlotte to call the theatre the Royal Coburg. It was rumoured that he was one of a very small number of subscribers and he was soon out of his depth. By July 1819 the shortfalls in takings were such that his debts relating to the costs of decoration could only be cleared by a bond forfeiting any future income from the theatre, which survives to this day as the Old Vic. However, Serres' association with it was over, and he faced prosecution for recovery of assessed taxes.

His position became increasingly desperate as the fantastic pretensions of his unstable wife increased. Her public pursuit of her claims could not but affect her husband. He had embarked in Royal Yachts for earlier royal journeys to Germany and Ireland, but he was refused permission to accompany the royal squadron to Scotland in 1822,[210] and in the same year King George IV discontinued his patronage. The post of Marine Painter in Ordinary to the King passed to J.C. Schetky, Professor of Drawing at the Royal Naval College, Portsmouth. When he wrote his will in December 1823 Serres cited Olive's pretensions to royal blood alongside her repeated adultery as grounds for disinheriting her.[211] He had again been declared bankrupt and committed to debtor's prison, where he attempted to earn some money through teaching and through the production of a large set of watercolours depicting his wretched surroundings. His fortunes never recovered.

Around this time he developed a painful abscess under an arm. In 1825, concerned at the frail state of his health, some friends saved him from a further imprisonment by removing him into the rules of the King's Bench, which allowed him to reside more comfortably under their guarantee of security. However, a cold winter journey exacerbated his illness and he died on 28 December of that year, aged 66. His friend and fellow artist, the portraitist Sir William Beechey, obtained £20 from the Society of Arts to pay for his funeral.[212]

By this time his wife's claims to both British and Polish royal connection had also been discredited in no less a forum than Parliament where a motion of 1823 that they be seriously investigated was defeated. She too died within the rules of the King's Bench in 1835, but even that did not end the story since her pretensions were taken up by her daughter Lavinia, the self-styled 'Princess Lavinia of Cumberland and Duchess of Lancaster'. The fraudulence of these continued claims was only fully confirmed a few years before Lavinia's death in 1871.

The anonymous author of a tract intended to defend Serres' reputation and to raise funds to support his dependents, states that 'His duties as marine painter, in the exercise of which he was frequently employed during the last war, were to go into the harbours on the enemy coast, and make sketches to direct the consultations of the admiral . . . He was concerned in several engagements, and became on terms of familiarity with many naval officers of eminence.'[213] The writer suggests that Serres was employed occasionally on 'Government duties' for short periods during the later Napoleonic wars, but no products from this period have been identified and his seagoing reputation rests firmly on the products of the specific commission from the Admiralty Board which Nepean's letter launched in 1799.[214] As we have seen, in the course of the nineteenth century his views vanished from circulation.

The Hydrographic Office quickly adopted the charts in the *Pilote François* resulting from the work of Beautemps-Beaupré and his fellow *ingénieurs hydrographes*. These contained few 'appearances'. Chart 2694 of the channels between Ushant and the mainland contained new views taken from rocks rather than from the more usual positions chosen to be most advantageous to the navigator. Meanwhile, Serres' work lay in obscurity,[215] occasionally culled in more recent times for reproductions to present on special occasions. His endeavours to be the 'eyes' of the landsmen, as well as to improve guidance for the mariner, deserve greater prominence. His publications should also earn him notice in the story of the 'war artists' whose contribution to government information policy would be dramatically expanded in the major wars of the next century and a half, especially with the development of the illustrated newspaper and the emergence of cinematic film and public broadcasting.

Opposite **A 74-gun ship, used as an artistic device to add depth to one of Serres' panoramic views of the Biscay coast of Spain.**

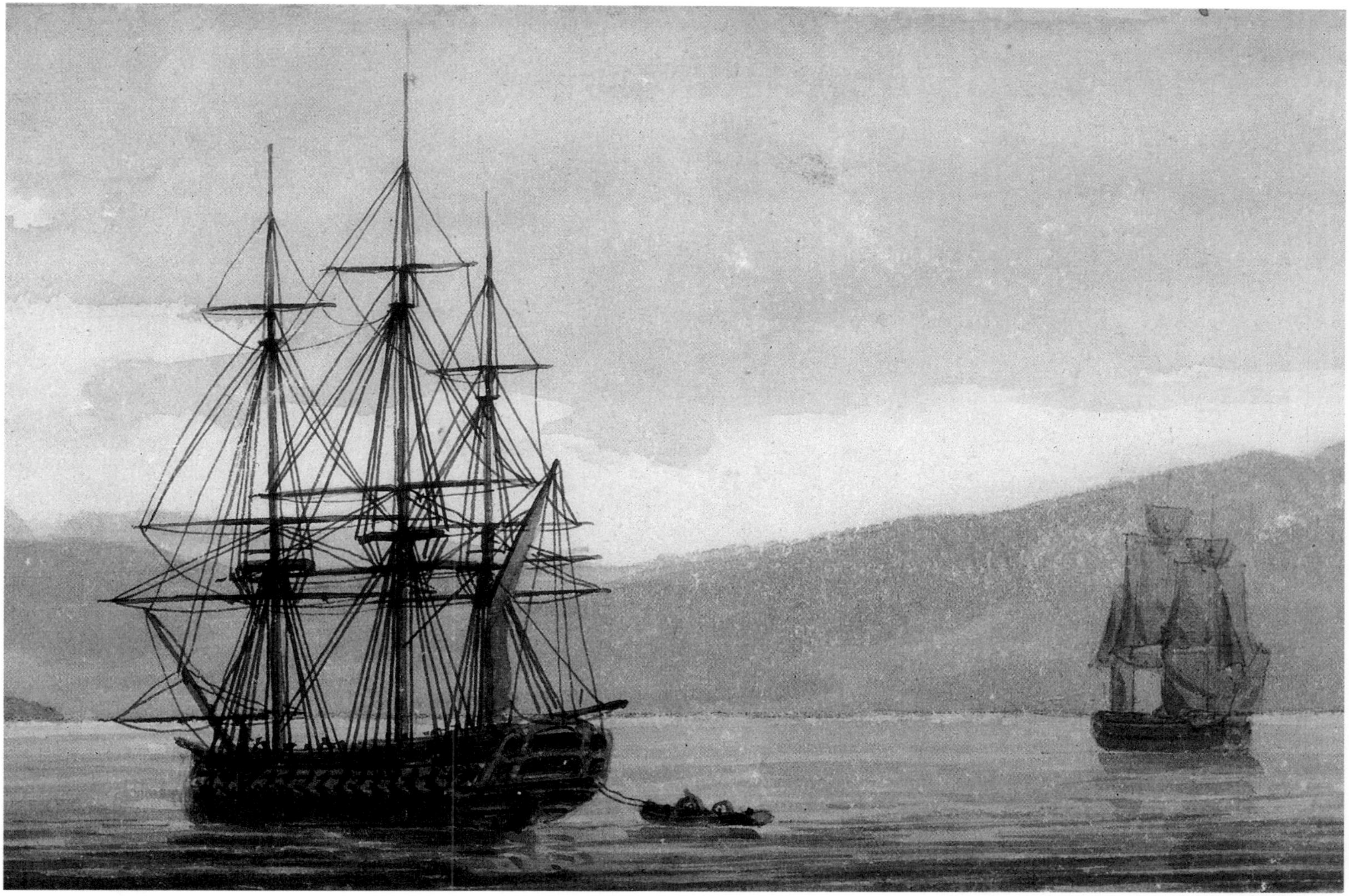

NOTES

Chapter One

1 J. C. Sainty, *Office-Holders in Modern Britain*, IV, Admiralty Officials 1660–1870, London (1975), p. 26.

2 R. Morriss (ed.), *The Channel Fleet and the Blockade of Brest*, N. R. S. 141 (2001), p. 13; NMM9 NEP/5, p. 144; M. A. Rae, *The Blockade of Brest and the French Atlantic Ports*, Exeter (2000), pp. 12–14.

3 Rear Admiral H. W. Richmond (ed.), *The Spencer Papers*, III, N. R. S. 58 (1924), pp. 117–25; P. Mackesy, *War without Victory: The downfall of Pitt 1799–1802*, Oxford (1984), p. 30.

4 N. R. S. 141, p. 403.

5 As had been done in 1759: *The Hawke Papers: A Selection, 1743–1771*, R. F. Mackay (ed.), N. R. S. 129 (1990), pp. 296–7.

6 NMM9 NEP/3, 6 Nov 1799.

7 Andrew S. Cook, unpublished thesis, 'Alexander Dalrymple (1737–1808) Hydrographer to the East India Company and to the Admiralty, as Publisher: A Catalogue of Books and Charts', St Andrew's (1992), pp. 158–61 and 186; G. S. Ritchie, *The Admiralty Chart*, London (1967), pp. 31–4; A. Day, *The Admiralty Hydrographic Service 1795–1919*, London (1967), p. 14. The illustrated plan, dating from the 1820s, is in UKHO MLP 5.

8 UKHO View Folio 2C pp. 2 and 5 contain the views around Brest, including that illustrated, annotated as copied in 1798.

9 N. R. S. 141, pp. 403 and 414. Serres had been one of the artists who had sketched the *Sans Pareil*, the largest of the prizes to be towed into Portsmouth harbour after the victory of the Glorious First of June (1794).

Chapter Two

10 The National Archives (TNA), Kew, ADM 36/324 *Bideford* Muster Book, in which Dominic Serres is No. 12 in the list of prisoners from the *San Antonio*; ADM 51/109 Part 2; ADM52/547 Part 3.

11 Extensive research in the TNA ADM 36 collection of Muster Books has not so far revealed the circumstances of any second capture.

12 Warwickshire County Record Office, Catalogue Ref. CR 1886, Boxes 674 and 677 contain bundles of Serres family correspondence. Some of these had been in the possession of W. J. Thoms, Librarian of the House of Lords, who conducted a correspondence on biographical information on J. T. Serres in *Notes and Queries*, 5th Series II, 1874, pp. 289, 364, 397, 410, 418, and 457.

13 Olive Serres (née Wilmot) is generally referred to as Olivia, a name she affected later in life. John Serres always called her Olive.

14 British Library Tracts 1091 No. 13 p. 16, also quoted by Alan Russet, *Dominic Serres RA, 1719–1793, War Artist to the Navy*, Antique Collectors Club (2001), p. 203.

15 Russet, *op. cit.*, p. 203; Warwickshire County Record Office, Catalogue Ref. CR 1886, 677/2, letter dated 11 June 1797.

16 Russet, *op. cit.*, pp. 21–81 and pp. 126–7; Roger Quarm and Scott Wilcox, *Masters of the Sea*, Oxford (1987), p. 24; Warwickshire County

Record Office, Catalogue Ref. CR 1886, Ryves Papers, Box 676/2.

17 David Joel, *Charles Brooking, 1723–1759, and the 18th Century British Marine Painters*, Antique Collectors Club (2000), pp. 77–8 and 81–2.

18 V. Duchêne et al., *Joseph Vernet: Les Vues des Ports de France, 1714–1789*, Musée Nationale de la Marine, Paris (2003). Vernet hinted to Dominic Serres that poor payment by the French court forced him to break off the commission (Russet, *op. cit.*, p. 172).

19 For Huë see *The Dictionary of Art*, Macmillan, (1996), and an example in Olivier Chapuis, *A la Mer comme au Ciel*, Paris (1999), p. 329. D. Cordingly, *Nicholas Pocock 1740–1821*, London (1986), pp. 66–9, quoted in N. R. S. 141.

20 Russet, *op. cit.*, p. 203; C. McCreery, *Ports of the World: Prints from the National Maritime Museum, Greenwich c.1700–1870*, London (1999), p. 33.

21 ADM 2/83 pp. 516–18.

22 ADM 1/3522 paper 239.

23 A. C. F. David et al. (eds.), *The Charts and Coastal Views of Captain Cook's Voyages*, I–III, Hakluyt Society (1988–97) especially vol. I, p. xxxviii; J. C. Beaglehole (ed.), *The Journals of Captain James Cook on his Voyages of Discovery, II*, Hakluyt Society Extra Series No. XXXV (1969), p. clviii.

24 For evidence of the influence of the naval members see P. Mackesy in *Statesmen at War: The Strategy of Overthrow 1798–1799*, London (1974), p. 17 and *op. cit.*, (1984), pp. 154–5. Nicholas Rodger, *The Admiralty*, Lavenham (1979), pp. 64–5, 88, notes that Evan Nepean handled all the correspondence of the Admiralty, consulting the Board only in contentious cases, using his knowledge, contacts and initiative to the full. No Terms of Reference and Instructions for Serres are apparent in either Nepean's papers (NMM9 NEP) or the formal Board records (ADM2 Out-letters, and 3 Minutes).

25 NMM9 NEP/5 p. 137.

26 ADM12/82 Digest 1799, S, dated 4 Sep 1799. The date is curious, since it is some three days after Serres embarked in the *Royal George*.

27 N. R. S. 58, pp. 127–8.

28 Russet, *op. cit.*, pp. 116 and 172–4.

29 The mysterious informant may have been a certain 'Wells' who provided details of ships and troops leaving Brest in September 1798, or John Cadman Etches, another agent mentioned frequently in the correspondence of the War Cabinet. Elizabeth Sparrow, *British Agents in France 1792–1815*, Woodbridge (1999), pp. 22, 176 and 180; *Dictionary of National Biography* (*DNB*), vol. 40, pp. 425–6; NMM 9 NEP/1–3.

30 DNB, pp. 1194–5; Warwickshire County Record Office, CR1886, Serres-Ryves Papers, Box 674; British Library Tracts 1091, No. 13, p. 20. Alan Russet notes that no official reference has yet been found to substantiate the statement that he was to receive an allowance of £100 per month (*pers. comm.*). This would have been a remarkably generous allowance by modern standards. In 1940 the watercolourist, Eric Ravilious, was employed for six months as a War Artist for the Admiralty at a rate of £325 for all the work he could produce, with assistance to procure uniform and art materials, and a daily allowance of £1, reducing to five shillings when onboard ship. Anne Ullmann (ed.), *Ravilious at War*, Huddersfield (2002).

31 NMM RCL/14 Number 9; British Library Tracts 1091, No. 13, pp. 50–1.

Chapter Three

32 N. R. S. 141, p. 408. Spencer took his son and his son's tutor with him for his 'sight-seeing' visit, the true purpose of which was to tackle Bridport and other flag officers on some delicate matters of reappointments.

33 Clearing bearings to keep the deeper draught vessels in safe water were shown on Lieutenant Murdoch Mackenzie's 1781 chart (UKHO Chart 26, Series A, No. 1).

34 N. R. S. 141, pp. 410–2. ADM51/1315, No. 1, Log of Captain William Dommett; ADM 36/12221 Muster Book for the *Royal George* 1 Sep–31 Oct 1799, in which Serres is Entry 2021.

35 *Naval Chronicle II* (hereafter cited as *NC*), p. 100.

36 ADM 51/1315, No. 1, and ADM 52/3376 No. 3, Master's Log of Mr John Douglas, are the source of the reconstruction of ship movements in this and subsequent paragraphs.

37 UKHO View Folio 2b*: JTS 9, 16, 23 (2 views) and View Folio 2a, p. 1.

38 UKHO View Folio 2b* 23 (2 views).

39 UKHO View Folio 2a, p. 1.

40 ADM 52/3376 No. 3 Log of Mr John Douglas.

41 N. R. S. 141, p. 420.

42 ADM 1/1627 f. 446.

43 E. G. R. Taylor, *The Haven-finding Art*, London (1956), pp. 168–9.

44 ADM 1/3523, p. 155.

45 ADM 1/3522, Dalrymple to Secretary to the Admiralty Board, 10 Oct 1807; S. Fisher, 'The Organisation of Hydrographic Information for English Navigators – Five Hundred Years of Sailing Directions and Charts', *Journal of Navigation*, 54 (May 2001), No. 2, pp. 157–66; W. H. Smyth, *The Mediterranean*, London (1854), p. 353; Cook, *op. cit.*, pp. 165–6.

46 The Mariner's Mirror (hereafter cited as M. M.) 75(4) (1989), p. 364.

47 N. R. S. 129, pp. 308 and 328–9.

48 Howard T. Fry, *Alexander Dalrymple (1737–1808) and the Expansion of British Trade*, London (1970), pp. 248–9; J. Leyland (ed.), *Despatches and Letters Relating to the Blockade of Brest*, I, N. R. S. 14 (1899), p. 120; Michael Lewis, *A Social History of the Navy, 1793–1815*, London (1960), pp. 348, 357.

49 The 'Examination of a Young Sea Officer' in J. W. Norie's *Complete Epitome of Practical Navigation*, first published in 1805, lays the emphasis on rote knowledge of marks, soundings and qualities of the bottom. The 'Description and Use of Charts' indicates clearly that they are reference sources and not plotting surfaces.

50 Chapuis, *op. cit.*, p. 150; M. M. 10(2) (1924), p. 193; J. Randier, *Marine Navigation Instruments*, London (1980), pp. 23–7; E. Fanning, *Steady as she Goes, a History of the Compass Department of the Admiralty*, London (1946), pp. xix–xx, xxii–xxiv, xxviii, 12; F. Marguet, *Histoire Générale de la Navigation du XVe au XXe Siècle*, Paris (1931), pp. 38–9, 86; B. Lavery, *The Arming and Fitting of English Ships of War, 1600–1815*, London (1987), p. 25; *NC* II, pp. 511–2.

51 T. Grocott, *Shipwrecks of the Revolutionary and Napoleonic Eras*, London (2002), pp. 235–6

52 ADM 36/12877, Entry 826.

53 ADM 36/12877 *Clyde* Monthly Book for September and October 1799, in which Serres is No. 75 on the Supernumeraries page; ADM 51/1296 No. 6 *Clyde*; ADM 36/12221; *DNB*, vol. 55, pp. 634–5; Anthony Bailey, *Standing in the Sun, A Life of J. M. W. Turner*, London (1997), pp. 50–1; E. Joll et al., *The Oxford Companion to J. M. W. Turner*, Oxford (2001), pp. 271, 286 and 312.

Chapter Four

54 William James, *Naval History of Great Britain*, III, London (1837), pp. 34–5; Dudley Pope, *The Devil Himself: the Mutiny of 1800*, London (1987); M. M. 74 (1988), p. 328.

55 N. R. S. 141, pp. 413, 416; pp. 432, and 462–4; p. 548; pp. 432–3; pp. 464–5.

56 Grocott, *op. cit.*, pp. 91–2.

57 J. Leyland (ed.), *The Blockade of Brest*, II, N. R. S. 21 (1902), p. 123.

58 *NC* VI, p. 108, 'RAB'.

59 N. R. S. 129, papers 218, 227–31, 293, and 303, and for the Black Rocks station pp. 129 and 235.

60 N. R. S. 141 p. 539. Morriss suggests (p. 536) that permanent moorings had been laid in the Black Rocks station. However, the report from Berkeley suggests rather that the squadron had been obliged to slip and buoy their anchor cables, leaving boats secured to the anchor-buoys. Neither the remarks of a subsequent senior officer of the advanced squadron, Captain John Knight (UKHO Miscellaneous Papers De 2, vol. 2, p. 579), nor his chart, give any indication of permanent moorings, nor does Hurd's *Nautical Description*, p. 18. Knight's own log records that his squadron returned to single anchor each day throughout most of July and August 1800, ready to slip at sight of enemy or change of weather (ADM 51/1309 No. 14), while the Master's log for 21 July notes: 'Saw 8 of the enemy's frigates coming out. Slipped the cable and left the launch fast to the buoy and cleared for action.' (ADM 52/3234 Part 8 21 July 1800).

61 Grocott, *op. cit.*, pp. 10–11

62 ADM 36/15370, *Superb*, Entry 217: Julien Galaise. The *Superb* also took out Julien Dantec, a pilot for the *Triton*. Dantec is a Breton name. In 1796, because of difficulty in procuring French pilots when ships were suddenly ordered onto the coast, Admiral Seymour had caused all those known to be serving in the fleet to be examined and based in the Portsmouth guardship (N. R. S. 141, pp. 150–1).

63 ADM 36/14444, *Mars*, Entry 604: Francois Adelize; ADM 36/14166, *Centaur*, Entry 3: Guillaume Queside; ADM 36/13897, *La Nymphe*, Entry 20: Joseph Qauntu, a Breton name; Nicholas Tracy (ed.), *The Naval Chronicle*

(Consolidated Edition), 1799–1804, London (1998), p. 324, hereafter cited as *NC* Consolidated.

64 *Montague* went without a pilot until Charles Carnella, another Breton, transferred from the *Saturn* on 8 Aug 1800. He was discharged to the *Captain* in Nov before that ship commenced the blockade of L'Orient (ADM 36/13688, Entry 1294; N. R. S. 141, p. 592).

65 Grocott, *op. cit.*, pp. 87–8.

66 UKHO Misc. Papers De 2, vol. 2, Admiral Knight's remarks and views off Brest. UKHO UB8, Hurd's Directions, p. 6.

67 NMM9 NEP/5, pp. 158–9; N. R. S. 141, p. 463 and N. R. S. 59, p. 6; NMM9 NEP/5, pp. 116–7; NMM9 NEP/8, pp. 23–4. NMM KEA/9 letter 1, dated 8 May 1800, records his determination to keep as close to the Black Rock station as possible.

68 ODNB, vol. 30, p. 68.

69 ADM 1/3523, First Report of the Committee, 29 Feb 1808; D. Howse and M. Sanderson, *The Sea Chart*, Newton Abbot (1973), p. 101.

70 Pascal Geneste, 'The Archivist and the Hydrographer', in Pieter van der Merwe (ed.), *Science and the French and British Navies, 1700–1850*, London (2003), pp. 37, 40; B. le Guisquet, 'Le Dépôt des Cartes, Plans et Journaux de la Marine sous l'Ancien Régime', *Annales Hydrographiques*, 5th series, vol. 18 (1992), No. 765, Paris, p. 24; Watkin Tench in G. Edwards (ed.), *Letters from Revolutionary France*, Cardiff (2001), pp. 37–8.

71 Howe and Sanderson, *op. cit.*, pp. 116–17, notes that one of the earliest charts to be published by the Admiralty was a French plan of Aboukir Bay which was printed with minimal changes.

72 UKHO Misc. Papers, vol. 103 (De 1), 101–11, HMS CLYDE. Remarks taken by Thomas Nott, Master of His Majesty's Ship *Clyde*, Charles Cunningham Esq. Captain, between the 15th Sep 1799 and the 14th Sep 1800 including Remarks, Bearings, Distances and Soundings where Mr Serris (*sic*, Nott's spellings have been preserved) Marine Painter drew the shape of the land on the Coast of France, Spain etc.

73 N. R. S. 141, p. 652.

74 Mackesy, *op. cit.* (1974), p. 215; N. R. S. 141, p. 19.

75 A. M. W. Stirling (ed.), *Pages and portraits from the Past: being the Private Papers of Sir William Hotham*, (1919), p. 123.

76 NMM9 NEP/8, p. 110; NMM9 NEP/7, pp. 54–5.

77 *Hotham Papers*, p. 53. NMM9 NEP/4, p. 115. On arrival in the Channel command, St Vincent made no secret of his views on prevailing standards: 'The waste of stores in this Fleet before I took command would beggar any description . . . the licentiousness of all the officers of the old Tenor is not to be credited.' The influence of St Vincent's Mediterranean captains, 'amongst whom I do not include Captain Knight', helped him to establish economy (NMM9 NEP/8, p. 109). See also NEP/5, pp. 160–1, and N. R. S. 59, pp. 12 and 16 for further disparagement of Knight. In the *ODNB*, vol. 31, p. 910, Susanna Fisher remarks that Knight had a poor record for maintaining discipline.

78 N. R. S. 58, p. 339; N. R. S. 141, p. 150. ADM 36/13688 shows that 22% of the men were Irish and that a substantial number of these were seamen. The books also record men from many countries of northern and southern Europe as well as America.

79 N. R. S. 59, p. 16.

80 J. Ralfe, *The Naval Biography of Great Britain*, III, London (1828), pp. 352–6; J. R. Sellers and P. M. Van Ee, *Maps and Charts of North America and the West Indies, 1750–89: A Guide to the Collections in the Library of Congress*, Washington DC (1981); P. J. Guthorn, *British Maps of the American Revolution*, Monmouth Beach, NJ (1972), pp. 32–3.

81 N. R. S. 141, p. 55; Raigersfeld's picture of the action with the French frigates is reproduced in R. Gardiner (ed.), *Nelson against Napoleon*, p. 125; Marshall *op. cit.* Supplement Part 3, p. 355, which records that Knight's son commanded one of the boats; *NC* IV, p. 145 reproduces the entry in the Gazette for a boat action which cut out eleven vessels from the port of Danene.

82 ADM 52/3234, Part 8, 12 July 1800.

83 A. Temple Patterson, *The Other Armada*, Oxford (1960), p. 207; N. R. S. 129, pp. 240–1, 246, 262–3, 289–90; M. M. 74 (4), p. 146.

Chapter Five

84 N. R. S. 141, p. 551.

85 N. R. S. 141, p. 556.

86 UKHO Miscellaneous Papers De 2, vol. 2, pp. 533–5, 577–81. The latter section has been bound in the wrong order. These 'General

Nautical Observations' were published with his charts by Faden in 1802 (BL Maps 15383).

87 UKHO Misc. Papers De 2, vol. 2, p. 577.

88 N. R. S. 141, p. 534.

89 Knight's skill in draughtsmanship should not be underestimated, and a fine view of the approaches to Toulon is illustrated in R. Gardiner (ed.), *The Campaign of Trafalgar 1803–1805*, London (1997), p. 109.

90 N. R. S. 58, pp. 333–4, 338; NMM9 NEP/5, p. 122; ADM 51/1302, No. 5, *Ville de Paris*; ADM 51/1338 *Indefatigable*; ADM 52/3710, No. 7 *Ville de Paris*; ADM 52/3261, No. 9 *La Nymphe*.

91 Saxby R. C., M. M. 46(2), pp. 113–19, contains a highly critical account of Fraser's performance, while acknowledging that the main body of the French squadron had escaped unseen before he made contact.

92 Some commentators have suggested that Fraser's career was now blighted. However, given that he was not a 'high-flyer', and that his correspondence suggests that he suffered from ill-health (ADM 1/1799, papers 153–6), this does not seem to be borne out by his subsequent record. He enjoyed two more commands, in the *Narcissus* (36) and the *Vanguard* (74), before being appointed successively as commissioner in Malta, Gibraltar and then on the Navy Board. He was to retire as a rear-admiral in 1823.

93 N. R. S. 20, p. 286.

94 N. R. S. 141, pp. 500–1; NMM9, NEP/5, 112, 6 May 1800; NMM9 NEP/8, p. 137; N. R. S. 141, pp. 439 (14 Mar 1800) and 502.

95 N. R. S. 141, p. 367; N. R. S. 141, p. 371; John Marshall, *op. cit.*, p. 47; NMM9 NEP/5, p. 159.

96 A year later, in September 1801, Captain T. Byam Martin closed le Goulet in *Fisgard* and drew a view and numbered plan which he used to report changes spotted in subsequent checks (Rae, *op. cit.*, pp. 23, 99).

97 NMM9 NEP/5, pp. 136–7; N. R. S. 141, p. 466; N. R. S. 20, pp. 284–5.

98 N. R. S. 141, p. 484; NMM9 NEP/8, pp. 135–6.

99 *A Nautical Description of the Bay of Brest with indications for its Navigation; also for A NEW CHANNEL into the FOUR*, London (1809). Hurd wrote: 'The particular use of this channel is, to enable our men of war to pass clear of the heavy batteries about St Matthew's and Conquet, from the Bay of Brest into the Four, either for the purpose of attacking or preventing the enemy's convoys and flotillas from getting into or out of Brest Harbour by this passage, as well as for enabling the ships of the inshore squadron to make their retreat through it, whenever, by the unexpected entrance of a superior force from the westward, and through the Raz Passage, they may find themselves cut off from all chance of escape by other means.'

100 N. R. S. 141, pp. 461–2, 506–7, 508–9, and 513–14.

101 The use of groups of seagulls to mark conspicuous objects, as shown on pp. 541, is evident in a view by Fraser illustrated in R. Gardiner (ed.), *Fleet Battle and Blockade, The French Revolutionary War 1793–1797*, London (1996), p. 8.

102 N. R. S. 141, p. 500.

103 UKHO View Folio 3***, 67–87.

104 N. R. S. 141, pp. 499–500, and 505.

105 *Steel's Naval Chronologist of the War*, facsimile reprint, London (1969), p. 43*.

106 ADM52/3261, No. 9.

107 It survives in UKHO View Folio 2c*.

108 British Library, Tracts 1091, No. 13, p. 21; ADM 12/85 Pro S letters. Sadly all promiscuous correspondence earlier than 1801 was destroyed in 1808. Mrs Serres appears to have left a distinct impression on the Admiralty clerks, since her name rather than that of her husband heads the brief summary in the Digest. Bills are recorded arriving on 8 June and 19 September.

Chapter Six

109 NMM CUN/4; G. E. Manwaring and Bonamy Dobrée, *The Floating Republic*, London (1937), pp. 166–8; illustrated in Gardiner (ed.), *Fleet Battle and Blockade*, p. 167; N. R. S. 141, p. 420.

110 N. R. S. 141, p. 607.

111 Chapuis, *op. cit.*, p. 147.

112 N. R. S. 138, pp. 26–7 and 124–5.

113 UKHO Misc. Papers, vol. 103 (De 1), p. 101.

114 N. R. S. 129, Papers 248–8a, 293.

115 UKHO Misc. Papers De 2, vol. 2, p. 577.

116 N. R. S. 141, p. 549; ADM 51/1309 Part 14 and ADM 52/3234 Part 8, 16 Sep 1800; N. R. S. 141, pp. 561–2; UKHO Vy 4.

117 NMM9 NEP/8, p. 54; UKHO Misc. Papers De 2, vol. 2, p. 535; NMM9 NEP/8, pp. 53–5.

118 *Nautical Description*, pp. 18–19.

119 N. R. S. 141, pp. 289–91; N. R. S. 58, pp. 374–6; N. R. S. 14, Paper 238, and N. R. S. 21, Papers 370 and 377. In 1804 Admiral Graves reported damaged anchors and cables and opined that the French telegraph system could enable ships in Brest to escape with a northerly wind. He also considered that a westerly swell could pin ships in Douarnenez Bay while not being a problem at Brest (ADM 1/124, Paper 176).

120 ADM 1/1629, Paper 420.

121 Captain Philip d'Auvergne, serving with the Channel Islands flotilla, was in close touch with Royalist exiles and contacts. N. R. S. 14, pp. 35–6.

122 NMM9 NEP/5, pp. 146–7.

123 NP 27 *Channel Pilot*, 6th edn., UK Hydrographic Office (2005), p. 262.

124 Admiralty Library Vy 4.

125 ADM 52/3234 Part 5, 18 Sep 1800; UKHO De 2, vol. 2, p. 581; UKHO UB8.

126 N. R. S. 141, p. 551; N. R. S. 141 p. 556; NMM9 NEP/8, pp. 38–9; NMM9 NEP/5, p. 182.

127 N. R. S. 141, p. 445; James, *op. cit.*, III, p. 4; Grocott, *op. cit.*, p. 92; *NC II*, (1998), p. 107.

128 UKHO Miscellaneous Papers 103 (De 1), p. 102.

129 N. R. S. 20, p. 290.

130 Grocott, *op. cit.*, p. 108.

131 N. R. S. 58, pp. 340–1, James, *op. cit.*, III, pp. 39–40.

Chapter Seven

132 N. R. S. 141, pp. 477–8, 553, 557, 560.

133 Grocott, *op. cit.*, p. 101.

134 N. R. S. 58, pp. 117–25.

135 N. R. S. 141, p. 474.

136 N. R. S. 58, p. 336.

137 Russet, *op. cit.*, pp. 34–8.

138 James, *op. cit.*, III, pp. 5–6, *NC* (Consolidated) II, p. 110.

139 N. R. S. 58, pp. 348–52.

140 N. R. S. 141, p. 533; *NC* (Consolidated) I, pp. 133–8; N. R. S. 141, p. 534; N. R. S. 58, p. 365; N. R. S. 129, Papers 226, 270, 334, and M. Steer, 'Blockade of Brest and the Victualling of the Western Squadron, 1793–1805', M. M. 76, (4), pp. 312–13.

141 James, *op. cit.*, II, pp. 341–4; Marshall, *op. cit.*, II, p. 80, *United Service Journal*, 1834, Part II, p. 88. The engagement is illustrated in R. Gardiner (ed.), *Nelson against Napoleon*, p. 128.

142 N. R. S. 141, pp. 278–9.

143 ADM 51/1332 *Clyde* 3 to 5 July 1800.

Chapter Eight

144 NMM KEA/9, letter 2, dated 12 May 1800, 'You will send your weekly accounts, which possibly may induce Lord St Vincent to relieve you from your present very fatiguing service.'

145 N. R. S. 141, p. 531.

146 NMM9 NEP/5, p. 147. St Vincent had known Dominic Serres and his sons for a quarter of a century. He had entered one of John's brothers on the books of *Foudroyant*, where he served for three months before turning his back on a sea career. Evan Nepean was Captain's Secretary and Purser of the ship at this time (Russet, *op. cit.*, pp. 148–51). St Vincent was proud of the position Nepean had attained 'by superior talents for business, unremitting diligence, and integrity' (N. R. S. 59, p. 8). Letters from St Vincent form the major part of the Nepean papers in the NMM.

147 British Library Tracts, 1091, No. 13, pp. 50–1.

148 UKHO View Folio 2c*. Mr Nott's Remarks mention the ship heaving to for views which are not in this folio.

149 ADM 52/2865, Part 3, 12 July.

150 C. D. Hall, *Wellington's Navy: Sea Power and the Peninsular War 1807–1814*, London (2004).

151 When the author visited Bayonne in 1988 in command of HMS *Bulldog*, the graves of some of the fallen British officers were being tended by a retired French naval officer.

152 ADM 51/1332 *Clyde*.

153 Hall, *op. cit.*, pp. 10–11, 62–3, and 214; NP 22 (2004), p. 277.

154 Spanish hydrographic efforts had been spurred by the example of France, especially after collaboration in Borda's survey of the Canaries and adjacent African waters in the *Boussolle*. Tofiño, as Director and Professor of Mathematics in the Naval Academy in Cadiz, had gained approval to select some cadets for additional training in astronomy and surveying. These students assisted him in rigorous controlled surveys of the Spanish coast between 1783 and

1786, the results of which were published in his Sailing Directions and the *Atlas Maritimo de España*. F. J. González and L. Martín-Merás, *La Dirección de Trabajos Hidrográficos (1797–1908)*, Barcelona and Madrid (2003), pp. 40–1, 49, 132 and 183.

155 *Atlas Marítimo de España*, reproduced by the Instituto Hidrografico de la Marina, Cadiz (1989); NP 22 *Bay of Biscay Pilot*, 9th edn., UKHO, (2004), p. 266.

156 N. R. S. 141, pp. 414–15, 419 and 428–30.

157 28 July the *Uranie* reported the capture of *La Revanche*, a schooner pioneer belonging to Bayonne, but operating from Vigo. N. R. S. 141, p. 540.

158 Hall, *op. cit.*, pp. 220–1.

159 Hall, *op. cit.*, p. 222. For a present-day description of the navigation in the approaches see NP 22 (2004), p. 283.

160 ADM 51/1332, 14–16 July.

161 UKHO Miscellaneous Publication 103 (De 1), p. 107.

162 *Spanish Ports throughout History*, Centro de Estudios Históricos de Obras Públicas y Urbanismo, Madrid (1994), p. 31.

163 A 74-gun ship in the view on the title-page has probably been added with artistic licence.

164 NP 22 (2004), p. 300.

165 *Spanish Ports throughout History*, Madrid (1994), p. 248; Hall, *op. cit.*, pp. 202–3, 209.

166 UKHO Miscellaneous Publication 103 (De 1), p. 108.

167 NMM 527.83(46):094 TOF *Spanish Coasting Pilot*, p. 31. This English translation did not become available until 1812, when Faden published it in response to demand from Royal Navy officers who had great difficulty in obtaining the original.

168 ADM 51/1332.

169 ADM 51/1341 Part 4 *Boadicea*; N. R. S. 141, p. 535.

170 N. R. S. 20 (1901), pp. 253–4.

171 ADM 51/1341 Part 4, 23–4 July.

172 NMM KEA/5, letter 1 dated 6 Jul 1800, from St Vincent.

173 N. R. S. 141, pp. 416–17, 531; NMM9 NEP/5, p. 137.

174 UKHO Miscellaneous Publication 103 (De 1), p. 110.

175 The *Clyde* captured two French schooners during the remainder of her cruise, one of which provided important intelligence of a threat on the African coast, and also recaptured a Guineaman from Liverpool. ADM 1/1629, Papers 427–8.

176 NMM9 NEP/5, pp. 164–5.

177 ADM 1/2691, letter 191.

178 ADM 12/86, Digest 5.1c.

Chapter Nine

179 British Library Tracts, 1091, No. 13, pp. 21–2.

180 The Admiralty Office Contingent Accounts show two guineas expended in 1800 as a half subscription to two sets of *The Little Sea Torch* (MM 55 (3) Query by P. K. Crimmin, p. 353).

181 ADM 12/85, 1800 Digest of Pro S letters.

182 H. S. Vaughan, 'Old Pilot Books and Sailing Directions', M. M. 6(2), (1920), p. 176.

183 Chapuis, *op. cit.*, p. 839. BL 795.e.12(2) is the 1st edn. of 1684, possibly from King George III's collection. BL 10498.aa.4 is a dog-eared copy of the 1789 edition, bought in a chandlery in Antwerp.

184 ADM 1/1631, Papers 346–89.

185 The view is in the Paul Mellon collection at the Yale Center for British Art.

186 ADM 36/15307.

187 Vaughan, *op. cit.*

188 He had already painted Belem Castle at Lisbon and scenes of Naples by 1790 (Russet, *op. cit.*, pp. 199–200), and he travelled between Marseilles, Nice, Genoa, Leghorn and Pisa, and widely within the Kingdom of Naples during his Grand Tour (British Library Tracts, 1091, No. 13, p. 12).

189 R. Walter (ed.), *A Voyage round the World in the Years 1740–4 by Lord Anson*, London (1911), pp. 6–10.

190 Andrew David, Geographical Listing of Views found in the Miscellaneous Papers Series. Manuscript in UKHO Archives.

191 ADM 1/3522, 23 Dec 1806; ADM 1/3523, 29 Feb 1808.

192 Day, *op. cit.*, pp. 35 and 217; A. David, Provisional unpublished draft notes on major changes of series, title, limits and format of Sailing Directions, 1820–1995, UKHO.

193 NMM P/30(6) Approaches to Brest, 1724 manuscript, shows le Boufoloc with the same hatching as the Black Rocks; Admiralty Library Vf 3/1 Chart of Brest and Adjacent Parts from a French Manuscript published by the HO in 1803 shows the rock as drying at half tide.

194 ADM/5365 28.3 × 31.1 cm, Court Martial aboard HMS *Salvador del Mundo*.

195 Admiralty Library Vy 4.

196 David et. al., *op. cit.*, vol. I., London (1988), p. xxix; ADM 1/3523, 29 Feb 1808; N. R. S. 14, Papers 237–8; S. Fisher, 'Captain Thomas Hurd's Survey of the Bay of Brest during the Blockade in the Napoleonic Wars', M. M. 79(3) (1993), p. 294. The Maritime Collection of King George III (BL MAR V.14) contains copies of the successive versions of Knight's charts of the Bay of Brest.

197 ADM 1/3522, Dalrymple to Secretary to the Admiralty Board, 10 Oct 1807; Chapuis, *op. cit.*, pp. 106–10, 128.

198 N. A. M. Rodger, 'Navies and the Enlightenment', in P. van der Merwe, *op. cit.*, p. 15; Chapuis, *op. cit.*, pp. 614–25; M. K. Barritt, review article on Chapuis, *op. cit.*, M. M. 87 (3) (2001), pp. 359–61.

199 The plate was subsequently destroyed. UKHO D.5 contains three proofs which were pulled as a record of it.

200 UKHO UB8. Hurd's survey remarks, from which the text was developed, are in RB103, commencing on p. 465.

201 UKHO View Folio 2c, 546–77, and 581–6.

202 The original drawing from which one of the views is derived is contained in UKHO View Folio 2c. It is dated as received in Jan 1887. The provenance is not given.

Chapter Ten

203 NMM CUN/4, correspondence with Lord Melville in 1820.

204 NMM CUN/1 and 4 Papers of Rear-Admiral Sir Charles Cunningham.

205 W. R. O'Byrne, *A Naval Biographical Dictionary*, London (1849).

206 N. R. S. 20 (1901), p. 231.

207 Warwickshire County Records Office, CR 1886, various papers in boxes 674 and 676 and box 677, paper 4; British Library Tracts T1091, No. 13, *op. cit.*

208 CR 1886, Box 676, transcripts of court hearings.

209 CR 1886, Box 677, Olive Serres – Legal Case, 1866, also some papers in Box 676.

210 British Library Tracts T1091, p. 41.

211 British Library Tracts T1091; Ryves Papers, CR 1886, Box 676/11.

212 British Library, *op. cit.*, pp. 47–8.

213 British Library, *op. cit.*, pp. 20–1.

214 British Library Tracts T10826 d.8 and T1091, No. 13, pp. 20–1 and p. 36.

215 The existence in the Admiralty Hydrographic Department of 'a series of Serres' water-colours of the Spanish coast and a magnificent panorama of the British blockade of Brest' was mentioned by Mary Blewitt in her pioneering work *Surveys of the Seas*, London (1957). Two reproductions, of part of the panorama, and of the view of Cape Torinana with the *Clyde* in the offing, graphically illustrate the limitations of the colour printing technology of the day.

BIBLIOGRAPHY

Manuscript Sources and other Archive Material

National Archives, Kew:

ADM 1 In-letters:

Commanders in Chief:

124, No. 176.

Captains:

1627 (C) for 1799, Nos. 432–48, Captain Charles Cunningham.

1629 (C) for 1800, Nos. 419–31, Captain Charles Cunningham.

1631 (C) for 1801, Nos. 340–89, Captain Charles Cunningham.

1799 (F) for 1800, Nos. 153–6, Captain Percy Fraser.

2018 (K) for 1798–9, Nos. 100–3 and 118, Captain John Knight.

2019 (K) for 1800–2, Nos. 51–2 and 86–98, Captain John Knight.

2691 (W) for 1800, No. 191, Captain Williams.

Correspondence of the Hydrographer to the Admiralty and the Admiralty Chart Committee:

3522–3.

Promiscuous S:

5015–23 have been examined and contain no correspondence from Serres.

ADM 2 Out-letters:

138 has been examined and it contains no reference to Serres' task.

ADM 3 Minutes:

123, 125, 142 and 143 also contain no reference to Serres' task or results.

ADM 12 Indices and Digests:

81 Index M–Z for 1799.

82–3 Digests for 1799.

85 Index M–Z for 1800.

86 Digest for 1800.

ADM 36 Muster Books:

137, 139–40 ARGYLE.

319–22 and 324 BIDEFORD.

542–4 CENTAUR.

629–31 and 633 CORNWALL.

716 and 719 DRAKE.

735–7 DEAL CASTLE.

1041–7 ENTERPRISE.

1080, 1088–9 EXPERIMENT.

1379–81 GOSPORT.

1860, 1866–8 LUDLOW CASTLE.

1919–21 LYME.

1934 LYNN.

1972–6 MARY GALLEY.

2019–20 MERLIN.

2074 MONTAGUE.

2642 PORCUPINE.

2887–8 RICHMOND.

3227–8 RYE.

3383 SAXON.

4454 VAINQUEUR.

4442–5 VULTURE.

4509 and 4511 WARWICK.

4530 WEAZLE.

4782–3 AUGUSTA.

12221 ROYAL GEORGE.

12877 CLYDE.

13687–8 MONTAGU.

13829 INDEFATIGABLE.

13897 LA NYMPHE.

14166 CENTAUR.

14444 MARS.

15306–7 CLYDE.

15370 SUPERB.

ADM 41 Muster Books of Hired Vessels:

6 FOWEY

11 LURCHER

ADM 51 Captains' Logs:

109 Part 2, BIDEFORD.

615 Part 4, MONTAGU.

1048 Part 6, WARWICK.

1271 Part 3, TRITON.

1296 Part 6, CLYDE.

1302 Part 5, VILLE DE PARIS.

1309 Part 12, LA NYMPHE.

1309 Part 14, MONTAGU.

1315 Part 1, ROYAL GEORGE.

1329 Part 5, TRITON.

1332 CLYDE.

1338 INDEFATIGABLE.

1341 Part 4, BOADICEA.

4018 JOSEPH.

ADM 52 Masters' Logs:

547 Part 3, BIDEFORD.

2865 Parts 2 and 3, CLYDE.

2866 CLYDE.

3115 Parts 4 and 10, INDEFATIGABLE.

3234 Parts 5–8, MONTAGU.

3261 Part 9, LA NYMPHE.

3376 Part 3, ROYAL GEORGE.

3710 Part 7, VILLE DE PARIS.

National Maritime Museum:

NMM CUN/1, 4 Papers of Rear Admiral Sir Charles Cunningham.

NMM9 NEP/1–5, 7–8 Papers of Sir Evan Nepean.

UKHO:

Original Documents:

View Folio 2a, West Coast of Europe, volume I.

View Folio 2b*, Views by J. T. Serres 1799–1800.

View Folio 2c, West Coast of Europe, volume III.

View Folio 2c*, Sketchbook of J. T. Serres 1800.

Miscellaneous Papers:

Volume 103 (De 1) pp. 101–11, HMS *Clyde* De 1, 'Clyde. Remarks on the Western Coasts of France with Mr Serres'.

Volume 105 (De2, vol. 2), pp. 533–4, 577–81. Remarks and views off Brest by Admiral Knight.

RB103 Remark Book including Hurd's remarks from his survey in the Bay of Brest.

Warwickshire County Record Office:

Greville of Warwick Castle. Serres/Ryves Papers, CR 1886, Boxes 674, 676 and 677.

Printed Sources

Primary

The British Library:

795.e.12(2) Bougard, R. *Le Petit Flambeau de la Mer*, 1684 edn.

10498.aa.4 Bougard, R. *Le Petit Flambeau de la Mer*, 1789 edn.

Tracts T1091 (13) and T10826.d.8(2) Copies of "Memoir of John Serres, late Marine Painter to His Majesty. By A Friend" published in London in 1826.

Maps 15383 Knight's Charts of the Bay of Brest. 2nd edn. (1802).

Maps K.MAR.V(14) Knight's Charts of the Bay of Brest. 1st (1800) and 2nd (1802) edns.

The Admiralty Library:

UB8 Book of remarks for the Western Station contains a copy of Captain Thomas Hurd's *A Nautical Description of the Bay of Brest with indications for its navigation; also for A NEW CHANNEL into the FOUR*, London (1809).

Vf 3/1 *Chart of Brest and Adjacent Parts*, published by the Hydrographer to the Admiralty, 31 Dec 1803.

Vy 4 Captain John Knight's four charts of the Bay of Brest, 2nd edn. published by Faden in 1802.

Vw10 A copy of *Le Neptune François* with interleaved Faden charts of Quiberon Bay and the Glenan Islands (the latter by J. Knight).

Vw10a A second copy of *Le Neptune François*.

Catalogue of the Admiralty Library 1859.

The National Maritime Museum:

527.83:094 R. Bougard. *Le Petit Flambeau de la Mer*, 1731 edn.

527.83(46):094 TOF Tofiño de San Miguel, Brigadier Don Vicente, transl. J. Dougal, *España Maritima or Spanish Coasting Pilot*, London (1812).

912.44 (26:46) "17": 094 *Atlas maritimo de España*, Madrid, (1789).

The Royal Geographical Society:

14 B 75 A-3 A copy of *The Little Sea Torch*.

The Navy Records Society:

Vols. 14 and 21: J. Leyland, (ed.), *Despatches and Letters Relating to the Blockade of Brest*, vols. I and II, (1899) and (1902).

Vol. 20: J. K. Laughton, (ed.), *The Naval Miscellany*, vol. I (1901).

Vol. 58: H. W. Richmond, (ed.), *The Spencer Papers*, vol. III (1924).

Vol. 129: R. F. Mackay, (ed.), *The Hawke Papers: A Selection, 1743–1771* (1990).

Vol. 138: B. Lavery, (ed.), *Shipboard life and organisation, 1731–1815* (1998).

Vol. 141: R. Morriss, (ed.), *The Channel Fleet and the Blockade of Brest* (2001).

Secondary

Alexander, G. K., *A Catalogue of the Admiralty Collection of Marine and Air Magnetic Compasses etc. in the Museum of ACO Slough*, (1930).

Bailey, Anthony, *Standing in the Sun, A Life of J. M. W. Turner*, London (1997).

Barritt, M. K., review article on Chapuis, *op. cit.*, M. M. 87(3) (2001).

Beaglehole, J. C. (ed.), *The Journals of Captain James Cook on his Voyages of Discovery*, vol. II, Hakluyt Society Extra Series No. XXXV (1969).

Blake, N., *Steering to Glory, a Day in the Life of a Ship of the Line*, London (2005).

Centro de Estudios Históricos de Obras Públicas y Urbanismo, *Spanish Ports throughout History*, Madrid (1994).

Chapuis, O., *A la Mer comme au Ciel*, Paris (1999).

Cook, A. S., unpublished thesis, 'Alexander Dalrymple (1737–1808), Hydrographer to the East India Company and to the Admiralty, as Publisher: A Catalogue of Books and Charts', St Andrew's (1992).

David, A. C. F. et al. (eds.), *The Charts and Coastal Views of Captain Cook's Voyages*, vols. I–III, Hakluyt Society (1988–97).

Dawson, L. S., *Memoirs of Hydrography*, London (1969).

Day, A., *The Admiralty Hydrographic Service 1795–1919*, London (1967).

Dictionary of National Biography, Oxford (2004).

Duchêne, V. et al., *Joseph Vernet: les Vues des Ports de France, 1714–1789*, Musée de la Marine, Paris (2003).

Fanning, A. E., *Steady as she Goes, A History of the Compass Department of the Admiralty*, London (1946).

Fisher, S., 'Captain Thomas Hurd's Survey of the Bay of Brest during the Blockade in the Napoleonic Wars', M. M. 79(3) (1993).

Fisher, S., 'The Organisation of Hydrographic Information for English Navigators – Five Hundred Years of Sailing Directions and Charts', *Journal of Navigation*, vol. 54(2) (2001).

Fry, H. T., *Alexander Dalrymple (1737–1808) and the Expansion of British Trade*, London (1970).

Gardiner, R. (ed.), *Fleet Battle and Blockade, The French Revolutionary War 1793–1797*, London (1996).

Gardiner R. (ed.), *Nelson against Napoleon, From the Nile to Copenhagen, 1798–1801*, London (1997).

Gardiner, R. (ed.), *The Campaign of Trafalgar 1803–1805*, London (1997).

Geneste, P., 'The Archivist and the Hydrographer', in P. van der Merwe (ed.), *Science and the French and British Navies, 1700–1850*, London (2003).

González, F. J., and Martín-Merás, L., *La Dirección de Trabajos Hidrográficos (1797–1908), Historia de la Cartografía Náutica en la España del Siglo XIX*, Barcelona and Madrid (2003).

Grocott, T., *Shipwrecks of the Revolutionary and Napoleonic Eras*, London (2002).

Guisquet, B. le, 'Le Dépôt des Cartes, Plans et Journaux de la Marine sous l'Ancien Régime', *Annales Hydrographiques*, 5th series, vol. 18, no. 765, Paris (1992).

Guthorn, P. J., *British Maps of the American Revolution*, Monmouth Beach, NJ (1972).

Hall, C. D., *Wellington's Navy: Sea Power and the Peninsular War 1807–1814*, London (2004).

Howse, D. and Sanderson, M., *The Sea Chart*, Newton Abbot (1973).

Instituto Hidrografico de la Marina, *Atlas Marítimo de España, Madrid MDCCLXXXIX*, Cadiz (1989).

James, W., *Naval History of Great Britain*, vol. III, London (1837).

Joel, D., *Charles Brooking, 1723–1759, and the 18th Century British Marine Painters*, Antique Collectors Club (2000).

Joll, E., Butlin, M., and Herrmann, L. (eds.), *The Oxford Companion to J. M. W. Turner*, Oxford (2001).

Lavery, B., *The Ship of the Line*, Vol. I: *The Development of the Battle-Fleet 1650–1850*, London (1983).

Lavery, B., *The Arming and Fitting of English Ships of War, 1600–1815*, London (1987).

Lewis, M., *A Social History of the Navy, 1793–1815*, London (1960).

Mackesy, P., *Statesmen at War: The Strategy of Overthrow 1798–1799*, London (1974).

Mackesy, P., *War without Victory: The Downfall of Pitt 1799–1802*, Oxford (1984).

Marguet, F., *Histoire Générale de la Navigation du XVe au XXe siècle*, Paris (1931).

Marshall, J., *Royal Navy Biography*, London (1823).

Naval Chronicle, London, 1799 onwards.

O'Byrne, W. R., *A Naval Biographical Dictionary*, London (1849).

Quarm, R. and Wilcox, S., *Masters of the Sea*, Oxford (1987).

Rae, M. A., 'The Blockade of Brest and the French Atlantic Ports, Including Ferrol, in the Revolutionary and Napoleonic Wars, 1796–1806, together with the use of Torbay as a Port of Refuge', MA dissertation, University of Exeter (2000).

Ralfe, J., *The Naval Biography of Great Britain*, vol. III, London (1828).

Randier, J., trans. Powell, J. E., *Marine Navigation Instruments*, London (1980).

Richards G. H., *A Memoir of the Hydrographical Department of the Admiralty*, London (1868).

Ritchie, G. S., *The Admiralty Chart*, London (1967).

Rodger, N. A. M., *The Admiralty*, Lavenham (1979).

Rodger, N. A. M., 'Navies and the Enlightenment' in P. van der Merwe (ed.), *Science and the French and British Navies, 1700–1850*, London (2003).

Rodger, N. A. M., *The Command of the Ocean*, London (2004).

Russet A., *Dominic Serres RA, 1719–1793, War Artist to the Navy*, Antique Collectors Club (2001).

Sainty, J. C., *Office-Holders in Modern Britain, vol. IV, Admiralty Officials 1660–1870*, London (1975).

Saxby, R. C., 'The Escape of Admiral Bruix from Brest', M. M. 46(2).

Sellers, J. R. and Van Ee, P. M., *Maps and Charts of North America and the West Indies, 1750–89: A Guide to the Collections in the Library of Congress*, Washington DC (1981).

Sparrow, E., *British Agents in France 1792–1815*, Woodbridge (1999).

Steel, David, *Steel's Naval Chronologist of the War*, facsimile reprint, London (1969).

Steer, M., 'Blockade of Brest and the Victualling of the Western Squadron, 1793–1805', M. M. 76, (4).

Stirling, A. M. W. (ed.), *Pages and Portraits from the Past: being the Private Papers of Sir William Hotham*, London (1919).

Smyth, W. H., *The Mediterranean*, London (1854).

Taylor, E. G. R., *The Haven-finding Art*, London (1956).

Tench, W., *Letters from Revolutionary France*, Cardiff (2001).

Tracy, N. (ed.), *The Naval Chronicle Volumes I and II*, Consolidated edn., London (1998).

Van der Merwe, P. (ed.), *Science and the French and British Navies, 1700–1850*, London (2003).

Vaughan, H. S., 'Old Pilot Books and Sailing Directions', M. M. 6 (2)(1920).

Walter, R. (ed.), *A Voyage round the World in the years 1740–4 by Lord Anson*, London (1911).

INDEX

Page numbers in italics indicate illustrations.

PICTURE ACKNOWLEDGEMENTS

All illustrations, except where stated below, appear by kind permission of the United Kingdom Hydrographic Office © British Crown Copyright/2008 UKHO

© National Maritime Museum, Greenwich, London, *pages* 10, 13, 18, 36, 46, 64,

Courtesy the author, *page* 8

Courtesy Royal Naval Museum, Portsmouth, *pages* 26, 39, 44, 48, 70, 114–15, 116

© Crown Copyright/MoD 2008/Government Art Collection, *page* 14

Illustrations from the collection of the National Maritime Museum may be ordered by writing to: Picture Library, National Maritime Museum, Greenwich, London SE10 9NF, fax: +44 (0)20 8312 6533, email: picturelibrary@nmm.ac.uk

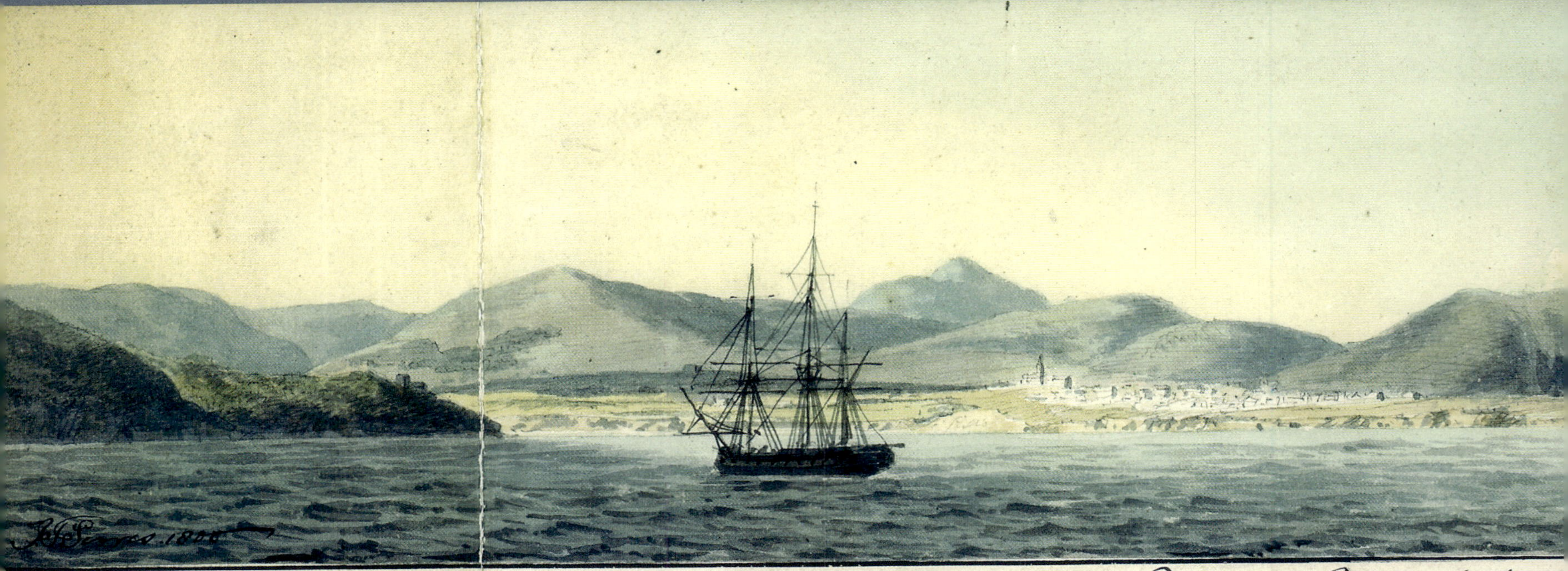

Quexo. on the coast of Spain. the Bluff bear